DEAR FUTURE EXAM SUCCESS STORY

First of all, **THANK YOU** for purchasing Mometrix study materials!

Second, congratulations! You are one of the few determined test-takers who are committed to doing whatever it takes to excel on your exam. **You have come to the right place.** We developed these study materials with one goal in mind: to deliver you the information you need in a format that's concise and easy to use.

In addition to optimizing your guide for the content of the test, we've outlined our recommended steps for breaking down the preparation process into small, attainable goals so you can make sure you stay on track.

We've also analyzed the entire test-taking process, identifying the most common pitfalls and showing how you can overcome them and be ready for any curveball the test throws you.

Standardized testing is one of the biggest obstacles on your road to success, which only increases the importance of doing well in the high-pressure, high-stakes environment of test day. Your results on this test could have a significant impact on your future, and this guide provides the information and practical advice to help you achieve your full potential on test day.

Your success is our success

We would love to hear from you! If you would like to share the story of your exam success or if you have any questions or comments in regard to our products, please contact us at **800-673-8175** or **support@mometrix.com**.

Thanks again for your business and we wish you continued success!

Sincerely,
The Mometrix Test Preparation Team

> **Need more help? Check out our flashcards at:**
> **http://MometrixFlashcards.com/GACE**

GACE

School Psychology
Secrets Study Guide

TABLE OF CONTENTS

Introduction

Thank you for purchasing this resource! You have made the choice to prepare yourself for a test that could have a huge impact on your future, and this guide is designed to help you be fully ready for test day. Obviously, it's important to have a solid understanding of the test material, but you also need to be prepared for the unique environment and stressors of the test, so that you can perform to the best of your abilities.

For this purpose, the first section that appears in this guide is the **Secret Keys**. We've devoted countless hours to meticulously researching what works and what doesn't, and we've boiled down our findings to the five most impactful steps you can take to improve your performance on the test. We start at the beginning with study planning and move through the preparation process, all the way to the testing strategies that will help you get the most out of what you know when you're finally sitting in front of the test.

We recommend that you start preparing for your test as far in advance as possible. However, if you've bought this guide as a last-minute study resource and only have a few days before your test, we recommend that you skip over the first two Secret Keys since they address a long-term study plan.

If you struggle with **test anxiety**, we strongly encourage you to check out our recommendations for how you can overcome it. Test anxiety is a formidable foe, but it can be beaten, and we want to make sure you have the tools you need to defeat it.

Secret Key #1 – Plan Big, Study Small

There's a lot riding on your performance. If you want to ace this test, you're going to need to keep your skills sharp and the material fresh in your mind. You need a plan that lets you review everything you need to know while still fitting in your schedule. We'll break this strategy down into three categories.

Information Organization

Start with the information you already have: the official test outline. From this, you can make a complete list of all the concepts you need to cover before the test. Organize these concepts into groups that can be studied together, and create a list of any related vocabulary you need to learn so you can brush up on any difficult terms. You'll want to keep this vocabulary list handy once you actually start studying since you may need to add to it along the way.

Time Management

Once you have your set of study concepts, decide how to spread them out over the time you have left before the test. Break your study plan into small, clear goals so you have a manageable task for each day and know exactly what you're doing. Then just focus on one small step at a time. When you manage your time this way, you don't need to spend hours at a time studying. Studying a small block of content for a short period each day helps you retain information better and avoid stressing over how much you have left to do. You can relax knowing that you have a plan to cover everything in time. In order for this strategy to be effective though, you have to start studying early and stick to your schedule. Avoid the exhaustion and futility that comes from last-minute cramming!

Study Environment

The environment you study in has a big impact on your learning. Studying in a coffee shop, while probably more enjoyable, is not likely to be as fruitful as studying in a quiet room. It's important to keep distractions to a minimum. You're only planning to study for a short block of time, so make the most of it. Don't pause to check your phone or get up to find a snack. It's also important to **avoid multitasking**. Research has consistently shown that multitasking will make your studying dramatically less effective. Your study area should also be comfortable and well-lit so you don't have the distraction of straining your eyes or sitting on an uncomfortable chair.

 The time of day you study is also important. You want to be rested and alert. Don't wait until just before bedtime. Study when you'll be most likely to comprehend and remember. Even better, if you know what time of day your test will be, set that time aside for study. That way your brain will be used to working on that subject at that specific time and you'll have a better chance of recalling information.

Finally, it can be helpful to team up with others who are studying for the same test. Your actual studying should be done in as isolated an environment as possible, but the work of organizing the information and setting up the study plan can be divided up. In between study sessions, you can discuss with your teammates the concepts that you're all studying and quiz each other on the details. Just be sure that your teammates are as serious about the test as you are. If you find that your study time is being replaced with social time, you might need to find a new team.

2

Secret Key #2 – Make Your Studying Count

You're devoting a lot of time and effort to preparing for this test, so you want to be absolutely certain it will pay off. This means doing more than just reading the content and hoping you can remember it on test day. It's important to make every minute of study count. There are two main areas you can focus on to make your studying count.

Retention

It doesn't matter how much time you study if you can't remember the material. You need to make sure you are retaining the concepts. To check your retention of the information you're learning, try recalling it at later times with minimal prompting. Try carrying around flashcards and glance at one or two from time to time or ask a friend who's also studying for the test to quiz you.

To enhance your retention, look for ways to put the information into practice so that you can apply it rather than simply recalling it. If you're using the information in practical ways, it will be much easier to remember. Similarly, it helps to solidify a concept in your mind if you're not only reading it to yourself but also explaining it to someone else. Ask a friend to let you teach them about a concept you're a little shaky on (or speak aloud to an imaginary audience if necessary). As you try to summarize, define, give examples, and answer your friend's questions, you'll understand the concepts better and they will stay with you longer. Finally, step back for a big picture view and ask yourself how each piece of information fits with the whole subject. When you link the different concepts together and see them working together as a whole, it's easier to remember the individual components.

Finally, practice showing your work on any multi-step problems, even if you're just studying. Writing out each step you take to solve a problem will help solidify the process in your mind, and you'll be more likely to remember it during the test.

Modality

Modality simply refers to the means or method by which you study. Choosing a study modality that fits your own individual learning style is crucial. No two people learn best in exactly the same way, so it's important to know your strengths and use them to your advantage.

For example, if you learn best by visualization, focus on visualizing a concept in your mind and draw an image or a diagram. Try color-coding your notes, illustrating them, or creating symbols that will trigger your mind to recall a learned concept. If you learn best by hearing or discussing information, find a study partner who learns the same way or read aloud to yourself. Think about how to put the information in your own words. Imagine that you are giving a lecture on the topic and record yourself so you can listen to it later.

For any learning style, flashcards can be helpful. Organize the information so you can take advantage of spare moments to review. Underline key words or phrases. Use different colors for different categories. Mnemonic devices (such as creating a short list in which every item starts with the same letter) can also help with retention. Find what works best for you and use it to store the information in your mind most effectively and easily.

3

Secret Key #3 – Practice the Right Way

Your success on test day depends not only on how many hours you put into preparing, but also on whether you prepared the right way. It's good to check along the way to see if your studying is paying off. One of the most effective ways to do this is by taking practice tests to evaluate your progress. Practice tests are useful because they show exactly where you need to improve. Every time you take a practice test, pay special attention to these three groups of questions:

- The questions you got wrong
- The questions you had to guess on, even if you guessed right
- The questions you found difficult or slow to work through

This will show you exactly what your weak areas are, and where you need to devote more study time. Ask yourself why each of these questions gave you trouble. Was it because you didn't understand the material? Was it because you didn't remember the vocabulary? Do you need more repetitions on this type of question to build speed and confidence? Dig into those questions and figure out how you can strengthen your weak areas as you go back to review the material.

 Additionally, many practice tests have a section explaining the answer choices. It can be tempting to read the explanation and think that you now have a good understanding of the concept. However, an explanation likely only covers part of the question's broader context. Even if the explanation makes perfect sense, **go back and investigate** every concept related to the question until you're positive you have a thorough understanding.

As you go along, keep in mind that the practice test is just that: practice. Memorizing these questions and answers will not be very helpful on the actual test because it is unlikely to have any of the same exact questions. If you only know the right answers to the sample questions, you won't be prepared for the real thing. **Study the concepts** until you understand them fully, and then you'll be able to answer any question that shows up on the test.

It's important to wait on the practice tests until you're ready. If you take a test on your first day of study, you may be overwhelmed by the amount of material covered and how much you need to learn. Work up to it gradually.

On test day, you'll need to be prepared for answering questions, managing your time, and using the test-taking strategies you've learned. It's a lot to balance, like a mental marathon that will have a big impact on your future. Like training for a marathon, you'll need to start slowly and work your way up. When test day arrives, you'll be ready.

Start with the strategies you've read in the first two Secret Keys—plan your course and study in the way that works best for you. If you have time, consider using multiple study resources to get different approaches to the same concepts. It can be helpful to see difficult concepts from more than one angle. Then find a good source for practice tests. Many times, the test website will suggest potential study resources or provide sample tests.

Practice Test Strategy

If you're able to find at least three practice tests, we recommend this strategy:

UNTIMED AND OPEN-BOOK PRACTICE

Take the first test with no time constraints and with your notes and study guide handy. Take your time and focus on applying the strategies you've learned.

TIMED AND OPEN-BOOK PRACTICE

Take the second practice test open-book as well, but set a timer and practice pacing yourself to finish in time.

TIMED AND CLOSED-BOOK PRACTICE

Take any other practice tests as if it were test day. Set a timer and put away your study materials. Sit at a table or desk in a quiet room, imagine yourself at the testing center, and answer questions as quickly and accurately as possible.

Keep repeating timed and closed-book tests on a regular basis until you run out of practice tests or it's time for the actual test. Your mind will be ready for the schedule and stress of test day, and you'll be able to focus on recalling the material you've learned.

Secret Key #4 – Pace Yourself

Once you're fully prepared for the material on the test, your biggest challenge on test day will be managing your time. Just knowing that the clock is ticking can make you panic even if you have plenty of time left. Work on pacing yourself so you can build confidence against the time constraints of the exam. Pacing is a difficult skill to master, especially in a high-pressure environment, so **practice is vital**.

Set time expectations for your pace based on how much time is available. For example, if a section has 60 questions and the time limit is 30 minutes, you know you have to average 30 seconds or less per question in order to answer them all. Although 30 seconds is the hard limit, set 25 seconds per question as your goal, so you reserve extra time to spend on harder questions. When you budget extra time for the harder questions, you no longer have any reason to stress when those questions take longer to answer.

Don't let this time expectation distract you from working through the test at a calm, steady pace, but keep it in mind so you don't spend too much time on any one question. Recognize that taking extra time on one question you don't understand may keep you from answering two that you do understand later in the test. If your time limit for a question is up and you're still not sure of the answer, mark it and move on, and come back to it later if the time and the test format allow. If the testing format doesn't allow you to return to earlier questions, just make an educated guess; then put it out of your mind and move on.

On the easier questions, be careful not to rush. It may seem wise to hurry through them so you have more time for the challenging ones, but it's not worth missing one if you know the concept and just didn't take the time to read the question fully. Work efficiently but make sure you understand the question and have looked at all of the answer choices, since more than one may seem right at first.

Even if you're paying attention to the time, you may find yourself a little behind at some point. You should speed up to get back on track, but do so wisely. Don't panic; just take a few seconds less on each question until you're caught up. Don't guess without thinking, but do look through the answer choices and eliminate any you know are wrong. If you can get down to two choices, it is often worthwhile to guess from those. Once you've chosen an answer, move on and don't dwell on any that you skipped or had to hurry through. If a question was taking too long, chances are it was one of the harder ones, so you weren't as likely to get it right anyway.

On the other hand, if you find yourself getting ahead of schedule, it may be beneficial to slow down a little. The more quickly you work, the more likely you are to make a careless mistake that will affect your score. You've budgeted time for each question, so don't be afraid to spend that time. Practice an efficient but careful pace to get the most out of the time you have.

Secret Key #5 – Have a Plan for Guessing

When you're taking the test, you may find yourself stuck on a question. Some of the answer choices seem better than others, but you don't see the one answer choice that is obviously correct. What do you do?

The scenario described above is very common, yet most test takers have not effectively prepared for it. Developing and practicing a plan for guessing may be one of the single most effective uses of your time as you get ready for the exam.

In developing your plan for guessing, there are three questions to address:

- When should you start the guessing process?
- How should you narrow down the choices?
- Which answer should you choose?

When to Start the Guessing Process

Unless your plan for guessing is to select C every time (which, despite its merits, is not what we recommend), you need to leave yourself enough time to apply your answer elimination strategies. Since you have a limited amount of time for each question, that means that if you're going to give yourself the best shot at guessing correctly, you have to decide quickly whether or not you will guess.

Of course, the best-case scenario is that you don't have to guess at all, so first, see if you can answer the question based on your knowledge of the subject and basic reasoning skills. Focus on the key words in the question and try to jog your memory of related topics. Give yourself a chance to bring the knowledge to mind, but once you realize that you don't have (or you can't access) the knowledge you need to answer the question, it's time to start the guessing process.

It's almost always better to start the guessing process too early than too late. It only takes a few seconds to remember something and answer the question from knowledge. Carefully eliminating wrong answer choices takes longer. Plus, going through the process of eliminating answer choices can actually help jog your memory.

Summary: Start the guessing process as soon as you decide that you can't answer the question based on your knowledge.

How to Narrow Down the Choices

The next chapter in this book (**Test-Taking Strategies**) includes a wide range of strategies for how to approach questions and how to look for answer choices to eliminate. You will definitely want to read those carefully, practice them, and figure out which ones work best for you. Here though, we're going to address a mindset rather than a particular strategy.

Your odds of guessing an answer correctly depend on how many options you are choosing from.

Number of options left	5	4	3	2	1
Odds of guessing correctly	20%	25%	33%	50%	100%

You can see from this chart just how valuable it is to be able to eliminate incorrect answers and make an educated guess, but there are two things that many test takers do that cause them to miss out on the benefits of guessing:

- Accidentally eliminating the correct answer
- Selecting an answer based on an impression

We'll look at the first one here, and the second one in the next section.

To avoid accidentally eliminating the correct answer, we recommend a thought exercise called **the $5 challenge**. In this challenge, you only eliminate an answer choice from contention if you are willing to bet $5 on it being wrong. Why $5? Five dollars is a small but not insignificant amount of money. It's an amount you could afford to lose but wouldn't want to throw away. And while losing

$5 once might not hurt too much, doing it twenty times will set you back $100. In the same way, each small decision you make—eliminating a choice here, guessing on a question there—won't by itself impact your score very much, but when you put them all together, they can make a big difference. By holding each answer choice elimination decision to a higher standard, you can reduce the risk of accidentally eliminating the correct answer.

The $5 challenge can also be applied in a positive sense: If you are willing to bet $5 that an answer choice *is* correct, go ahead and mark it as correct.

Summary: Only eliminate an answer choice if you are willing to bet $5 that it is wrong.

8

Which Answer to Choose

You're taking the test. You've run into a hard question and decided you'll have to guess. You've eliminated all the answer choices you're willing to bet $5 on. Now you have to pick an answer. Why do we even need to talk about this? Why can't you just pick whichever one you feel like when the time comes?

The answer to these questions is that if you don't come into the test with a plan, you'll rely on your impression to select an answer choice, and if you do that, you risk falling into a trap. The test writers know that everyone who takes their test will be guessing on some of the questions, so they intentionally write wrong answer choices to seem plausible. You still have to pick an answer though, and if the wrong answer choices are designed to look right, how can you ever be sure that you're not falling for their trap? The best solution we've found to this dilemma is to take the decision out of your hands entirely. Here is the process we recommend:

Once you've eliminated any choices that you are confident (willing to bet $5) are wrong, select the first remaining choice as your answer.

Whether you choose to select the first remaining choice, the second, or the last, the important thing is that you use some preselected standard. Using this approach guarantees that you will not be enticed into selecting an answer choice that looks right, because you are not basing your decision on how the answer choices look.

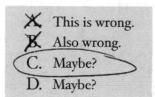

This is not meant to make you question your knowledge. Instead, it is to help you recognize the difference between your knowledge and your impressions. There's a huge difference between thinking an answer is right because of what you know, and thinking an answer is right because it looks or sounds like it should be right.

Summary: To ensure that your selection is appropriately random, make a predetermined selection from among all answer choices you have not eliminated.

Test-Taking Strategies

This section contains a list of test-taking strategies that you may find helpful as you work through the test. By taking what you know and applying logical thought, you can maximize your chances of answering any question correctly!

It is very important to realize that every question is different and every person is different: no single strategy will work on every question, and no single strategy will work for every person. That's why we've included all of them here, so you can try them out and determine which ones work best for different types of questions and which ones work best for you.

Question Strategies

⊘ READ CAREFULLY

Read the question and the answer choices carefully. Don't miss the question because you misread the terms. You have plenty of time to read each question thoroughly and make sure you understand what is being asked. Yet a happy medium must be attained, so don't waste too much time. You must read carefully and efficiently.

⊘ CONTEXTUAL CLUES

Look for contextual clues. If the question includes a word you are not familiar with, look at the immediate context for some indication of what the word might mean. Contextual clues can often give you all the information you need to decipher the meaning of an unfamiliar word. Even if you can't determine the meaning, you may be able to narrow down the possibilities enough to make a solid guess at the answer to the question.

⊘ PREFIXES

If you're having trouble with a word in the question or answer choices, try dissecting it. Take advantage of every clue that the word might include. Prefixes and suffixes can be a huge help. Usually, they allow you to determine a basic meaning. *Pre-* means before, *post-* means after, *pro-* is positive, *de-* is negative. From prefixes and suffixes, you can get an idea of the general meaning of the word and try to put it into context.

⊘ HEDGE WORDS

Watch out for critical hedge words, such as *likely, may, can, sometimes, often, almost, mostly, usually, generally, rarely,* and *sometimes*. Question writers insert these hedge phrases to cover every possibility. Often an answer choice will be wrong simply because it leaves no room for exception. Be on guard for answer choices that have definitive words such as *exactly* and *always*.

⊘ SWITCHBACK WORDS

Stay alert for *switchbacks*. These are the words and phrases frequently used to alert you to shifts in thought. The most common switchback words are *but, although,* and *however*. Others include *nevertheless, on the other hand, even though, while, in spite of, despite,* and *regardless of*. Switchback words are important to catch because they can change the direction of the question or an answer choice.

⊘ FACE VALUE

When in doubt, use common sense. Accept the situation in the problem at face value. Don't read too much into it. These problems will not require you to make wild assumptions. If you have to go beyond creativity and warp time or space in order to have an answer choice fit the question, then you should move on and consider the other answer choices. These are normal problems rooted in reality. The applicable relationship or explanation may not be readily apparent, but it is there for you to figure out. Use your common sense to interpret anything that isn't clear.

Answer Choice Strategies

⊘ ANSWER SELECTION

The most thorough way to pick an answer choice is to identify and eliminate wrong answers until only one is left, then confirm it is the correct answer. Sometimes an answer choice may immediately seem right, but be careful. The test writers will usually put more than one reasonable answer choice on each question, so take a second to read all of them and make sure that the other choices are not equally obvious. As long as you have time left, it is better to read every answer choice than to pick the first one that looks right without checking the others.

⊘ ANSWER CHOICE FAMILIES

An answer choice family consists of two (in rare cases, three) answer choices that are very similar in construction and cannot all be true at the same time. If you see two answer choices that are direct opposites or parallels, one of them is usually the correct answer. For instance, if one answer choice says that quantity x increases and another either says that quantity x decreases (opposite) or says that quantity y increases (parallel), then those answer choices would fall into the same family. An answer choice that doesn't match the construction of the answer choice family is more likely to be incorrect. Most questions will not have answer choice families, but when they do appear, you should be prepared to recognize them.

⊘ ELIMINATE ANSWERS

Eliminate answer choices as soon as you realize they are wrong, but make sure you consider all possibilities. If you are eliminating answer choices and realize that the last one you are left with is also wrong, don't panic. Start over and consider each choice again. There may be something you missed the first time that you will realize on the second pass.

⊘ AVOID FACT TRAPS

Don't be distracted by an answer choice that is factually true but doesn't answer the question. You are looking for the choice that answers the question. Stay focused on what the question is asking for so you don't accidentally pick an answer that is true but incorrect. Always go back to the question and make sure the answer choice you've selected actually answers the question and is not merely a true statement.

⊘ EXTREME STATEMENTS

In general, you should avoid answers that put forth extreme actions as standard practice or proclaim controversial ideas as established fact. An answer choice that states the "process should be used in certain situations, if…" is much more likely to be correct than one that states the "process should be discontinued completely." The first is a calm rational statement and doesn't even make a definitive, uncompromising stance, using a hedge word *if* to provide wiggle room, whereas the second choice is far more extreme.

11

⊘ BENCHMARK

As you read through the answer choices and you come across one that seems to answer the question well, mentally select that answer choice. This is not your final answer, but it's the one that will help you evaluate the other answer choices. The one that you selected is your benchmark or standard for judging each of the other answer choices. Every other answer choice must be compared to your benchmark. That choice is correct until proven otherwise by another answer choice beating it. If you find a better answer, then that one becomes your new benchmark. Once you've decided that no other choice answers the question as well as your benchmark, you have your final answer.

⊘ PREDICT THE ANSWER

Before you even start looking at the answer choices, it is often best to try to predict the answer. When you come up with the answer on your own, it is easier to avoid distractions and traps because you will know exactly what to look for. The right answer choice is unlikely to be word-for-word what you came up with, but it should be a close match. Even if you are confident that you have the right answer, you should still take the time to read each option before moving on.

General Strategies

⊘ TOUGH QUESTIONS

If you are stumped on a problem or it appears too hard or too difficult, don't waste time. Move on! Remember though, if you can quickly check for obviously incorrect answer choices, your chances of guessing correctly are greatly improved. Before you completely give up, at least try to knock out a couple of possible answers. Eliminate what you can and then guess at the remaining answer choices before moving on.

⊘ CHECK YOUR WORK

Since you will probably not know every term listed and the answer to every question, it is important that you get credit for the ones that you do know. Don't miss any questions through careless mistakes. If at all possible, try to take a second to look back over your answer selection and make sure you've selected the correct answer choice and haven't made a costly careless mistake (such as marking an answer choice that you didn't mean to mark). This quick double check should more than pay for itself in caught mistakes for the time it costs.

⊘ PACE YOURSELF

It's easy to be overwhelmed when you're looking at a page full of questions; your mind is confused and full of random thoughts, and the clock is ticking down faster than you would like. Calm down and maintain the pace that you have set for yourself. Especially as you get down to the last few minutes of the test, don't let the small numbers on the clock make you panic. As long as you are on track by monitoring your pace, you are guaranteed to have time for each question.

⊘ DON'T RUSH

It is very easy to make errors when you are in a hurry. Maintaining a fast pace in answering questions is pointless if it makes you miss questions that you would have gotten right otherwise. Test writers like to include distracting information and wrong answers that seem right. Taking a little extra time to avoid careless mistakes can make all the difference in your test score. Find a pace that allows you to be confident in the answers that you select.

⊘ KEEP MOVING

Panicking will not help you pass the test, so do your best to stay calm and keep moving. Taking deep breaths and going through the answer elimination steps you practiced can help to break through a stress barrier and keep your pace.

Final Notes

The combination of a solid foundation of content knowledge and the confidence that comes from practicing your plan for applying that knowledge is the key to maximizing your performance on test day. As your foundation of content knowledge is built up and strengthened, you'll find that the strategies included in this chapter become more and more effective in helping you quickly sift through the distractions and traps of the test to isolate the correct answer.

Now that you're preparing to move forward into the test content chapters of this book, be sure to keep your goal in mind. As you read, think about how you will be able to apply this information on the test. If you've already seen sample questions for the test and you have an idea of the question format and style, try to come up with questions of your own that you can answer based on what you're reading. This will give you valuable practice applying your knowledge in the same ways you can expect to on test day.

Good luck and good studying!

Data-Based Decision Making and Accountability

Problem Identification

CONSIDERATIONS REGARDING INTERVIEWS

School psychologists can get information from students' parents through questionnaires or interviews—in person or via phone and/or video. They can use both methods to get information directly from students too, although interviews have greater advantages for counseling purposes whereas questionnaires can be suitable for gathering information only. Two major differences between the two are that questionnaires are less expensive, because they do not require interviewer training; and interviews involve social interaction while questionnaires do not. If a psychologist wants to research school truancy or other sensitive subjects, questionnaires may be preferable since people are more comfortable privately completing them. Some interviewers use a set of prepared questions, called an interview schedule, with a standardized format wherein they ask each interviewee the same questions in the same sequence. Other interviews may include closed questions, which generate fixed responses; or open questions, which let respondents use their own words to express their thoughts. Psychologists can record interviews and write up transcripts of the data to analyze later. Additional considerations include using language compatible with individual interviewee age, ethnicity, social class, education level, etc.; keeping interviews short for younger children's attention spans; and sensitivity to children's vulnerability.

STRUCTURED INTERVIEWS

A structured or formal interview features questions asked in a standardized, set sequence without probing beyond the responses given or deviating from the fixed interview schedule. The questions asked are closed-ended and structured. Advantages of structured interviews include that closed-ended questions in fixed sets are more easily quantified, making it easy to test an interview for reliability—i.e., being able to replicate it and obtain the same/similar results across administrations. Another advantage is that structured interviews can be conducted fairly quickly, enabling multiple interviews within shorter time periods. Thus, a psychologist doing research as well as counseling can gather large samples of data efficiently. Larger data sample sizes make findings more representative of the sampled population, hence also more generalizable to that larger population. Disadvantages of structured interviews include their lack of flexibility: the interviewer cannot ask new/different questions spontaneously, change the order of questions, or pursue a response by probing further. Another disadvantage is that since structured interview questions are closed, the answers are quantitative and lacking in detail, preventing the psychologist from determining respondent motivations for behaviors.

UNSTRUCTURED INTERVIEWS

Unstructured or "discovery" interviews are like guided conversations rather than following a strict sequence of fixed questions like structured interviews. The interviewer may not use an interview schedule. When using one, it will include open-ended questions the interviewer can ask in any order. Skipping and/or adding questions during interviews are permitted. Advantages of unstructured interviews include greater flexibility: interviewers can change or adapt questions based on respondent answers. Rather than only the quantitative data that structured interviews generate, unstructured interviews yield qualitative data by asking open-ended questions that enable respondents to use their own words and speak in depth, facilitating the psychologist's

15

determining the interviewee's understanding of situations and behavioral motivations. Letting the interviewee guide the interview's direction and letting the interviewer request clarification and probe for deeper insights give unstructured interviews greater validity, i.e., they obtain the intended information/understandings. Weaknesses of unstructured interviews include their taking more time to conduct and to analyze the qualitative data obtained; and the cost of training and employing interviewers with rapport-building and probing skills, etc.

INTERVIEWER EFFECT

In-person interviews—and indeed, even phone or video interviews—involve social interaction between the interviewer and interviewee. Therefore, the presence of the interviewer can influence the responses that the interviewee gives. This can be problematic in both counseling and research. In counseling, the student might not represent his/her circumstances and feelings accurately due to an interviewer effect. In research, a study's results can be biased, and therefore invalid, due to an interviewer effect. Some factors that can cause interviewer effects include the interviewer's age, ethnicity, gender, social status, and body language—and how these interact with those same attributes of the interviewee. As an example, if a female interviewer were researching sexism in males, the male participants might try to represent themselves as not sexist by lying to the interviewer to flatter her, impress her, avoid offending her, and/or "look better." This would constitute an interviewer effect, biasing the results. To design interviews, the psychologist must first choose a structured vs. unstructured interview; and ten consider the gender, age, personality traits, appearance, speaking dialect/accent, and ethnicity of both interviewer and interviewee, and how these could interact.

FREQUENCY/EVENT RECORDING VS. DURATION RECORDING

Frequency/event recording counts behavior occurrences observed during specified time periods. When observation period durations vary, observers convert frequency to averaged behavior rates per minute/hour/time unit to enable comparison across periods. Event/frequency recording is best for behaviors with distinct beginnings and ends, e.g., hand-raising, out-of-seat, hitting, throwing things, etc. Persistent/continuous behaviors are harder to observe with event recording. However, if a behavior is operationally defined including duration, e.g., audible pencil-tapping for at least five seconds, which enables recording frequency, not actual number of taps. If episode durations vary and duration is important, event recording is contraindicated. Low-frequency yet serious/intense behaviors are amenable to event/frequency recording—with the caveat that missing even one occurrence destroys reliability. Duration recording, wherein observers measure both individual and cumulative length of behavioral occurrences with a stopwatch, lends itself to discrete school behaviors like thumb-sucking, social isolation, tantrums, aggressive episodes, and studying; and for interventions targeting changing behavior duration. Observers can calculate total and average episode durations. When observation session durations vary, observers compute percentages of behavior duration to session duration.

OBSERVATIONAL STRATEGIES

Latency recording measures the time elapsed after giving a direction, signal, or other stimulus before the student initiates the behavior specified. Its best use is for educator concerns with how long a student takes to respond to stimuli. It requires both stimulus and behavior to have distinct starting points. As with duration recording, the observer times latency with a stopwatch and can compute both total and average latency times. Drawbacks, as with frequency and duration recording, are complications with operationally identifying some behaviors' exact initiation and cessation; insufficient time; and/or observer availability. Time-sampling interval recording divides observation periods into equal intervals (e.g., 120 15-second intervals per 30-minute session), identifying behavior occurrence/absence within each interval. Time-sampling includes whole-interval, partial-interval, and momentary recording. Since it only yields approximate measures, it is unsuitable when behavior's precise duration/latency/frequency is important. It is the best alternative for recording moderate-to-high-frequency/steady-rate/simultaneous multiple behaviors. Whole-interval recording requires a behavior's occurrence throughout each specified time interval to score its presence. Thus, it is better for short durations/continuous behaviors. A drawback is underestimating occurrence: if a behavior occurred for 13 seconds of a 15-second interval, its absence is scored. Interventions to increase behaviors are amenable to whole-interval recording.

PARTIAL-INTERVAL RECORDING VS. WHOLE-INTERVAL RECORDING

While whole-interval recording requires a behavior to continue throughout each interval specified to score it as occurring, partial-interval recording scores a behavior if it occurs anytime during the interval—regardless of whether it starts after the interval begins/ends before the interval ends, or occurs multiple times within one interval, in which case it is still counted as one occurrence. Partial-interval recording hence is better for relatively low-rate behaviors or those whose durations are somewhat inconsistent. While whole-interval recording tends to underestimate real-time behavior occurrences, partial-interval recording tends to overestimate them. This makes it more compatible with interventions designed to decrease the frequency of undesired behaviors, whereas whole-interval recording is more compatible with interventions designed to increase the frequency of desired behaviors. Momentary time-sampling records a behavior's presence or absence during only the moment when a timed interval starts, regardless of any behavior's presence or absence observed during the remainder of that interval. Though this is based on the smallest behavioral sample, momentary time-sampling still gives the least biased estimate of a behavior's actual real-time occurrence, in contrast to the less accurate estimates of whole-interval and partial-interval time-sampling procedures.

SALIENT CHARACTERISTICS AND ADVANTAGES OF THE BOSS AND THE ADHDSOC

The Behavior Observation of Students in Schools (BOSS) is an observation code to assess student academic behavior in classrooms. Basically, it measures on-task and off-task behavior levels. While several other codes incorporate behaviors representing academic engagement, only the BOSS classifies two separate categories of engagement: (1) active engagement (answering questions, hand-raising, writing) and (2) passive engagement (listening to the teacher, looking at a worksheet). Moreover, it divides off-task behaviors into three groups: (1) motor (fidgeting, out-of-seat, playing with pencils/other objects); (2) verbal (talking to classmates against prohibitions, calling out); and (3) passive (looking out the window/around the room, not attending to the task). The BOSS additionally incorporates a teacher-directed instruction (TDI) measure. The Attention Deficit Hyperactivity Disorder School Observation Code (ADHDSOC) is for both screening and evaluating intervention effects and can be applied across classrooms, cafeterias, playgrounds/other school settings. It identifies seven classroom behavior categories: interference; motor movement; noncompliance; verbal aggression; symbolic aggression; object aggression; and off-task. Aggression scores can be individually coded or (as the authors suggest) combined into "nonphysical aggression." Cafeteria/playground categories include: appropriate social behavior; noncompliance; nonphysical aggression; verbal aggression; physical aggression. Observing 3-4 average peers for comparison is recommended.

PSYCHOLOGICAL EVALUATION REPORTS ON STUDENTS

In a psychological evaluation report, the school psychologist typically includes the reason for referral; assessment procedures used; background information; behavioral observations; test results; interpretations; conclusions; and recommendations. Background information includes a summarized history of the student's physical, social, cognitive, and academic development and a brief medical history. Typically the school psychologist obtains this information by interviewing the student, the student's parents, and the student's teachers; and by reviewing any pertinent health and school records. Such background data help to inform the school psychologist's interpretation of the student's performance, both on certain testing instruments and in school. As an example, if two students are identified with low scores on receptive language or listening skills assessments, the school psychologist will interpret these test results differently when one student has a history of chronic middle-ear infections and the other student does not. As another example, if the background information includes a reference to earlier student evaluations, the school psychologist can compare findings from his/her current evaluation to the earlier ones to identify patterns or trends in the student's behavioral and/or learning characteristics and progress.

STUDENT ASSESSMENT CONSIDERATIONS FOR SCHOOL PSYCHOLOGISTS

Rapidly growing demographic diversity in American school districts dictates greater needs to implement new standards and guidelines to enable non-discriminatory student assessment procedures. Although no single, clear means exists for evaluating bias in assessing linguistically and culturally diverse students, school psychologists need to consider every individual situation to develop suitable hypotheses to apply in assessment. They must be able to make useful decisions based on the psychometric data their assessments yield. This ability can be compromised by any personal or professional bias; hence they must eliminate any such biases. Proven by best practices, linguistically and culturally competent school psychologists communicate to students and parents in their native languages more effectively, obviating needs for interpreters. School psychologists must also consider standardized tests, which are culturally biased or loaded for assessing students from low-income and minority populations. The school psychologist must be able to recognize incorrect test score interpretations based on standardized student samples not representative of minority students, which do not reflect these students' aptitudes or abilities. Also, administering well-designed, theoretically comprehensive tests in English to ESL students is preferred over poorly-designed, limited tests in their native languages.

TYPES OF BACKGROUND INFORMATION THAT SCHOOLS MAY COLLECT ABOUT STUDENTS

Specifying any primary and secondary disabilities making a student eligible for special education services, e.g., intellectual disability and level; learning disability; autism; developmental delay; deafness/hearing impairment; blindness/visual impairment; emotional disturbance; behavior disorder, etc. informs school psychologists which assessment instruments and procedures are appropriate, and which treatment modalities and methods are likely to be most effective. Time spent in regular education and whether support is provided informs student frustration, resulting disruptive behaviors; lack of comprehension, resulting inattention; peer interaction problems, etc. Medical diagnoses inform IQ test results, activity limitations, behavior, etc. Test results and/or teacher reports of current student vision and hearing status inform student learning, achievement, and behavior levels and characteristics, as well as information about any required assistive technology/devices, which also informs their use during assessment and treatment as well as instruction. The dates and results of the most recent previous psychological assessment(s) enable school psychologists to compare these to current assessment results. Dates, scores, and grade levels of the most recent achievement tests inform the student's performance level relative to age/grade peers. Recent assessments of adaptive behavior, including instrument(s) used and results, inform student strength and need areas.

USING STUDENT BACKGROUND INFORMATION

Assessment results of student reading, writing, and visual, visual-motor and auditory processing skills inform academic needs and strengths as well as current assessment and treatment methods and modalities. For students enrolled in functional training programs and those with pre-academic

18

status, schools may provide information such as alerting to sounds; showing object permanence; showing understanding of causality; anticipating routines; identifying familiar objects/people; imitating motor and/or vocal behaviors within the student's abilities; matching objects/pictures to samples; sorting; demonstrating functional object use; the approximate number of words in the student's sight vocabulary, if any; and the length of time the student attends to a task. This information informs the school psychologist about which kinds of stimuli the student can respond to during evaluation and treatment and at what levels, and can inform functional behavior analysis of some maladaptive behaviors based on cognitive development levels. Results from formal and informal measurements of receptive and expressive communication skills, modes, and impairments inform student behavior, academic performance, peer and teacher interaction levels and characteristics, how students can communicate during assessment and treatment, and remediation of communication deficit-based maladaptive behaviors.

SCREENING AND RESPONSE TO INTERVENTION (RtI)

Response to Intervention (RtI) is a framework for a multi-level preventative system to promote maximal student learning and achievement and prevent or decrease student problem behaviors. This system incorporates assessment and intervention. It includes screening; data-based decision-making; and progress monitoring as well as prevention to improve student outcomes. When examining screening tools, psychologists should look for evidence of their validity and reliability. Validity is whether the screener tests what it is supposed to test; reliability is whether its results are consistent across administrations. Classification accuracy is how well a screening tool can classify students accurately into categories of at-risk or not at-risk for reading/math disabilities. Generalizability is how well a screening tool's results with one population can be applied to different population. Studies using a screening instrument with larger, more representative samples indicate that the screening instrument has greater generalizability.

TYPES OF RELIABILITY IN SCREENING TOOLS

Reliability indicates an instrument's consistent results across administrations. Test-Retest Reliability compares screening test scores obtained during administration at two different times, and thus also measures the extent of time-sampling error. Parallel-Forms, Equivalent-Forms, or Alternate-Forms Reliability compares the results of two equivalent forms of a screening tool that measures the same quantity or attribute, and thus also measures the tool's extent of item-sampling error. Split-Half Reliability compares two halves of a screening test to see how well they compare to one another, and hence measures the test's amount of internal consistency error. Split-Half Reliability is a type of Internal Consistency Reliability. Interrater Reliability is an important type of reliability to evaluate if the psychologist wants multiple different trained raters, scorers, judges, or observers to be able to administer the same screening tool and obtain similar results. It compares results of the same screening instrument across different administrators. Thus it measures the instrument's amount of observer differences error.

TYPES OF VALIDITY TO EVALUATE IN SCREENING TOOLS

Validity is how well an instrument measures what it is meant to measure. Content validity is how well a test represents the domain addressed; e.g., measures everything it is intended to measure about reading/math, etc. Criterion validity is how much a test's results correspond to a specific criterion measurement; e.g., whether a screening tool can predict overall reading proficiency as measured by a state standardized reading test or national/global computerized assessment, like the MAP (Measures of Academic Progress) for reading from Northwest Evaluation Association (NWEA), used by some state education departments. Construct validity is how well an instrument reflects the construct it is intended to measure; it includes aspects of both content and criterion validity and is necessary when no body of content or criterion is adequate for defining the construct measured.

Face validity, though many reject it as an official validity evidence source, can be a significant factor when considering which screening tools to use with certain teachers, grades, and schools. For example, even if a screener does not directly test everything a teacher has taught about reading/math, a teacher might consider whether it can predict student risk for poor performance on a state/national standardized test.

INTERPRETATIONS AND EXPLANATIONS OF STUDENT SCREENING AND TEST SCORES

To help teachers and parents (and older students) understand screening and other test scores, school psychologists can refer to target scores, such as criterion-referenced and norm-referenced targets. For example, with criterion-referenced measures, the school psychologist can use benchmark performance indicated in reading or math probes, such as those from AIMSweb (Pearson, 2015) a Response to Intervention (RtI) assessment system, or Northwest Evaluation Association (NWEA)'s Measures of Academic Progress (MAP) reading or math tests, to predict the probability of student proficiency on state reading or math tests. With norm-referenced targets, the school psychologist can refer to both local and national norms. For example, regardless of student performance in a given school during a given year, identifying students below the 25th percentile compared to local norms will always yield 25% of students. Identifying students below the 25th percentile compared to national norms may yield 25%, more, or less of students depending on performance in the given school during a given year. School psychologists can explain/refer to the normal distribution to identify and explain such common scores as IQ and achievement test subscale scores, standard scores, and percentile ranks; behavior rating scales T-scores; and some state test stanine scores.

Assessment and Problem Analysis

SPEARMAN'S "G FACTOR" THEORY OF INTELLIGENCE

Charles Spearman (1863-1945), a British psychologist, was among the early pioneers of research into intelligence testing. Spearman conducted an examination of multiple tests being used at the time to assess mental ability. He used factor analysis, a statistical technique, to compare these tests and the scores that the same individuals would receive on the different test instruments. From his factor analysis, Spearman came to the conclusion that individuals tended to receive very similar scores on different tests. Individuals who scored poorly on one intelligence measure usually scored equally poorly on the other intelligence measures, and people who achieved good performance on one test typically performed equally well on the other tests. Because of this similarity, Spearman proposed that intelligence was a generalized cognitive ability, which he dubbed *g* (or the "g factor" as some have called it), and that this general intelligence could be quantitatively measured and expressed in numerical terms.

THURSTONE'S PRIMARY MENTAL ABILITIES THEORY OF INTELLIGENCE

Louis Thurstone (1887-1955), an American psychologist who was roughly contemporary with British psychologist Charles Spearman (1863-1945), viewed intelligence differently from Spearman, who proposed that intelligence consisted of *g*, which he defined as a general cognitive ability that could be measured and represented numerically. Rather than seeing intelligence as one single general capacity, Thurstone identified seven different skills that he described as "primary metal abilities." These seven primary mental abilities, which Thurstone proposed were the components of intelligence, were as follow: verbal comprehension (understanding spoken and written language); reasoning (thinking logically); perceptual speed (how quickly an individual registers and interprets sensory input); numerical ability (skill in understanding and performing mathematical computations); word fluency (ability to produce connected speech smoothly at normal speeds); associative memory (capacity for recalling information related to stimuli presented); and spatial visualization (ability to form mental imagery related to the location, position, organization, and movement of objects in space).

GARDNER'S THEORY OF MULTIPLE INTELLIGENCES

American developmental psychologist Howard Gardner (b. 1943) departed from earlier theories of intelligence by not basing his idea of intelligence on analyzing scores from standardized tests as other theorists had commonly done. Gardner found that expressing human intelligence solely through numerical measures was not an accurate or complete representation of an individual's cognitive skills. Instead, Gardner proposed that people have eight distinct, different intelligences, and that people have higher or lower degrees of each. Gardner defined (1) Visual-spatial intelligence, i.e., skills with visual images and objects in space; (2) Verbal-linguistic intelligence, i.e., skills with words and spoken/written language; (3) Bodily-kinesthetic intelligence, i.e., skills with physical movement; (4) Logical-mathematical intelligence, i.e., skills with logical structures and numbers; (5) Interpersonal intelligence, i.e., skills in interacting with other people; (6) Intrapersonal intelligence, i.e., skills in self-knowledge, introspection, metacognition, and independence; (7) Musical intelligence, i.e., skills with musical melodic, harmonic, and rhythmic forms, listening, appreciation, composition, and expression; and (8) Naturalistic intelligence, i.e., skills for appreciating, understanding, and interacting with the natural world. Gardner found that if educators identified individual students' highest intelligence(s), they could optimize their learning by using corresponding instructional modalities.

STERNBERG'S THEORY OF INTELLIGENCE

American psychologist Robert Sternberg (b. 1949), who has conducted research into creativity and proposed a theory of learning styles and a "Triangular" theory of love, is also well-known for his Triarchic theory of intelligence. Sternberg found that "successfully intelligent" individuals determine their strengths and weaknesses and how to capitalize on the strengths and remediate or compensate for the weaknesses. He also found that striking a balance among a "triarchy of abilities," as well as developing them all further, contributed to intelligent people's success. He defined intelligence as "mental activity directed toward purposive adaptation to, selection and shaping of, real-world environments relevant to one's life." Though he agreed with Howard Gardner and disagreed with Charles Spearman that intelligence encompasses much more than one general capacity, he found that some of Gardner's eight intelligences were better characterized as individual talents. Sternberg's three factors of "successful intelligence" are: Analytical intelligence, i.e., problem-solving skills; creative intelligence, i.e., applying past experiences and current skills to address new situations; and practical intelligence, i.e., the capacity for adapting to environmental changes.

ACADEMIC ACHIEVEMENT TESTS

Tests of academic achievement measure individual student's specific academic skills and compare them to the skills of other, similar students at the same age or grade levels as indicated by their scores on the same standardized achievement test. Academic achievement tests not only assess students' broader skills in reading, writing, oral language, and math; but also measure more specific components of these domains. For example, within the domain of reading, an achievement test will typically include a subscale or task to measure reading comprehension; one to measure reading fluency; one to measure recognition of sight words; and one to measure word decoding abilities. Within the domain of writing, most achievement tests typically include subscales or tasks to measure writing fluency; spelling; and skills for expressing oneself in written language. Within the domain of mathematics, typical achievement tests include tasks or subscales to measure mathematical computation skills, mathematical fluency, and mathematical reasoning abilities.

ACADEMIC ACHIEVEMENT TESTS VS. CLASSROOM ASSESSMENTS

Whereas classroom assessments are designed to measure how well a student has acquired a specific skill that the teacher has just taught, academic achievement tests measure a student's more general, basic academic skills. These tests are typically norm-referenced, meaning they compare an individual student's scores to the average scores of other students the same age or in the same grade, selected as a sample representative of the identified population. For example, the scores attained on an achievement test by a student who just turned 10 will be compared to the average scores of students who also just turned 10 in the normative sample. This provides a measure of the student's skill levels relative to "typical" students his/her age. On most standardized academic achievement tests, the "Average" range of scores that most students attain are typically between 90 and 109, with 100 being the mean or average. The further a student score deviates from the mean, the less typical it is. In regular education classrooms, most students score in the Average range, the Low Average range of 80-89, or the High Average range of 110-119.

STUDENT SCORES ON ACADEMIC ACHIEVEMENT TESTS AND COGNITIVE ABILITY TESTS

While cognitive assessments yield an overall IQ score as well as subscale scores measuring different processing skills (e.g., processing speed, working memory, verbal ability and nonverbal ability on the Wechsler Intelligence Scale for Children or WISC); academic achievement tests do not measure cognitive ability but rather basic academic skills in domains like reading, writing, oral language, and mathematics skills. Within these areas, academic achievement tests also contain subscales measuring more specific components of each domain, e.g., reading comprehension, fluency, sight word recognition and word decoding within the reading domain; spelling, fluency, and self-expression within the writing domain; and computations, fluency, and reasoning within the mathematics domain. Most students typically attain similar cognitive ability and academic achievement test scores. If achievement scores are much lower than cognitive scores, one factor that can cause this discrepancy is a learning disability, which does not impair intelligence but does impair certain processing abilities. Additional factors that can cause discrepancies include emotional disturbances, mental disorders, behavior disorders, family dysfunction, and other environmental factors interfering with learning and/or performance.

MOST COMMONLY USED TESTS OF ACADEMIC ACHIEVEMENT

The Wechsler Individual Achievement Test (WIAT), Woodcock-Johnson Tests of Achievement (WJ), and Kaufman Test of Educational Achievement (KTEA) are among the most commonly administered academic achievement tests. The only nationwide academic achievement test, the National Assessment of Educational Progress (NAEP) from the U.S. Department of Education (ED)'s National Center for Education Statistics (NCES), tests student reading, math, science, civics, arts, writing, economics, U.S. history, and geography performance, comparing it to representative nationwide student sample norms. The National Assessment Governing Board (NAGB), appointed by the U.S. Secretary of Education following a national search, rating, and nomination process, develops and administers these tests and the procedures for evaluating and reporting their results. The NAEP reports test data by urban areas and/or overall scores, computed from administrations to fourth-grade, eighth-grade and twelfth-grade students at "critical" academic achievement levels. To receive federal funding, the U.S. government requires public schools to administer standardized achievement tests; each state has its own, evaluating vocabulary, reading comprehension, word analysis, listening skills, language, math, and social studies by grade levels.

WOODCOCK-JOHNSON TESTS OF ACHIEVEMENT, WECHSLER INTELLIGENCE SCALES FOR CHILDREN

Regarding content features of independent composite scores on measures of lower-order cognitive skills, the Woodcock-Johnson (WJ) includes Long-Term Retrieval, i.e., recalling information stored in long-term memory; and Short-Term Memory, i.e., ability to retain information temporarily. The WISC has a subscale in this category that tests Working Memory, i.e., the ability to manipulate information temporarily retained in short-term memory. Regarding how these tests cover the underlying "Broad" and "Narrow Cognitive Abilities" as defined by the Cattell-Horn-Carroll (CHC) theory of cognitive abilities: Under the broad cognitive factor of Long-Term Storage and Retrieval, the WJ Visual-Auditory Learning and Visual-Auditory Learning-Delayed tests measure the primary narrow ability of associative memory; the Retrieval Fluency test measures ideational fluency. Under Visual Processing, the Picture Recognition test measures visual memory. Under Short-Term Memory, the Numbers Reversed and Auditory Working Memory tests measure working memory and memory span; Memory for Words tests memory span. Under Short-Term Memory, the WISC's Digit Span subscale tests memory span; Letter-Number Sequencing tests working memory and memory span; and Sentences tests memory span (as well as language development).

STANDARDIZED MEASURES OF EXECUTIVE FUNCTION (EF) FOR USE IN SCHOOLS

The Behavior Rating Inventory of Executive Function (BRIEF) tests ages 5-18, has a preschool form, and includes teacher and parent versions. Scale scores for Metacognition include planning/organizing, working memory, initiation, materials organization and monitoring. Behavior regulation index scores and global score include emotional control, shifting, and inhibition scales. The Child Behavior Checklist (CBCL)-Teacher Report Form generally assesses emotional/social attentional functioning. The Neuropsychological Assessment (NEPSY), individually administered to ages 3-4 and 5-16, tests Executive Functioning/Attention, Sensorimotor Functioning, Visual-Spatial Processing, Social Perception, Memory and Learning, and Language. The Cognitive Assessment System assesses planning and attention using six subtests. The Children's Category Test (CCT) for ages 6-16 nonverbally evaluates categorization and mental flexibility; can be combined with IQ and achievement tests, administered during the delayed recall section of the California Verbal Learning Test®-Children's Version (CVLT®-C) or independently; meets federal requirements for evaluating students with suspected TBIs; and is compatible with color vision deficits and severe motor disabilities. Standardized with a national normative sample and co-normed with the CVLT-C, CCT is based on the Halstead-Reitan Category Test for Children.

FORMAL MEASURES OF STUDENT EXECUTIVE FUNCTION (EF)

The WISC-IV Advanced Clinical Interpretation can research/screen EF via four subtests, based on 1 WISC-IV subtest from each modality: Comprehension Multiple Choice, Elithorn Mazes, Spatial Span Forward, Cancellation Random, with normative and clinical EF group research information. In classrooms, assess student emotional self-regulation during boring/demanding tasks; problem-solving strategies; response/idea perseveration; task/goal persistence; task/idea flexibility in problem-solving; attention maintenance and span; memory for specific words/previous learning; working memory of steps/sequences/directions/information for problem-solving; organization; time management; theory of mind/perspective-taking; and task latency/initiation. Observe: having materials ready to begin lessons; starting/stopping work when classmates do; switching between/among tasks; acknowledging equal importance of peer feelings/thoughts with one's own. Writing difficulties: Planning how writing fits on a page; motor control; automatic writing; content organization; idea retrieval and use; thought manipulation; execution. Math difficulties: Progress monitoring; self-correction; idea maintenance, strategy organization, step retrieval; information organization, storage, retrieval and step execution in learning/applying memorized information.

23

Reading difficulties: Planning, retrieval, decoding; fluency; comprehension and application of longer text; comprehension strategies; inferring. Study skills difficulties: Organizing backpacks, desks; timely homework completion and submission; obtaining information needed from reading/listening; correct assignment interpretation; classroom study strategies.

ASSESSMENT INSTRUMENTS FOR EVALUATING STUDENT PHONEMIC AWARENESS

The Recognizing Rhyme Assessment tests whether children can identify rhyming words (e.g., cat-fat) vs. non-rhyming (e.g., cat-mop). Isolating Beginning Sounds and Isolating Final Sounds tests identifying word-initial and word-final phonemes. The Phoneme Blending Assessment tests combining phonemes spoken separately (e.g., /d/, /ɔ/, /g/ = dog). The Yopp-Singer Test of Phonemic Segmentation assesses separating spoken words into their individual phonemes. The Phonological Awareness and Literacy Screening (PALS) includes PALS-PreK; PALS-K with a rhyming subtest, beginning sound-picture sorting, concept of work testing print word awareness level; spelling involving oral word segmentation and phoneme-letter matching. PALS 1-3 tests spelling; oral phoneme blending; sound-to-letter matching. The standardized Phonological Awareness Test (PAT) for grades K-4/ages 5-9 subtests include discriminating and producing rhymes; segmenting phonemes, syllables, sentences; isolating word-initial/word-medial/word-final phonemes; deleting/manipulating phonemes, syllables, root words in words/compound words; substituting phonemes in words to form new words with manipulatives; blending phonemes and syllables to form words; knowing graphemes and sound-letter correspondence with consonants, vowels, consonant blends, consonant digraphs, r-controlled vowels, vowel digraphs, diphthongs; decoding sound-letter correspondence to blend phonemes into nonsense words; and (optional) invented spelling: writing dictated words, testing encoding skills.

ADAPTIVE VS. MALADAPTIVE BEHAVIORS

Adaptive behaviors involve skills for adapting to the environment through everyday living activities like talking, walking, dressing, meal preparation, house cleaning, going to school or work, etc. Because they are mainly developmental, adaptive behaviors can be measured using age equivalents. Maladaptive behaviors, which interfere with everyday activities and independent living, are not as developmental, are expressed variably across settings and times, and do not steadily increase or decrease with age; however, they can also be reliably measured. The Scales of Independent Behavior-Revised (SIB-R) contains several distinctive features. In addition to an assessment of adaptive behaviors, it includes a scale for behavior problems. It also yields a unique score that combines maladaptive and adaptive behaviors to reflect the individual's overall independence. It also includes norms for age groups ranging from three months to 80+ years old. Assessors can administer the SIB as either a questionnaire or a carefully structured interview. For use as a structured interview, special materials are provided to assist in the process. It includes a short form, a short form for children, and an adapted short form for blind examinees.

VINELAND ADAPTIVE BEHAVIOR SCALES (VABS)

Originally the Vineland Social Maturity Scale, the revised VABS has high-quality psychometrics, norms for ages up to 18 years, and a reputable history. Semi-structured interviews—one edition with 577 items, another with 297—collect personal and social skills information. Both contain an optional Maladaptive Behavior Domain for children aged 5-18 and a Motor Skills Domain for children younger than 6 years. The VABS Manual requires administration by a psychologist/social worker/other professional with training and a graduate degree in interviewing techniques. While assessment items are well-organized and straightforward, the interviewing process is somewhat time-intensive and complicated. Individual item scoring criteria are included. Administrators are directed never to read items to/let examinees read items, but ask general questions, with additional probes as needed. The maladaptive behavior section lists 27 minor behaviors (e.g., "sucks thumb/fingers") and nine more serious ones, not normed for respondents with disabilities, which can be described "severe"/"moderate" and scored by frequency. The VABS Classroom form for ages 3-12, a questionnaire booklet which teachers complete directly, does not require a graduate degree or interviewing training. It has no maladaptive behavior section. Its standard error of measurement is smaller than for the interview forms.

AAIDD Adaptive Behavior Scale

The American Association for Intellectual and Developmental Disability (AAIDD, formerly AAMR), the oldest professional organization in the United States dedicated to the area of intellectual disability, developed the AAIDD Adaptive Behavior Scale (ABS). Two versions of this adaptive behavior scale are available: one is for School settings, and the other is for Residential and Community Settings. In both forms, the ways in which an individual copes with the natural and social demands of his/her environment are evaluated. The adaptive behavior domains in the AAIDD ABS include two item types: yes/no items, and items for which the examiner circles the highest level. Some items can be a bit confusing by their negative wording; e.g., the item phrased as "Does not use a napkin" is rated "No" if the child does use a napkin. Although ratings for maladaptive behavior items are "never," "occasionally," or "frequently," they do not include any comparative severity indices. For example, items as different as "Chokes others" and "Blames own mistakes on others" are given equal weight. Several AAIDD ABS domains are not unidimensional; for example, in the Physical Development Domain, items on vision, hearing, walking, running, balance, and arm-hand use are all scored collectively, making interpretation difficult.

ICAP as a Standardized Measure of Adaptive and Maladaptive Behaviors

The Inventory for Client and Agency Planning (ICAP), a 16-page booklet, not only measures adaptive and maladaptive behaviors; in addition, it collects a concise yet comprehensive body of information that includes the demographic characteristics of the examinee; the diagnoses the examinee has received; the services that the individual needs; the services that the individual has received; and the social and leisure activities in which the individual has taken part. The ICAP incorporates scoring and database software, which prints reports and can store and maintain historical and current information for as many as 10,000 individuals. The sections on adaptive and maladaptive behavior in the ICAP consist of items selected from the Scales of Independent Behavior-Revised (SIB-R), including norms for ages from infancy through adulthood. The ICAP also provides a Service Score the same as the SIB does. This score is a combination of adaptive and maladaptive behavior that indicates the individual's overall need for supervision, training, and/or care. Although the ICAP's shorter length compared to the SIB makes it slightly less reliable, its reliability compared to other tests' is nevertheless excellent.

Evaluating Social and Emotional Skills and Language

The Social Emotional Evaluation® (SEE) for ages 6.0-12.11 is a norm-referenced test with high validity and test-retest reliability and inter-rater reliability. Its standardization samples comprise more than 800 children with characteristics closely resembling the most recently available U.S. Census Bureau data. It assesses higher-level language and social skills students need for successful everyday interactions in the home, school, and community. Identifying the social and emotional language needs of students with autism spectrum disorders, attention deficit disorders, learning disabilities, and emotional disorders is described as an ideal use of SEE. It presents common emotional responses and typical social situations that students in elementary and middle school often experience. The Teacher/Parent Questionnaire is a quick screener to show whether confirming test results or administering the full evaluation is necessary. The accompanying audio CD ensures consistent administration of auditory stimuli in the third and fourth subtests. Five subtests, all using pictures, are: Recalling Facial Expressions; Identifying Common Emotions;

Recognizing Emotional Reactions; Understanding Social Gaffes (with audio); and Understanding Conflicting Messages (with audio), including lies, sarcasm, and humor. The online Qualitative Response Analyzer calculates parent/caregiver and educator/specialist questionnaire percentages, saving time; and produces qualitative reports to help set treatment goals.

SCREENING INSTRUMENTS FOR SOCIAL-EMOTIONAL DEVELOPMENT

The Ages & Stages Questionnaires: Social-Emotional (ASQ:SE) is an instrument completed via parental reporting. It can be used for children from infancy to 5 years old and is available in multiple languages. It does not require direct observations at the time of the screening. The Brief Infant Toddler Social Emotional Assessment (BITSEA), like the ASQ:SE, is not an observational instrument but a screening instrument completed by parental report. It cannot be used with infants younger than one year of age, but does apply to toddlers aged 1-3 years old. However, it is not for use with preschoolers from 3-5 years of age. The BITSEA is available in multiple languages. The Pediatric Symptom Checklist (PSC), like the ASQ:SE and the BITSEA, is a parental report instrument that does not require observations at the time of screening. It is not designed for use with infants below one year of age or toddlers aged 1-3 years old. It can be used with four-year-old preschoolers, and also with older children or students up to 18 years old. The PSC is also available in multiple language formats.

EMOTIONAL INTELLIGENCE (EI)

EI, or EQ as psychologist Daniel Goleman dubbed it (Goleman co-authored the most widely used and validated behavioral test of emotional and social intelligence, the Emotional and Social Competency Inventory or ESCI), is a rather specific competence involving an individual's connection of knowledge processes to emotional processes. It is thus distinct from emotions, emotional traits, emotional styles, and traditional intelligence assessments that are based on general cognitive or mental ability, i.e., IQ. EI involves being able to monitor emotions in oneself and others; discriminate among various emotions; and apply this information to guide one's thoughts and behaviors. EI skills can be classified into five domains: (1) Self-awareness – observing oneself and identifying an emotion as it occurs. (2) Emotional management – understanding what underlies an emotion; finding ways to cope with anxiety, fear, sadness, and anger; and handling feelings to make them appropriate. (3) Self-motivation – controlling impulses; delaying gratification; channeling feelings to help meet goals; emotional self-control. (4) Empathy – appreciating individual differences in how people feel about things; taking others' perspectives; sensitivity to others' concerns and feelings. (5) Handling relationships – social competence, social skills, and managing others' emotions.

EVALUATING AND SELECTING TESTS TO ASSESS EMOTIONAL INTELLIGENCE (EI OR EQ)

School psychologists should consider an instrument's validity. Research has found that ability-based EI tests help in predicting performance, especially when it depends on positive interpersonal interactions. Face validity can be evaluated via examinee reactions; for example, tests often contain items wherein individuals must identify emotions from viewing photos of people's facial expressions. The school psychologist should know whether an EI/EQ test can be administered electronically, using paper and pencil, or both/either. It can be informative and interesting to consider subgroup differences; for example, some research evidence suggests that females have more skill in reading facial expressions for the emotions they express than males, and thus tend to score better than males on EI/EQ measures. Development costs are a consideration: typically it costs much more to develop a customized EI/EQ test than it does to purchase a published one that is proven valid and reliable. In general, administration of EI/EQ tests is inexpensive as they typically do not require trained/skilled administrators or many resources to administer them. Since interpersonal skills are necessary to social success in school and work, EI testing has high utility and can be used anywhere cooperation, teamwork, and social interaction are important.

FUNCTIONAL BEHAVIOR ASSESSMENT (FBA)

According to leading psychological and behavioral experts, all behaviors have a purpose or function. Individuals do not exhibit behaviors randomly or for no reason. As some psychologists have described it, any behavior has the purpose or function of either getting something (reward/positive reinforcement) or getting away from something (escape, avoidance or relief/negative reinforcement). For example, an individual may engage in a behavior to get basic needs met, e.g., for food, liquid, shelter, rest, comfort, etc.; get attention the individual desires/needs; get a desired object; or get away from loud noises, bright lights, strong odors; uncomfortable temperatures, rooms, or seats; crowds/too many people, too much attention/undesired kinds of attention, school/work task demands, boring activities/settings, unstimulating situations, or overstimulating ones. Individuals with autism spectrum disorders frequently have difficulty with excessive sensory stimulation, for example. It is important to analyze the functions of maladaptive behaviors to design interventions that substitute more adaptive replacement behaviors; and analyze the functions of adaptive behaviors to identify replacement behaviors that motivate the individual. Also, the IDEA mandates FBA by IEP teams in response to school disciplinary actions before developing behavior intervention plans.

CONDUCTING A FUNCTIONAL BEHAVIOR ANALYSIS (FBA)

Multiple assessment methods and sources are required for FBA; a single information source usually does not yield accurate enough information, especially since the same behavior can serve multiple functions. For instance, making inappropriate comments during lessons/lectures can help a student avoid having the teacher call on him/her in some situations, and garner classmates' attention in others. In addition to observable behaviors, cognitive and affective states that cannot be directly observed outwardly by others can be behavioral antecedents/triggers. Determining these requires indirect assessment, e.g., interviewing the student. For example, if receiving a worksheet triggers a tantrum, the cause may not be the worksheet but the student's expectation of ridicule or failure based on his/her not knowing/understanding what is required. Psychologists/IEP team members should consider if the behavior is related to a skill deficit, i.e., its function is to avoid/escape tasks requiring the deficient skill(s). FBA can determine whether the student understands situational behavior expectations; understands a behavior is unacceptable, or merely does it out of habit; can control the behavior or requires support; and has the skills needed to perform new, expected behaviors.

PERFORMANCE DEFICITS VS. SKILL DEFICITS IN MALADAPTIVE BEHAVIORS

In conducting FBA, the school psychologist and other IEP team members can determine if a student engages in a maladaptive behavior because of some skill deficit, i.e., s/he cannot perform certain tasks and thus engages in the behavior to avoid or escape them. FBA can also determine a performance deficit, i.e., the student possesses the skill but does not apply it consistently across all settings or situations. The student may not be sure about the appropriateness of certain behaviors in different situations. For example, yelling, screaming, and applauding loudly are accepted behaviors at football games and other sports events; but the student may not realize these are usually not acceptable during classroom academic games. The school psychologist and other IEP team members should also analyze whether the student gets any value (i.e., reward) from engaging in appropriate behaviors; whether certain environmental or social conditions are related to the problem behavior, e.g., the student is trying to avoid or escape demanding or boring tasks; and/or whether the student finds certain expectations, rules, or routines irrelevant.

Indirect and Direct Assessment to Collect Data for FBA

Indirect assessment depends primarily on gathering information from students, teachers, parents, and other adults responsible for the student through structured interviews. Examples of questions that to ask include: Settings where the informant observes the problem behavior; any settings wherein the behavior is absent; who is there when the behavior happens; which interactions, activities, and/or events occur just before the behavior (antecedents); what kinds of things typically happen immediately following the behavior (consequences); and whether the informant can think of a more acceptable behavior to replace the problem behavior. The school psychologist can also use a less structured interview with the student to identify his/her perceptions and motivations; e.g., what the student was thinking just before the behavior; how an assignment/other trigger/antecedent made the student feel; how the teacher expects the student to contribute in class; and what usually happens after the behavior. Direct assessment entails observing and recording the behavior's situational antecedents and consequences. In data analysis, the IEP team analyzes and compares information collected to identify patterns, e.g., the student hits somebody whenever s/he does not get his/her way. The hypothesis statement predicts general antecedent conditions for the behavior and likely maintaining consequences.

Student Portfolio Contents That May Be Used in Portfolio Assessment

Student portfolios can contain writing samples with varying content, genres, and styles; lab reports of science experiments; written journals; audio or video recordings of musical, dance, or gymnastics performances; art works; physical constructions and other projects; photographs; interview transcripts; conference transcripts; quizzes; tests; observations; and reflections. Teachers should use explicit instruction to make clear to students all policies or principles guiding what they can or cannot include in their portfolios. Teachers must provide clear, unambiguous evaluation criteria. Specific assignment rubrics should clearly define entry goals, requirements, and prohibitions. Comprehensive rubrics should include structured information regarding required components; organization; and content and length of reflections and entries. The greater a rubric's comprehensiveness and precision is, the more objective the assessment will be. Teachers must clarify any new vocabulary, and ensure mutual teacher-student understanding of the task's theoretical foundations, in advance. Comprehensive portfolio assessment includes reflection, which enables students to analyze their accomplishments, compare them to class standards, and evaluate their products; identify their needs and growth; and develop/use metacognition to ascertain how they know what they know about their learning and hence, also take responsibility for it.

Types of Student Portfolios Used for Portfolio Assessment and Their Purposes

Showcase portfolios highlight a student's best products within a given course/time period. As examples, in a business class, a showcase portfolio might contain a resume, a marketing project, sample business letters, and a cooperative learning project showing the student's teamwork skills. In an English composition class, it might contain a poem, a short story, an essay, a biographical piece, and/or a literary analysis to provide the best examples of various writing genres. Students can frequently choose their best products. Process portfolios emphasize learning processes more than end products. For example, in composition class, the student might include the outline, first draft, teacher and peer feedback, early revisions, and an edited final draft of a paper to show various stages of the process. Evaluation portfolios contain course evaluations and student accomplishments/learning/performance relative to pre-established goals/criteria. Tests, quizzes, written problem solution explanations might be found in a math evaluation portfolio. Lab experiments, photos/artifacts from science projects, and research reports in addition to tests and quizzes might be in a science evaluation portfolio. These can show student difficulties as well as best work. Online/e-portfolios can be any of the above or a combination, with all contents accessible online.

BENEFITS OF PORTFOLIO ASSESSMENT AS AN EVALUATION METHOD

Students frequently receive grades for projects/papers without understanding what they need to do to improve their work. Portfolio assessment can establish a student-teacher dialogue concerning their individualized work and products. By combining such conferencing with required student reflections, teachers can clarify the assessment and corresponding improvement actions for students. This 1:1 interaction also benefits both students afraid/shy about initiating conversations with teachers, and students with verbal learning styles who like discussing their work and may understand its effective/ineffective elements better through verbal interchanges. Portfolio assessments raise student awareness of learning strategies and processes. They involve students in the evaluation process; yield more individualized assessment; can show a wide range of accomplishments; and can be used together with norm-referenced/standardized tests/other required assessments. When students select portfolio contents collaboratively, they develop decision-making and goal-setting skills regarding what they achieved and what to improve, which can benefit them in many life activities. Portfolio assessments offer authentic means to demonstrate skills and accomplishments; require organization, decision-making, and metacognition in real-life experiences; and when carefully, thoughtfully planned by teachers, can develop positive student attitudes toward achievement and learning.

PERFORMANCE TASKS INVOLVING GRAPHING TO INFORM PERFORMANCE-BASED ASSESSMENT

K-2: The teacher demonstrates placing 10 caterpillars in a box, folding the top over at one end to darken it, putting a flashlight at the other end. The teacher has the students observe whether the caterpillars move toward the dark or the light more and graph the number of each. The teacher informs the class their graphs will be displayed at the upcoming Open House. Grades 3-5: The teacher assigns students specified times to observe and count vehicles passing through a nearby intersection for a specific length of time and graph vehicle numbers at certain times of day, telling the class the police department is considering assigning a crossing guard/installing a traffic light at this intersection, and they need the students' help from their graphs. The teacher informs students the Chief of Police will receive copies of the best graphs. Middle/High School: The teacher gives students a copy of a speeding ticket indicating how the fine was assessed; asks students how their state determines speeding fines; and assigns them to graph speeding fine costs to local teenagers, telling them excellent graphs will be displayed in the Driver Education classroom(s).

ASSUMPTIONS, PROCEDURES, AND CHARACTERISTICS OF CURRICULUM-BASED ASSESSMENT

According to some experts, CBA refers to any measurement that informs instructional decisions by collecting information based on directly observing and documenting a student's performance with the local curriculum. Direct assessment of academic skills is also an expert description of the CBA process. Among various models of CBA, they all commonly share the assumption that educators should test what they teach. Another commonly shared assumption of CBA is that to know whether students are making progress, educators must observe and count their curriculum-related school behaviors, and gather such data as frequently as possible in order to ascertain timely whether a student is falling behind or progressing well. Traditional CBA procedures have typically placed emphasis on repeatedly conducting direct assessments of the academic behaviors that the educators are targeting. In each academic subject or area, educators develop probes. These may be samples of math items from the curriculum; short spelling lists; brief reading passages, etc. Teachers develop these probes from the materials and/or textbooks that comprise the curriculum and use them to gather student performance data. Thus CBA affords a structured means to evaluate how well students perform with teacher-assigned materials.

EXPERT DESCRIPTIONS OF CURRICULUM-BASED ASSESSMENT (CBA) PROCEDURES

Regardless of the specific curriculum type and the individual CBA model, some experts describe the general construction of a CBA as following a common type of procedure. The educator first either selects sample items from the curriculum or creates items that match with the curriculum. Then s/he organizes these items in order of difficulty and compiles them into a single test. The educator administers this test on Day 1 of the assessment. The educator then constructs two or more forms of the same test. These should contain items similar to those in the first test, and should follow the difficulty sequence identical to that of the first test. The educator administers these additional test forms on Days 2 and 3 of the assessment. Testing with at least three different forms on three separate occasions is strongly advised to control for the inconsistent responses that are particularly characteristic of special education students. Educators test students across several curriculum levels when administering CBA. Student responses are assessed not only for accuracy but also for proficiency or speed. Educators develop assessment forms to record student responses. Classroom teachers, special education teachers, and learning specialists/consulting teachers should collaborate to establish performance criteria for acceptable mastery levels.

ESTABLISHING CRITERIA FOR STUDENT CURRICULUM MASTERY

A helpful procedure to establish criteria for student mastery of the curriculum in CBA, particularly for classes that combine regular education students with mainstreamed special education students, is to conduct normative sampling. In this procedure, the educator takes samples from the mainstreamed class of acceptable student performance and average student performance. Based on these samples, the educator decides what should be designated as the absolute criteria for mastery of the curriculum. In classes that mainstream special education students, which are continuing to become more prevalent, it is not unusual for a student to demonstrate performance levels that are so far beneath the designated levels of acceptable performance that s/he will not be able to satisfy the established performance criteria within the school year or term. In these cases, educators can implement changing criterion designs. For example, the criteria for mastery would reflect the class average, but could then be lowered for subsequently instructing these students; and then would be gradually increased until these students attain the changed class average. After completing this social validation and establishing mastery criteria, educators administer CBA to individual students or student groups.

CHARACTERIZATION OF THE CURRICULUM-BASED ASSESSMENT (CBA) APPROACH

Some educational experts characterize CBA as an approach to connecting assessment and instruction. They identify the purposes of CBA as being: (1) to determine student eligibility for special education and related services; (2) to develop goals for the instruction of each student; and (3) to evaluate the progress a student is making in the curriculum. Teachers and other professionals can specify instructional goals on the basis of student performance on a CBA instrument. Since assessment and instruction are so closely related, teachers can conducts CBAs often as a means of ascertaining whether they need to make any changes to the curriculum or their instructional methods. Essential components of CBA include collecting data, interpreting the data collected, and designing interventions based on the data and interpretations. CBA is also known as continuous curriculum measurement; curriculum-embedded measurement; curriculum-referenced measurement; frequent measurement; and therapeutic measurement. Advantages that make CBA useful include its connection of instruction to curriculum; the ability to administer it frequently; its assistance in determining what to teach; its sensitivity to short-term academic improvements; its assistance in evaluating student progress and instructional programs, its assistance in improving student achievement; and its potential for statistical validity and reliability.

HOW AN ECOLOGICAL ASSESSMENT APPLIES TO EVALUATING SPECIAL EDUCATION STUDENTS

In an ecological assessment, assessors conduct a comprehensive process to collect data about the way a student functions in different settings or environments. This informs evaluating and instructing special-needs students because they may demonstrate good performance and/or behavior in some settings, but difficulty in other settings. As examples, one student might behave calmly during classes but always become upset in the lunchroom. Another student may act out in the classroom but not in the gym. Some students might behave well during art and music classes, but poorly during math and science classes, or vice versa. Some students may have school phobia, wherein they feel persistent, irrational fears about attending school. They may seem otherwise happy and demonstrate normal behaviors and interactions at home and in the community; yet whenever they have to go to school, they consistently experience anxiety, fear, and/or depression. Because in all of these examples, the student's behavior and functioning varies among settings, ecological assessment is helpful for identifying why these variations exist. As such, ecological assessment can contribute to functional behavior analysis, i.e., determining individual reasons for maladaptive and adaptive behaviors.

COLLECTING INFORMATION FOR AN ECOLOGICAL ASSESSMENT

School psychologists, educational specialists, and others may gather data for an ecological assessment through direct observations of a student in different settings, and also through reviewing student records and interviewing the student, parents/family, teachers, etc. For example, the assessor might observe a student in all his/her classes; in breaks during the school day; and at home and in the community; and then gather additional data by interviewing the student, teachers, and parents. Some of the types of information included in an ecological assessment are about the physical environment; student activity and behavior patterns; interactions between the student and authority figures; interactions with other students; and parent, teacher, and peer expectations of the student. The ecological assessment can help psychologists and educators discern why the student behaves/functions differently in different environments. For example, authority figures' expectations may vary dramatically from one setting to another. Some students misbehave in environments overstimulating to them. Some students with behavior disorders may act out regularly at the same time every day, regardless of setting/place. Knowing these things is critical to identifying and meeting individual student needs, including developing special education IEPs.

RELATIONSHIPS OF ASSESSMENTS AND ANALYSIS, SETTING DEVELOPMENTALLY APPROPRIATE GOALS

When developing ABA intervention programs for students with autism spectrum disorders (ASDs) or other disabilities, professionals utilize many approaches for setting goals. For example, some use the *Verbal Behavior Milestones Assessment and Placement Program* (VB-MAPP); the *Assessment of Basic Language and Learning Skills-Revised* (ABLLS-R), or other criterion-referenced assessment instruments. Some use informal observations; checklists; interviews with students, teachers, parents; and other informal assessment methods. However, according to experts (cf. Leach, 2012), they usually fail to utilize ecological assessments sufficiently. Ecological assessment observes the skills a student needs to succeed in specific settings, e.g., in general education classroom reading group; the playground; the cafeteria, auditorium; at home at dinner; in libraries, movie theaters, restaurants; or workplaces. The observer uses task analysis to list all skills needed for each setting, observe the student in each, and document skills demonstrated/not demonstrated. Necessary but undemonstrated skills are the bases for intervention goals. Goals must be developmentally appropriate. For example, if the task analysis identifies the restaurant skill of verbally ordering from a waitperson, but the student is nonverbal, the goal must specify pointing at a picture/description of something on a menu.

NEEDED SKILLS IDENTIFIED IN AN ECOLOGICAL ASSESSMENT

As an example of an ecological assessment of student participation in a small-group reading activity: The student did not demonstrate the skill of silently reading along while someone read aloud; a goal was set for the student to move his/her finger along text words while someone read aloud. Being nonverbal, this student could not demonstrate the skill of reading aloud when called on; a goal was set for the student, when called on, to press a switch activating a voice recording of a text passage. The student's nonverbal status also prevented demonstrating the skill of answering comprehension questions; a goal was set for the student to respond to literal comprehension questions by pointing to one correct picture out of each set of four. For the skill of predicting, which the student could not demonstrate verbally, a goal was set that given a communication board including an "I have an idea" symbol, the student would hold up this symbol; and then use pictures, gestures, or an AAC device to express the prediction.

WHY DECISION-MAKING IN SCHOOLS REQUIRES THE DATA COLLECTION ENABLED BY TECHNOLOGY

Accountability mandates are requiring school districts to follow business examples and base their decisions on the data that technology enables collecting. As experts point out, decision-making without data is akin to a pilot's "flying blind" without navigation instruments during a stormy night. In fact, some experts in school testing and research explain that lacking information is the reason for frequent policy changes in school systems: administrators cannot make good decisions due to insufficient data. The nature of D3M does not involve a specific technology, but a process. Although traditional D3M solutions have revolved around central data repositories/warehouses amassing data from varied sources, combined with data reports and queries generated by high-end decision-support tools, D3M processes can be supported by a broad range of solutions and technologies. For example, one school superintendent uses NWEA (Northwest Evaluation Association) test data to analyze instructional strategies and inform professional development decisions. In another school, a principal uses Microsoft Access database software to analyze school data, and the Pearson SuccessMaker management system for on-demand reports and student assessments. Over four years, he and his staff have enabled soaring test scores by mapping, benchmarking, and predicting student and teacher progress.

HOW DATA-DRIVEN DECISION-MAKING (D3M) CHANGES SCHOOLS

D3M increases accountability and quality in instruction and school leadership. It shifts school culture from always having answers to asking the right questions. However, appropriate questions and data interpretation do not equal finding solutions. Data are the means, i.e., tools; the ends are educators' abilities for effectively addressing problems. School administrators must also expect increased, not decreased expenses when implementing D3M. These come from time invested—a year for district and community goal-setting, another for roll-out and implementation; and a total of 3-4 years before seeing results—and expenses for training, data validation and cleanup, and maintenance for quality assurance. Users must be trained not only in tool use, but moreover in data use for analysis, in understanding how data warehouses structure data, and in data warehouse security. Although D3M refocuses time use, it does not save time. One school district data analyst compares D3M to action research: both involve continuous method refinement and interpretation informed by new insights gained through the process. More work is required of both administrators and teachers as they take ownership of the process.

ISSUES RELATED TO DATA CLEANLINESS AND PLANNING BEFORE CHOOSING SOLUTIONS FOR DATA-DRIVEN DECISION-MAKING (D3M)

Every day, district-wide school staff members use and update student information and instructional management systems, testing applications, financial software and other transactional systems supplying data to warehouses. This makes data-entry errors common. Also, some data "pools" are overlooked; without regular updating, they become stagnant. Such examples of "dirty" data can render a D3M initiative useless unless schools clean them up. According to experts, cleaning transactional data and exporting them to data warehouses are often time-intensive and complex. In fact, experts find educational data the most complicated kind. Because working with data appears deceptively easy, the largest problem in implementing D3M solutions is that users greatly underestimate the challenges. Schools must ensure in written contracts that vendors they select have data-cleansing expertise. Before choosing to build a D3M solution using components or purchase a turnkey system, educators must determine exactly what answers they want from data. Some districts build their own data warehouses when no commercial applications meet their needs. They can closely coordinate these with student information systems, enabling teachers to access past and current student information, state and district test results, and daily schedule updates/changes.

EXPERT ADVICE ABOUT INITIAL EXPENSES FOR DATA-DRIVEN DECISION-MAKING (D3M) SOLUTIONS

Experts advise schools not to spend a lot of money up-front for D3M solutions, because the larger the investment, the harder it is to abandon an unsatisfactory system when necessary. Changes in D3M solutions should be affordable: both data product features and school district needs change; thus it is necessary to consider not only interoperability, but also initial expenses. However, experts also note that D3M tools frequently have multipurpose applications. For example, while the executive director of evaluation, testing, and student information in one school district uses NWEA (Northwest Evaluation Association) item banks to produce tests aligned with local and state standards, the superintendent of another school district uses NWEA's product to inform professional development decisions with teaching strategy analyses. While federal accountability mandates (NCLB) have prompted D3M use, experts advise school districts to go beyond comparing each grade this year to last year and comparing average test scores across sites, and use D3M for system-wide/district-wide school improvements enabling every student's progress toward higher standards. In one example of D3M benefits, a superintendent, asked at a school board meeting about student math progress, used the district's web-based data system to answer within two minutes.

EDUCATIONAL PROGRESS MONITORING USING DATA COLLECTION AND ANALYSIS

Educational progress monitoring is a continuous process involving collecting and analyzing data to assess student progress toward general outcomes, specific skills, or both; and making instructional decisions based on student data review and analysis. The progress-monitoring cycle begins with initial assessment of historical data; standardized, diagnostic, and curriculum-based assessments; direct intervention; and parental input. Informed by assessment findings, the next step is instructional design, which includes developing goals and objectives; identifying specially designed instruction (SDI) and alignment with general curriculum; instructional scheduling and grouping; and identifying progress monitoring. The third step implements instructional design, including using SDI to deliver instruction corresponding with goals and objectives; collecting data on student progress; and monitoring student feedback and response. This leads to the fourth step, ongoing evaluation, which includes evaluating instructional effectiveness through progress monitoring; data recording and use for progress assessment and decision-making; adjusting goals, objectives, SDI, and other instruction as indicated; and reporting to parents. This step connects to revisiting instructional design, and the cycle repeats.

GOALS, BENEFITS, AND ESSENTIAL ELEMENTS OF SCHOOL DATA-BASED STUDENT PROGRESS MONITORING

The goals of data-based student progress include furnishing data to help schools make decisions about their students, including for guiding instructional decisions; supplying student performance data for identifying current student levels of performance, behavior, and/or learning and for measuring and reporting school and student progress toward goals; and providing data for the process of reevaluation, to ascertain whether students still meet eligibility requirements for special education services and whether they still require specially designed instruction (SDI). The benefits of data-based student progress monitoring include letting students and their parents know what the school expects of its students; providing teachers with organized records of student performance; letting teachers know what elements of their instruction are working and not working, indicated by the data; demonstrating student and school progress to parents in a way that is easy for them to understand; and providing IEP teams with comprehensive student performance data to inform their decisions. Essential progress-monitoring elements include: Data-driven monitoring; measurable outcomes/goals; sensitivity to student growth increments; effective, efficient classroom use; user-friendly formats; and connection with appropriate activities and general education curriculum.

TWO-PRONGED APPROACH TO DATA-DRIVEN STUDENT PROGRESS MONITORING

Some state education departments (e.g., Pennsylvania) use a two-pronged approach to monitoring student progress using data collection and analysis. One prong is progress toward general outcomes, the other toward specific skills. Monitoring progress toward general outcomes is appropriate for every student in the general education reading and math curriculum, including those at risk. Its goals and objectives are founded in the general education curriculum. Monitoring progress toward specific skills is appropriate for all students with IEPs, especially those having significant disabilities. Its goals and objectives make reference to the general education curriculum. Assessment of general outcomes is more efficient, while assessment of specific skills is more representative; educators must achieve a balance between the two. Outcome measures share the following characteristics in common: They are viewed as so critical to effective operations that they are conducted routinely. They are reasonably cost-effective and time-effective, accurate, and simple. They are collected frequently, and on an ongoing basis. A range of important decisions are informed and/or shaped by outcome measures.

CURRICULUM-BASED ANALYSIS (CBA) USED FOR MONITORING STUDENT AND/OR SCHOOL PROGRESS

When CBA is used to measure student/school progress toward general outcomes, it has the following features: The measures used are standardized and statistically valid and reliable. They indicate growth in the general curriculum across a broad variety of skills and over time. They may measure the curriculum of instruction directly, or they may not. While they do imply the need for modifying instruction, they do not specifically suggest doing so. Some state education departments and school districts use a process for monitoring progress toward both general outcomes and specific skills that follows these seven steps: (1) Establishing measurable yearly goals and objectives; (2) making decisions about data collection; (3) identifying the schedule and tools to use for collecting data; (4) representing the data collected; (5) evaluating the data collected; (6) making adjustments to instruction based on the data analysis; and (7) communicating the students' and school's progress toward the goals and objectives identified.

Knowledge of Measurement Theory and Principles

COLLABORATIVE PROBLEM-SOLVING (CPS) FRAMEWORKS

According to the Program for International Student Assessment (PISA, 2015) among others, CPS is a required and critical skill in all educational settings, as well as in employment. Collaboration affords advantages over individual problem-solving because it enables effective division of labor; incorporates information from multiple contributors as sources of experiences, perspectives, and knowledge; and fellow group members' ideas stimulate enhanced quality and creativity in solutions. Although social interaction is necessary for collaborating, it is not sufficient by itself: collaboration additionally requires shared goals, accommodating various perspectives, and organized efforts toward achieving identified goals, whereas not all social interactions also include all of these conditions. Research shows that national and state education systems are increasingly emphasizing inquiry-oriented and project-based learning. These incorporate designing curriculum and instruction toward problem-solving, critical thinking, self-management, and collaboration skills. In project-based assignments, students must frequently work together to attain group goals, e.g., producing joint presentations, integrated analyses, final reports, etc. Schools typically do not teach collaborative problem-solving as a discrete skill apart from specific content areas. Consequently, schools tend to integrate collaborative learning activities into history, math, sciences, and other subject courses.

TRENDS THAT SUPPORT THE USE OF COLLABORATIVE PROBLEM-SOLVING (CPS) FRAMEWORKS IN SCHOOLS

Teaching and evaluating 21st-century skills have recently received greater focus in approaches to curriculum and instruction reform. Such skills include information and communication technology (ICT) skills; self-management, problem-solving, and critical thinking skills; and communication and collaboration skills. Numerous curriculum and assessment reports name communication and collaboration skills as central among 21st-century skills. Also, today's careers increasingly require skills for effectively working in groups and applying problem-solving skills in social contexts, which requires schools to teach and assess collaborative problem-solving skills in order to prepare students for employment. In large part, today's problem-solving work is executed by teams, in an increasingly digital and global economy. Not only has commerce obviously shifted emphasis from manufacturing to information services; but even in manufacturing industries, collaboration and teamwork are more common than individual work. Additionally, as computer networks become more available, employers increasingly expect individuals to use collaborative technology to work across widespread locations with diverse teams.

TEACHING STUDENTS COLLABORATIVE PROBLEM-SOLVING SKILLS AND TECHNOLOGIES

The University of Phoenix Research Institute have identified one of the key skills for future employment as virtual collaboration, defined as the "ability to work productively, drive engagement, and demonstrate presence as a member of a virtual team" (Davis, Fidler, & Gorbis, 2011). According to a survey of decision-makers in knowledge and information management from 921 North American and European businesses, 94% of these companies had implemented or were planning to implement team workspaces, web conferencing, e-mail, instant messaging, videoconferencing, and/or other types of collaboration technologies (Forrester report, Q4 2009). In addition to collaboration in the coming workforce, collaborative problem-solving (CPS) skills are necessary for transactions with public services, administration; community life participation; volunteerism; social networking; and other civic contexts. Therefore, students must be provided with instruction in CPS skills, and in using suitable technology to collaborate. As they move from school to public life and employment, they will be expected to have and be able to apply CPS skills, and to know how to use the associated technology for doing so.

35

NORM-REFERENCED TESTING (NRT)

NRT is an integral part of psychological and educational testing practices. It assumes that intelligence, academic achievement, behavior, and other human characteristics/traits are distributed along a normal probability curve. The normal curve/bell curve shows the norm, i.e., the average of a population's performance plus scores above and below it. Test norms include statistics for a test's standardization sample/norm group, e.g., standard scores, percentile ranks, etc. Individual student test scores are described, from superior to deficient, based on the range where they fall. NRT compares student performance to that of age peers from the test's norm group, enabling interpreting scores more meaningfully. Norm groups can represent national populations or local, e.g., all students in a school district/single school. Comparison is made through converting raw scores to derived scores, which correspond to the normal distribution curve, supplying a framework for interpretation. Among many, the most commonly used derived scores include standard scores, standard deviations (SDs), scale scores, T-scores, percentile ranks, age-equivalent and grade-equivalent scores. A standard score corresponds to a statistical average/mean of 100; on an IQ test, 15 is one SD, so a score of 115 is one SD above the mean, i.e., High-Average.

NUMERICAL SCORE EXAMPLES FOR NORM-REFERENCED TESTS

Scale scores indicate test performance on NRT subscales/subtests/sub-domains. The average/mean of scale scores is 10; the standard deviation (SD) is 3. Therefore, a scale score of 7 is one SD below the mean, placing it in the Low-Average range. T-scores are typically reported by NRTs assessing behavior. T-scores distribute standard scores differently; i.e., the average/mean is 50 and the SD is 10. Therefore, a behavior rating scale T-score of 60 is one SD above the mean, placing it in the High-Average/At-Risk range. Percentile ranks reflect the test-taker's position relative to the norm group/standardization sample. Percentile rank is an individual score's place in the normal distribution, below which the corresponding percentage of other scores is found. For example, if a student takes an IQ test and receives a percentile ranking of 85, this does NOT mean the student got 85% of the test items correct, as some people incorrectly assume. It means, rather, that 85% of the student's age peers in the test's norm group scored below that student's score. Thus the student's score is equal to/higher than 85% of scores received by students the same age in the normative sample.

INTERPRETING GRADE-EQUIVALENT, AGE-EQUIVALENT SCORES ON NORM-REFERENCED TESTS

Although grade-equivalent and age-equivalents represent two types of scores most often used for reporting NRT results, they are also often misinterpreted. They compare a student's test score to the average score of students in the test's normative/standardization sample who are in specific grades or at specific ages. They show how a student's raw scores, i.e., number of correct item responses, compare to the norm group in terms of grade/age level. For example, a grade-equivalent score of 4.5 means the student (regardless of grade) scored the same as the average student in the fifth month of the fourth grade in the test's normative sample. It does NOT mean the student showed the same proficiency level as the average student in his/her school in the fifth month of the fourth grade according to curricular expectations. Similarly, an age-equivalent score of 8.0 years does NOT mean the student scored the same as the average eight-year-old student in his/her school in the context of expected curriculum proficiency; rather, it means the student (regardless of age) got the same raw score as the average eight-year-old in the test's norm group. Grade-equivalent and age-equivalent scores must not be literally interpreted: misinterpretation can cause misclassification/misdiagnosis/unsuitable educational services/placements.

SELF-REPORT INVENTORIES

Self-report inventories, frequently used for personality assessment, present statements or questions, to which the examinee responds by indicating his/her agreement/disagreement and/or degree of agreement/disagreement. Administration may be in computerized or paper-and-pencil format. The Minnesota Multiphasic Personality Inventory (MMPI) is probably the best-known self-report personality inventory. It includes over 500 statements assessing psychological health, interpersonal relationships, abnormal behaviors; social, religious, sexual, and political attitudes and other widely varied topics. Raymond Cattell's 16 Personality Factor Questionnaire, based on his trait theory of personality, produces personality profiles, frequently used for career counseling and employee evaluation. The California Personality Inventory, based on the MMPI and drawing almost half its questions from it, assesses self-control, independence, empathy and similar characteristics. Self-report inventory strengths include enabling administration of many tests in short times at low costs; standardization; use of pre-established norms; and greater validity and reliability than projective tests. Limitations include the potential for respondent deception; long, tedious administration—e.g., the MMPI takes about three hours—and lack of examinee self-knowledge and/or honest self-expression.

MULTIPLE-CHOICE TESTS AS ASSESSMENT INSTRUMENTS

Strengths: MC tests are versatile across numerous subjects and educational objectives and adaptable to different learning levels, from simple information recall to more complex cognition, e.g., concept/principle comprehension; application/transfer/generalization; analysis; distinguishing opinion vs. fact; interpreting graph/charts; cause-and-effect; inference; judging relevance; problem-solving. Testers can control item difficulty by changing choices: more homogeneous choices require finer distinctions to choose correct answers. MC enables item analysis: teachers can improve items by replacing ineffective distractors; and/or use wrong/distractor choices to diagnose student misconceptions/teacher weaknesses. Students can answer MC questions much faster than essay questions: teachers can cover more content in the same test/time, making test scores more representative of students' overall course achievement, hence more valid. MC items are less influenced by guessing than true-false items, making them more reliable. Scoring is more clear-cut than scoring short-answer questions: MC has no partial or misspelled answers. Objective scoring, unlike with essay tests, prevents scorer inconsistencies. Writing ability and bluffing have no influence. Also unlike essays, MC tests can be machine-scored and reported, expediting instructional adjustments. Limitations: MC tests do not allow/assess student explanations, thought process demonstration, information/example provision, thought organization, specific task performance, or original ideas. Also, guessing affects reliability somewhat.

STRENGTHS AND LIMITATIONS OF INTERVIEWS AS ASSESSMENT PROCEDURES

Interviews can provide empowering experiences for some respondents by letting them express their opinions in their own words. Examinees hesitant about writing down their thoughts or completing questionnaires are frequently more likely to respond to interested interviewers. The tendency of some respondents to get off the subject and ramble is a limitation, requiring (polite) interviewer redirection. Interviews in households can be limited by interruptions from children, phone calls, visitors, TVs, etc. Public places can be noisy and uncomfortable for interviews. The interpersonal interaction of interviews makes them more subject to bias than more objective methods. Interviewers may unconsciously discourage/encourage interviewees from expressing certain opinions and information. Social desirability is another caveat: respondents may say what the interviewer wants to hear/what they think s/he wants to hear/what is most socially acceptable. Because people often say one thing but do another, survey data can be unreliable for predicting behavior. Interviewer training and time for transcribing responses, coding open-ended question answers, and analyzing interviews are expensive; self-report questionnaires take a fraction of the money and time. However, clinicians skilled in interviewing and analysis may discover more about individualized aspects of psychological problems from interviews.

STATISTICAL RELIABILITY

Reliability applies to tests as well as scientific experiments. For a test to be reliable, other examiners must be able to replicate/administer the same test under the same conditions and obtain the same/consistent results as the original administration. The ability to replicate an assessment and generate consistent results supports those results' dependability. A simple way to test an assessment instrument's reliability and stability over time is test-retest reliability. IQ tests and surveys are amenable to this since IQs and opinions are unlikely to change suddenly and significantly; educational tests are less so, because students learn more between test administrations. Inter-rater reliability reflects how consistently different people score the same test or assessment activity. For instance, dog shows and the Olympics require high inter-rater reliability; and school examiners are regularly assessed to assure their adherence to the same standards. Internal consistency reliability shows whether individual items assessing different constructs within one test are consistent with one another. Ways of testing it include using two halves of a test (split-half) or statistical procedures like Kuder-Richardson, Cronbach's Alpha, etc. Parallel-Forms Reliability uses two equivalent yet independent forms of a test; between-forms correlation estimates reliability.

STATISTICAL VALIDITY

Validity is a concept applied to tests and other assessment instruments, methods, and procedures as well as to the experimental design of research studies. Validity means that a test instrument measures what it was intended or claims to measure. For example, if a psychological test is supposed to measure anxiety, but contains items also identifying depression symptoms, it is not a valid anxiety measure. External validity reflects whether/how much a test's results can be generalized to other populations, settings, and treatment and measurement variables. One type of external validity is population validity: whether sampling used acceptable methodology and a sample represents the whole population. Another is ecological validity: whether test results can be generalized to real-life/usual conditions via testing conditions' not influencing them. Internal validity is high if test results cannot be attributed to other, confounding variables than those identified for testing. With low internal validity, correlation between/among variables may be established but not causation. Content validity reflects how representative test items are of the subject content assessed. Construct validity reflects how well a test measures a construct, e.g., IQ, pain, etc., i.e., whether the instrument's operational definition of the variable tested matches the concept's actual theoretical meaning.

SPECIFIC KINDS OF VALIDITY

If a test measures what it means or purports to measure, it is valid. Criterion validity reflects whether a test measures a specified set of skills. Assessing this by comparing a test with an established standard, e.g., comparing a new test to an existing, proven test of the same construct (like IQ), is called concurrent validity because the two are typically compared simultaneously or close together in time. Assessing criterion validity by administering the same test over a period of time is called predictive validity. As an example of predictive validity, universities commonly use applicants' high school grades to predict similar post-secondary grades, and make admissions decisions accordingly. A famous example involving criterion and predictive validity is the Coca-Cola company: when changing the original Coke flavor, their market research showed people loved it, so they rushed it into production—and it was a resounding failure. The researchers' mistake was not asking respondents whether they liked the new flavor *better* than the original one, which would have assessed concurrent validity. Also, their positive market research findings did not correlate with the poor subsequent sales, indicating poor predictive validity.

PERSONAL PHYSICAL AND MENTAL FACTORS THAT CAN AFFECT ASSESSMENT PROCESSES

When conducting assessments of students, school psychologists must consider the individual student's personal factors and how they can influence the assessment process and results. For example, if a student has vision or hearing impairment, s/he will not be able to perceive and interpret test stimuli the same way as other students; and if s/he has other physical disabilities, s/he will not be able to respond to testing the same way as others. Students with intellectual or cognitive disabilities may neither comprehend nor respond to assessment items the same as those for whom many assessment instruments were designed. In these cases, adaptations, modifications, accommodations, or alternative forms of assessment may be indicated to obtain valid results for individual students. Health conditions in students without disabilities can also affect assessment: a student with a temporary (e.g., flu, cold, head lice, etc.) or chronic (e.g., otitis media, asthma, etc.) illness may not attend or comprehend as usual; students who did not get a good night's sleep and/or did not eat breakfast are also likely to perform less than optimally.

SOCIAL FACTORS RELATED TO HOME LIFE THAT CAN INFLUENCE STUDENT ASSESSMENTS

When assessing students directly, or reviewing/interpreting existing assessment results, school psychologists should take social factors into account. Some factors related to the home include whether the student enjoys a happy home life or one troubled by child abuse, neglect, marital discord, parental substance abuse; insecurity caused by absent or uninvolved parents, or parents rarely available due to long work hours. Socioeconomic status can affect students when parents lack the financial and material resources needed to support their education. Parents with limited formal education themselves may not provide necessary stimulation by talking and reading to children regularly. Homes without books, internet access, TV, etc. are likely to provide inadequate stimulation for learning. It also matters whether students can get help at home with their homework. In addition, whether or not or to what degree parents are interested and involved in their children's education will influence students' participation in their own learning and assessment.

SOCIAL/ENVIRONMENTAL FACTORS WHICH CAN INFLUENCE STUDENT ASSESSMENT

To gauge the influence of environmental factors related to the school setting on the procedures and results of assessment, school psychologists should consider a number of factors. For example, they should note whether a student is significantly older or younger for his/her grade; whether instruction is generally at a level suitable for the student; and whether the student seems interested in instructional content and activities. They should observe whether subjects that a student finds most difficult are given adequate time or not. The school psychologist should evaluate whether a student appears well-adjusted emotionally, or displays signs of insecurity, anxiety, fear, frustration, depression, being or feeling rejected, compulsive behaviors, disruptive behaviors, self-stimulating behaviors, self-injurious behaviors, social withdrawal, etc. School psychologists should ascertain whether the school program is challenging for the student or is too easy, too difficult, irrelevant, or boring. Knowing the student's study and work habits will also inform assessment and the accuracy and validity of its results. The psychologist should also consider whether educators are setting realistic expectations for the student; and whether the student experiences a personality clash with the teacher.

TEST BIAS IN PSYCHOLOGICAL ASSESSMENT

In psychological assessment today, the issue of using standardized tests with minority students is one of the most polarizing among both clinicians and laypersons. For clinicians, clients, students, and parents, the main concern is that when average test scores vary among ethnic groups, e.g., African-Americans, Hispanics, Native Americans, Asian Americans, etc., long-term consequences may result such as overdiagnosis of psychiatric disorders; disproportionate placement of students in special education classes; and unfair denials of college admission and/or employment to applicants based on scores on standardized tests that some claim are biased. While researchers are also polarized about test bias, among them conflicts appear more influenced by alternative explanations for test score variation. One researcher (Reynolds, 2000a, 2000b) has categorized the four most prevalent types of reasons: (1) genetic factors; (2) environmental factors of social, educational, and economic disadvantages; (3) the interaction of genetic and environmental influences; and (4) systematic underrepresentation of the real abilities of minority groups by biased tests. The controversy over test fairness has included a California ban on using IQ tests to identify and place African-American students; and truth-in-testing laws in New York, which can interfere with professional practice according to some clinicians.

BIAS RELATIVE TO STANDARDIZED TESTS

In inferential statistics, bias means that the estimation of some value contains systematic error. In other words, a test that systematically underestimates or overestimates the value of the variable that it is designed to evaluate is a biased test. If the bias is a function of ethnicity, gender, or another cultural variable, this is described as cultural test bias. As an example, David Wechsler's series of intelligence scales for preschool and primary-grade children (WPPSI), elementary-grade children (WISC), and adults (WAIS) have yielded differences in average scores of about one standard deviation, i.e., 15 points, between Black and White Americans. Now if this variation indicates a real difference between these two groups, then the tests are not biased. But if the variation can be attributed to systematic overestimation of White Americans' intelligence and/or systematic underestimation of Black Americans' intelligence, then the tests would be culturally biased. Research into potential IQ test bias has yielded inconsistent findings.

TAXONOMY OF THREE TYPES OF BIAS IN STANDARDIZED TESTING INSTRUMENTS

In studying the issue of cultural bias in standardized testing instruments, some researchers (Van de Vijver and Tanzer, 2004) have proposed a taxonomy of three types of bias. This classification identifies: (1) Construct bias – different cultures have overlapping definitions of the same construct; different behaviors related to the construct are considered appropriate in different cultures; and related behaviors relevant to the construct are poorly sampled. (2) Method bias – bias in sampling; for example, standardization or norming samples have not been matched to the population they are to represent in all characteristics (which, in reality, is virtually impossible); bias in instrumentation; for example, how familiar examinees from different cultures are with test items; or bias in administration; for example, the observer/interviewer/tester effects or ambiguous test-taking instructions. (3) Item bias – test items are ambiguous; items are poorly translated into other languages; item content is inappropriate or unfamiliar for some cultures; or word connotations, nuisance factors, or other culture-specific factors influence test items.

Assessment of Special Populations

PURPOSE AND ROLE OF SCREENINGS, INAPPROPRIATE USE, AND AGE GROUPS

Screening tools are mainly for identifying developmental areas needing additional evaluation, NOT determining special education eligibility. They may not identify all children needing referral due to the small number of behaviors they sample, so they should be combined with parent interviews, caregiver information, and ongoing observation for greater accuracy. Screening measures are typically more reliable with children 3-5 years old than infants and toddlers. Systematic observations and standardized tests are among traditional assessment procedures. Norm-referenced assessments evaluate child development during specific activities by comparing it with average scores/results for a norm group of age peers. They are not found very valid or reliable with preschool ages. School psychologists often adapt them and use item analysis to interpret results, requiring validation through multiple assessment instruments plus interview and observational data. Criterion-referenced assessments evaluate children's performance against specific criteria to determine functioning levels in developmental domains, typically reporting results within age ranges and tasks the child can/cannot perform. Curriculum-based assessments are also criterion-referenced, but use natural environments, materials, and activities to collect data. They compare skills to previous performance according to instructional objectives along a developmental continuum, ideally to plan instructional interventions/programs. Typically, observational data are collected at specific times (not ongoing) to identify child learning styles, generalization ability, and learning rates.

TRADITIONAL ASSESSMENT PROCEDURES TO EVALUATE INFANTS AND YOUNG CHILDREN

For children 0-5 years old, experts highly recommend using alternative approaches to assessment in order to procure valid, accurate, and realistic information regarding the abilities, skills, and knowledge of this population. This is because traditional assessment instruments—e.g., standardized norm-referenced tests, criterion-referenced tests, and curriculum-based assessments—are designed such that they often do not apply to early childhood. Recurring practical issues that cause error in ascertaining early childhood abilities are characteristic of traditional assessment approaches that utilized structured questions or tasks. For example, young children are limited in their ability to understand the cues provided in such assessments. Their capacities for perceptual-motor and verbal responses are also developmentally restricted. Some kinds of test items or questions in traditional assessments demand complex information-processing skills which young children have yet to develop. In formal assessment situations, young children may be unable to control their behavior to meet assessment demands, and/or to understand what they are asked to do. Additionally, young children with disabilities may not develop in typical sequences. These are all indications for using alternative assessment procedures in childhood.

PLAY-BASED ASSESSMENT AND PORTFOLIO-BASED AUTHENTIC ASSESSMENT

Experts recommend play-based assessment as an alternative for young children because they are more likely to show their actual abilities in play situations; all developmental domains can be assessed through play; play-based assessments provide information for developing intervention plans, recommending outcomes/goals for children and families, evaluating progress, and both assessment and intervention. Play is related to emotional, social, and relationship development. Assessors can collect data in different play settings. Play-based assessment can be conducted in an established formal assessment setting and/or in natural settings through direct observations. Portfolio-based authentic assessment integrates assessment into preschool curriculum, collecting data from everyday events. Information from these natural settings more accurately represents children's abilities and skills. Formal and informal observations include recording general daily interactions and/or specific developmental/learning domains/concepts. Developmental profiles collect data within curriculum, not artificial testing situations; and document child development in physical, cognitive, emotional, and social domains, including anecdotal records. Portfolios can include developmental profiles; fine motor skill development examples; audio/video/photos documenting activities; materials demonstrating numeracy, literacy, and language development and interest; personal and social development notes; parent-teacher conference notes; child self-observations, and teacher observations. Performance assessments combine assessment and intervention in one procedure set.

Assessing English Language Learner (ELL) Students

(1) Linguistic backgrounds: Although most speak Spanish, ELLs in America speak an estimated 400 different native languages. Since this can make it impossible for states/school districts with large populations to furnish assessments in every L1, testers may need to provide interpreters. (2) English-language proficiency (ELP) levels: These vary widely among ELLs; and individual students can have different oral vs. written ELP levels. Testers should not assume ELLs with fluent conversational English have equal English reading comprehension of printed standardized test directions: basic Interpersonal Communication Skills (BICS) are acquired much earlier and more easily than cognitive academic language proficiency (CALP; Cummins, 1979). Also, ELP levels influence processing speeds: ELLs typically need more time to complete tasks in English. Assessment design, scoring, and accommodations must be informed by this fact. (3) L1 proficiency levels: ELL proficiency and literacy in their native languages also vary. So testers cannot assume ELLs can understand printed test directions in their own languages. Indeed, a large number of ELLs were actually born in the United States, and may never have had any formal education in their native languages. Testers considering using native language accommodations need to keep this information in mind as well.

Factors Affecting How ELL Students Are Assessed

(1) L1 formal education: Wide variation exists among ELLs in native-language proficiency and native-language formal education, including both L1 literacy and content-area knowledge and skills levels. For instance, refugee students may enter American school systems with zero/little formal education in any language. They must simultaneously learn English, academic subject content, and socialization in unfamiliar school settings. ELLs with more formal content-area instruction in their L1s still must transfer their content knowledge to English. Assessors must consider these factors in testing accommodation decisions. (2) English formal education: time in English-language schools varies among ELLs. Some learned English as a foreign language in their native countries, others only in America. Also, they may have received ESL, bilingual, full-immersion, or other English instructional programs; and even within programs, implementation varies widely. Additionally, children of migrant workers may attend English-language schools for many years, but are repeatedly relocated and interrupted, which can affect both their English-language proficiency (ELP) and their content knowledge. (3) Standardized test exposure: in some countries, multiple-choice or constructed-response questions are unknown. Even well-educated, high-ELP students may be unaccustomed to large-scale standardized tests, putting them at a disadvantage.

Cultural Factors Influencing the Appropriate Assessment of ELL Students

ELL students come from a broad variety of cultural backgrounds, and their acculturation to mainstream American culture varies among individuals. In standardized testing situations, ELLs may be put at a disadvantage because of cultural differences. ELL students' test scores can be affected by their not being familiar with mainstream American cultural elements and characteristics. Students who have different cultural beliefs and values; different life experiences and background knowledge; different assumptions about the educational environment in general and/or the testing situation in particular; and are unacquainted with U.S. culture may respond differently to test questions, which can place them at a disadvantage compared to their American peers. As one example, students from Asian, Latin American, Native American, or other collectivist cultures, which value cooperation above competition, can encounter disadvantages in the U.S. individualist culture, which values competition above cooperation and where testing situations commonly expect each student to perform at his/her best independently. As another example, students from socioeconomically disadvantaged milieus may have different background knowledge and experiences than what test developers assume, and may respond differently to test items.

ASSESSMENT OF STUDENTS WITH HEARING LOSS

Assessment of Deaf or hearing-impaired students must take conditions into account that can determine a student's needs, including residual hearing amount; etiology of hearing loss; age of onset; communication skills; any co-occurring disabilities; the student's first language; and linguistic and cultural background. Standardized tests not standardized specifically for the Deaf population must be administered in non-standardized modes. Specialist assessment techniques and instruments have also been developed particularly for very young children with hearing impairment. Assessment teams must include audiologists having experience in assessment and intervention with infants, toddlers, and preschool-aged children with hearing loss. Some sensorineural hearing losses caused by rubella, meningitis, neurological conditions, etc. can affect the vestibular system, which can impair visual-motor functioning, equilibrium (balance), and body awareness. Regular audiological assessments are recommended for children aged 0-3 years—more frequently if they have chronic otitis media and/or speech/language problems. Experts also deem parental involvement in the assessment process critical to information quantity and quality, including how parents communicate with children, for making optimal communication and educational decisions for children with hearing loss.

ASSESSING STUDENTS WITH VISUAL IMPAIRMENTS

A school nurse's brief vision assessment may be the first step in ascertaining a young child's visual status. When nurses/others suspect visual impairment, they should refer the child to a pediatric ophthalmologist or other eye specialist. Schools should obtain further information from the pediatrician and other medical providers. Some state guidelines (e.g., California) recommend functional vision assessment for all children 0-3 years old who fail initial vision assessments. Children who cannot respond to traditional assessment procedures, or children with multiple disabilities, also benefit from this assessment. Assessment teams must include someone having expertise and knowledge in assessment and intervention with blind and low-vision infants, toddlers, and preschoolers. This person conducts the functional vision assessment determining how the child uses his/her sight (if any); the child's needs related to vision; and which accommodations, modifications, adaptations, and interventions are necessary for the child's most independent functioning. Sensorimotor development, adaptive development, communication skills, concept development, emotional development, and social development should also be assessed in children 0-5 years old.

ASSESSING STUDENTS WITH SEVERE ORTHOPEDIC IMPAIRMENTS

Children with severe orthopedic impairments may have been identified and/or referred by state or county children services or other agencies. If the impairment is caused by a neuromuscular or musculoskeletal condition that might indicate a need for physical therapy and/or occupational therapy, a physician may refer the child to the children services agency. A physical therapist and/or occupational therapist must assess the child's functional gross and fine motor skills and orthopedic function areas. When a child is referred to a school program, school personnel should collaborate with other agencies in further assessment, current information sharing, and child and family program planning. Assessment teams must include somebody with knowledge of orthopedic impairments and training in providing interventions for these disabilities. Because children with orthopedic impairments may not demonstrate typical motor responses, it is especially important for assessors to consider assessment accommodations such as positioning, technological devices, other adaptive equipment, and additional time. For children who cannot produce motor, movement, or speech responses required by most traditional assessment instruments, using alternative assessment methods will not invalidate the findings.

COMPONENTS OF GIFTEDNESS AND THEIR RESPECTIVE CHARACTERISTICS

Renzulli (1986) describes a "three-ring conception of giftedness" based on major conclusions and concepts generated by many researchers and theorists studying them over time: Well above-average ability, task commitment, and creativity. Their interaction is more important than any one. General ability includes abstract thinking; verbal and numerical reasoning; memory; word fluency; spatial relations; adaptation to novel environmental circumstances; rapid, accurate, selective information retrieval; information-processing automaticity. Specific ability includes applying general abilities to specialized knowledge/performance areas; acquiring and applying advanced formal and implicit knowledge, logistics, strategies, and specialized problem-solving/performance techniques; distinguishing relevant/irrelevant information in study/performance areas/problem-solving. Task commitment includes interest, enthusiasm, and engagement in a specific study area/problem/form of expression; determination, hard work, endurance, perseverance, dedication, practice; self-confidence, self-efficacy, achievement drive; problem identification; ability for accessing discipline-specific communication channels and new developments; high work standards; openness to external and self-criticism; aesthetic sense of quality and taste in one's and others' work. Creativity includes original thought, fluency, flexibility; openness to experience; receptivity to new/different, even irrational thoughts, actions, and products; curiosity, adventurousness, speculation, mental playfulness; willingness for risk-taking; uninhibitedness; sensitivity to aesthetics, details; willingness to react to/act upon external and internal stimulation.

IDENTIFYING GIFTED AND TALENTED STUDENTS

In Renzulli's (1986) identification system, test scores are the first step or way of nominating students for educational programs for the gifted/talented. Although simply selecting all students scoring above the 85th percentile (with local norms) would be easiest, because standardized tests do not necessarily reflect all students' potentials, a process that guarantees the inclusion of "bright underachievers" divides the "Talent Pool" in half, automatically selecting all students scoring at/above the 92nd percentile for half and leaving room in the other half for students excelling in some but not other areas or aptitudes (e.g., verbal/nonverbal, mechanical, spatial; athletics, leadership, the arts, etc.); those identified by non-test criteria; primary-grade students; culturally diverse populations; or disadvantaged groups. Teacher nominations are the second step: teachers often observe student gifts/talents not identified by tests. The third step is alternate pathways—local school district options including parent nominations, peer nominations, self-nominations (e.g., by high school students considering advanced courses), creativity tests, product evaluations, etc. While test scores and teacher nominations are automatic, alternate pathway nominations are reviewed by screening committees, who conduct case studies including school records examinations, interviews, and individual assessments to make selection decisions; program placement may be on a trial basis.

In Renzulli's (1986) system for identifying gifted/talented students, three steps/methods are test scores, teacher nominations, and alternate pathways. Three more steps/methods are: Special nominations – Lists of all students nominated via Steps 1-3 are distributed to all teachers, including from previous years and resource teachers, allowing them to nominate students not nominated by current teachers; make recommendations for students already in the "Talent Pool"; or nominate students they know from regular classroom enrichment activities. This enables total school population review and bypasses opinions of current teachers who may not appreciate individual student abilities, style, or personality; identifies underachievers; and helps overcome under-nominator/non-nominator teacher biases. Parent and student notification and orientation – These do not label students as "gifted," but explain the conception of giftedness, how admission is determined, program policies, procedures, services, and activities; and depict developing gifted behaviors to students as their responsibility as well as a program goal. Action information

44

nominations – Derived from the performance-based assessment concept; to identify overlooked students, orientation helps teachers spot dynamic interactions involving student excitement/fascination in some topic/learning aspect within regular curriculum. Schoolwide Enrichment Model (Renzulli & Reis, 1983) programs also provide varied classroom enrichment activities, which can identify candidates for gifted/talented services.

Research and Program Evaluation

EVALUATING RESEARCH

The U.S. Department of Education (ED) Institute of Education Sciences (IES) What Works Clearinghouse (WWC) contracted with the National Center for Education Evaluation and Regional Assistance to produce a guide for educators to identify and implement rigorous evidence-based educational practices. However, it is impossible to evaluate how effective every policy, practice, program, or product that schools may utilize; as a result, educators are increasingly expected to be research evaluators. Yet many educators lack the research background required for expert research evaluation. ED identifies four properties educators should seek in evaluating educational research:

- Educational relevance – the research should involve settings, participants, interventions, and outcomes representing the needs and interests of the specific school.
- Objective, systematic, rigorous methodology – the research should provide evidence of the highest quality for variables causing changes in measured outcomes. ED finds the best means of obtaining this evidence is the "gold standard" of research—conducting experiments.
- Enough detail for replication – researchers should describe their instruments and methods in detail sufficient to enable other researchers to replicate their studies to determine reliability.
- Independent expert review – publication in a refereed journal or other proof that content and research experts independently reviewed a study.

According to experts (Redfield, T.H.E. Journal, 2004), one question for educators to ask when evaluating research is whether a study claims that a specific product or program causes some outcome like improved student achievement, improved teacher skills, etc. If the answer is yes, evaluators should then determine whether the study's participants were randomly selected from the same population to which its findings will be generalized. For example, if a study claims an intervention improves achievement for sixth-graders in low-income urban schools, did the researchers randomly select their study participants from a low-income urban school population(s)? Were participants assigned randomly to experimental vs. comparison/control groups? The U.S. Department of Education (ED) emphasizes random assignment over random selection. Also, was there a comparison/control group? If both answers are yes, the study's design was experimental. If it also used valid, reliable measures and other rigorous practices, it can claim causation—particularly if its results have been replicated. If the first answer is no and the second is yes, the design was quasi-experimental. For quasi-experimental designs, ask whether researchers took all possible steps to match the experimental and control groups excepting the experimental treatment/intervention (e.g., similar student backgrounds, equal teacher qualifications, etc.).

When evaluating educational research, educators should ask whether a study used reliable procedures and instruments for measuring its results; and whether the authors described the procedures clearly enough for other researchers to replicate them. They should ask whether the researchers provided information about the instruments they used sufficient for readers to conclude reasonably that with all conditions remaining equal, the instrument would produce the same measurement if it were administered again. In addition, the evaluator should ask whether the procedures and instruments used valid for the purpose(s) of that particular study. Validity means that an instrument, test, procedure, or test measures what it claims to measure. As an example, if a test purports to measure mathematical reasoning, but only measures the ability to make accurate mathematical computations, it is not valid. Standardized test manuals provide data on a test's validity and reliability, expressed as r, i.e., the correlation coefficient. Usually, $r = 0.7$ or higher is considered acceptable; the closer to perfect validity/reliability or $r = 1.00$, the better. Validity and reliability must be especially high for instruments used as bases for high-stakes educational decisions.

According to experts (Redfield, 2004), when an educator needs to evaluate any research study in the field of education, s/he should ask herself or himself whether the study dealt with the question that the educator had when s/he selected the study. The educator should ask herself or himself whether there are any other variables that could potentially explain the results reported in the research study. She should also ask herself or himself how the researchers interpreted the results that they reported in their research study. Another question to ask about any educational research study is whether multiple (i.e., more than one) other research studies of high quality have been conducted and published that support the claims made by the authors of the research study that the educator is evaluating. In addition, the educator evaluating a research study should ask whether expert researchers other than the authors of the research study have independently reviewed the study. Moreover, if the answer to this question is yes, then the educator evaluating the research should ask whether these independent expert reviewers supported the research methods that the investigators used, and the conclusions that they drew based on their findings.

COMPETENCIES REGARDING RESEARCH-BASED PRACTICE

According to NASP, school psychologists should know a variety of evaluation/assessment methods for data-based decision-making and accountability; use assessment to identify student strengths and needs, estimate current student status, develop effective interventions based on assessment results, evaluate outcomes, and inform future interventions. In other words, all assessment procedures should be related to prevention and intervention. School psychologists should be able to apply learning theory and cognitive strategies to improve instruction—including alternative methods; develop student cognitive skills and achievement; help educators translate critical emerging research to instructional practice; and assure treatment integrity/correct intervention implementation. A NASP expert (Tilly, 2014) identifies four "thematic questions" to guide science-based school psychology practice, regardless of specific model or approach: (1) Is there a problem, and what is it? (2) Why is the problem occurring? (3) What can we do about the problem? And (4) Did the intervention work? These questions constitute the problem-solving method. (1) equals problem identification; (2) is problem analysis; (3) equates to intervention planning; and (4) represents evaluation of the intervention.

PROBLEM IDENTIFICATION AND PROBLEM ANALYSIS

Educational problem identification often defines a problem as a discrepancy between teacher expectations and student performance. The discrepancy—not the behavior on which problem-solving focuses—is the problem. For instance, physical aggression is not a problem if its rate is 0 as expected. But if a student expected to submit 70% of homework to pass a course is submitting 20%, a significant discrepancy exists. Discrepancies force problem-solver objectivity and agreement among all problem-solving members about related variables; enable directly scaling problem size; and typically allow direct analysis and intervention by being based on naturally occurring behavioral acts/incidents/units. Analyzing a problem's cause enables identifying interventions with direct, empirical connections to the problem's occurrence and high probabilities for successful

46

results. Thus, school psychologists/educators measure performance to identify not student disabilities, but conditions enabling student learning. Instead of published test instruments, the best problem analyses use students' actual school situations and materials for the most valid performance assessment through operationalizing current environmental performance demands. Data-based assessment analysis is then used to develop individualized, needs-specific interventions for each student. School psychologists need comprehensive content knowledge, experience, and professional judgment to analyze problem etiologies.

DESIGNING EDUCATIONAL INTERVENTIONS

After operationally defining an educational problem and analyzing its cause, the third step school psychologists and other educators take in science-based problem-solving is planning interventions. This involves planning how to modify the environment to change specific student behaviors. This includes setting a specific, measurable intervention goal; identifying and setting in place procedures for monitoring intervention effectiveness; procuring or producing materials or supports required to implement the intervention; training implementers as needed; and specifying who will do what, when, and in what way. Intervention components include antecedents, i.e., making changes in the environment to prevent a problem's occurrence, e.g., eliminating events/conditions triggering the problem; alternative skills instruction, i.e., teaching the student needed skills to decrease the problem's occurrence; instructional consequent strategies, i.e., changing the teaching process to decrease problem occurrence and reinforce the student's acquiring new skills; reduction-oriented consequent strategies, i.e., introducing consequences to decrease problem occurrence; long-term prevention strategies, i.e., supporting other situational and/or individual variables to enhance student functioning; and team member support, i.e., providing whichever supports will enable team members to make optimal contributions to the intervention.

PROGRESS MONITORING

Since school psychologists can help other educators design and implement educational interventions but cannot predict for certain how effective they will be in advance of implementation, to evaluate intervention effectiveness they must establish a process for monitoring progress. Being able to depict progress over time accurately is the significant characteristic of progress-monitoring systems. When educators collect data many times during each week, eventually a behavior pattern will emerge. A common practice is to graph this pattern. School psychologists and other educators analyze performance patterns using systematic procedures and decision rules to assess how effective an intervention has been. Progress monitoring commonly shares similar procedures with the earlier scientific research problem-solving steps of problem identification and problem analysis. For example, professionals measure student performance; compare it against a criterion of acceptable performance; and identify a discrepancy between the two. One addition is that now, discrepancy size can be compared to the baseline discrepancy as well as to the performance criterion. Program evaluation corresponds to hypothesis evaluation in scientific research. From intervention effectiveness, one can infer accurate problem analysis or supported hypotheses. When applying science to practice, student behavior changes improving performance outcomes are more important than universal hypotheses application.

RESEARCH

Quantitative research measures findings numerically; qualitative research describes phenomena in more depth but less precisely. Descriptive statistics organize and describe data collected from a population or sample. They only describe the group studied and cannot be generalized to larger groups; and can show correlation/relationship, but cannot infer/predict causation. Inferential statistics infer/predict that one variable causes another, in both the sample studied and the larger population. In experimental designs, researchers select a variable as the independent variable, which they hypothesize will have an effect on another variable, which they select as the dependent variable. For example, if the hypothesis is that the amount of sleep students get the night before a test will affect their test scores, amount of sleep is the independent variable and test score is the dependent variable. Because scientists want the conclusions they draw from experimental research to generalize to a large population but cannot test the whole population, they draw a sample. Random sampling—choosing sample members by chance, like flipping a coin—ensures every member of the population has an equal chance of being selected, making the sample more likely to represent the population accurately.

In research experiments, investigators want to know whether one variable causes effects in another variable. The presumed cause, or independent variable, affects the dependent variable. Experimenters manipulate the independent variable to see whether it affects the dependent variable. The independent variable could be a new medication/instructional intervention, etc.; the dependent variable could be medical symptoms/student achievement, etc. In experiments, the experimental/treatment group receives the drug/intervention/ independent variable; the control group does not. With drugs, control groups receive a placebo—a sugar pill/non-drug appearing identical to the drug. With educational interventions, control groups receive the same interventions already used, not the new one being studied. Confounding variables interfere with/confuse experiment results by also affecting the dependent variable. For example, getting more sleep/eating better could improve medical symptoms/student achievement instead of the new drug/instructional intervention. Researchers control for confounding variables by making experimental conditions as equal as possible, and applying statistical procedures. Longitudinal designs compare effects on the same group over time, typically years. Cross-sectional designs compare effects between/among different groups concurrently. Cross-sequential designs (Schaie, 1965) combine longitudinal and cross-sectional methods, testing different age cohorts at different times to account for cohort effects and normative history-graded effects.

DISTRIBUTION AND MEASURES OF CENTRAL TENDENCY

Distribution is an arrangement of the number values of a given variable showing how frequently they occur. For example, the scores on the same test of individual students in a group can be shown in a distribution. A normal distribution is graphed as a bell-shaped curve, with the largest number of scores/values falling in the center and progressively smaller numbers falling progressively farther away. A distribution with many low scores and a few unusually high scores is positively skewed; a distribution with many high scores and a few unusually low ones is negatively skewed. In positively skewed distributions, the mean is bigger than the median, being raised by the unusual high scores; in negatively skewed distributions, the mean is smaller than the median, being lowered by the unusual low scores. Measures of central tendency include the mean, or average, of all scores/values; the median, or middle, score; and the mode, or most frequent score. The range, a very approximate measure which disregards most scores, is obtained by subtracting the smallest from largest score.

SAMPLING AND SAMPLING ERROR, CONFIDENCE INTERVALS, AND STATISTICAL SIGNIFICANCE IN INFERENTIAL STATISTICS

Since it is impossible to experiment with or test all members of a large population, researchers select smaller samples that are representative of the larger group. Random samples are selected by chance, assuring every population member an equal possibility of being chosen to prevent selection bias. The difference between the values obtained for the sample and values of the same variable(s) for the corresponding population is called sampling error. The smaller the sampling error, the more accurately the sample represents the larger population. The larger the sample selected, the smaller the amount of sampling error. Random selection also minimizes sampling error. Confidence intervals are statistical percentages showing how often the researchers will be incorrect in predicting population results from sample results. For example, the most commonly used confidence interval is .05, meaning population estimates based on samples will be wrong only 5% of the time. Statistical significance, expressed as the value of p, indicates whether an experiment's result is due to chance or to a relationship between/among specific variables.

DATA COLLECTION AND ANALYSIS, ACCOUNTABILITY, AND TECHNOLOGY RESOURCES IN SCHOOL PSYCHOLOGY PRACTICE

According to the National Association of School Psychologists (NASP) *Model for Comprehensive and Integrated School Psychological Services,* making measurements, collecting data, analyzing data, accountability, and using technology resources for program evaluation are "practices that permeate all aspects of service delivery." As a part of a comprehensive, systematic, effective problem-solving and decision-making process, school psychologists have the skills to conduct psychological and educational assessments; know strategies for collecting data; make use of technology resources; and apply the results they obtain for designing, implementing, and evaluating student responses to psychological and educational programs and services. For example, for all professional activities, school psychologists use a problem-solving approach. They consider classroom, family, and community characteristics and other ecological factors, and collect data systematically from multiple sources to establish foundations for decision-making and contexts for general education and special education assessment and intervention. After analyzing assessment data to identify and implement evidence-based mental health and instructional programs and services, they collect further student assessment data to evaluate whether the programs and services implemented are effective in improving student learning, performance, and/or behavior.

Once school psychologists have used data collection and analysis to identify and implement instructional and mental health programs, they then utilize assessment techniques that have been proven valid and reliable to assess student progress toward the academic and behavioral goals that they or other educators have established for them. In Response to Intervention (RtI) approaches, school psychologists use these valid and reliable assessment methods to measure student responses to specified interventions after these have been implemented. They then analyze the data from assessment results and use this information to modify instructional or mental health interventions as needed to make them more effective if they have not already proven so. To enhance the precision, efficiency, and quality of data collection and data-based decisions, school psychologists make use of available information technology resources. For example, computer programs can perform computations to add up, divide, average, aggregate, disaggregate, compare, contrast, and otherwise manipulate data far more rapidly and accurately than humans can. Spreadsheet programs organize and display data for better examination and comprehension.

TREATMENT FIDELITY, INTERVENTION EVALUATION AND MODIFICATION, AND SELF-EVALUATION

After they have collected, analyzed, and applied student data to determine which mental health and instructional interventions to recommend, school psychologists help other educators to design and implement the most suitable assessment procedures for determining how correctly the educators have implemented the interventions that the school psychologists recommended. This is known as treatment fidelity. In order to evaluate how effective the school-based programs and interventions that the school has implemented have been, school psychologists use valid, reliable, and systematic procedures for collecting data. They also use these data collection procedures to determine whether the school programs and interventions need to modified, and in what ways, to increase their effectiveness if they have not worked well enough thus far. Additional ways in which school psychologists use valid, reliable, and systematic procedures in collecting data is to evaluate how effective their own services have been, and to document their own service effectiveness.

MAINTAINING OR ATTAINING ACCOUNTABILITY FOR EDUCATING STUDENTS

Ever since federal legislation has mandated that public schools be accountable for providing students with educations that will enable them to succeed in school, higher education, employment, and life, schools must provide the education departments of their state government and the federal government with documentation that they are giving proper educations to all students. For example, Adequate Yearly Progress (AYP) is a requirement wherein schools must show that their students have learned and achieved enough during each school year to meet the mandated standards. They document AYP by submitting figures showing student scores on high-stakes standardized testing instruments, which are compared both to established criteria and to previous years' results. If a school cannot demonstrate its accountability for achieving this progress, it is required to develop and implement a School Improvement Plan (SIP) and report the results on an ongoing basis to continue to receive federal funding. School psychologists help their fellow educators by collecting and analyzing student data using available information technology resources to inform SIPs, as well as other instructional and mental health school programs; and to evaluate and report student and school progress in these and other plans.

STUDENT-LEVEL SERVICES
INSTRUCTIONAL SUPPORT AND COGNITIVE AND ACADEMIC SKILL DEVELOPMENT

School psychologists develop and implement evidence-based instructional strategies to improve student achievement, based on assessment data. They promote student-centered learning principles to help students develop self-regulated learning; collaborate with other school staff to assure all students meet state and local academic benchmarks; apply current, empirical research on cognition and learning to developing effective instructional strategies that promote student learning at individual and group levels; collaborate with other school staff in developing, implementing, and evaluating interventions to increase the time students spend engaged in learning; incorporate all available assessment data to develop instructional strategies that address individual students' learning needs; share curriculum and instruction research information with educators, parents, and communities to support improving teaching, student performance, and healthy lifestyles; expedite designing and delivering curricular and instructional strategies, e.g., teacher-directed instruction, literacy instruction, peer tutoring, planning/organization interventions, self-regulation interventions, etc., which promote academic achievement; utilize assistive technology and information technology resources to improve student cognitive and academic skills; and, when developing, implementing, and evaluating instructional interventions, address treatment fidelity and acceptability.

MH SERVICES AND INTERVENTIONS FOR DEVELOPING STUDENT SOCIAL AND LIFE SKILLS

School psychologists integrate MH services and behavioral supports into learning and academic goals for students; help design and deliver curricula helping students develop planning, organization, self-regulation, self-monitoring, empathy, healthy decision-making, and other effective behaviors; apply systematic decision-making processes to consider antecedents, consequences, functions, and possible etiologies of behavioral problems that can interfere with socialization and/or learning; evaluate the fidelity and acceptability of interventions as they develop, implement, and evaluate them; provide a continuum of developmentally appropriate MH services including schoolwide and classroom emotional and social learning programs, positive behavioral support, behavioral coaching, individual counseling, group counseling, parental support and education, and addressing personal safety and life skills for lower-functioning students; develop and implement individual and group student-level behavior change programs using appropriate ecological and behavioral methods like social skills training, positive psychology, positive reinforcement, etc.; and evaluate the implementation and results of MH and behavioral interventions for individual students and student groups.

PROFESSIONAL PRACTICES TO PROMOTE SCHOOLWIDE LEARNING

School psychologists' professional practices to promote schoolwide learning include: Applying current, empirical research into learning to develop instructional strategies effectively promoting student learning at the systems level; developing and implementing schoolwide behavior change programs using suitable ecological and behavioral approaches like positive psychology, social skills training, positive reinforcement, etc. to classroom management and student discipline; collaborating to design, implement, and evaluate effective policies and practices regarding instructional support, staff training, student discipline, school improvement, improvement of other agencies, program evaluation, student transitions at all educational levels, grading, home-school partnerships, etc. incorporating evidence-based strategies; applying systems and organizational development theory to help schools provide supportive, respectful, collaborative climates for decision-making and commitment to quality services and instruction; actively help develop school improvement plans; incorporate evidence-based strategies into student transition intervention programs; promote learning environments supporting academic growth, resilience, high academic engagement time rates, and decreasing adverse influences on behavior and learning; help design and implement universal screening programs to identify student needing more behavioral/instructional support, and progress-monitoring systems; collaborate in providing multi-tiered service continua; and apply problem-solving processes to systems-level problems and research, identifying influential factors, evaluating systems-level initiative outcomes, and implementing decision-making practices for accountability.

EFFECTIVE SCHOOL PSYCHOLOGIST PRACTICES IN SYSTEMS-LEVEL PREVENTIVE AND RESPONSIVE SERVICES

School psychologists raise awareness/recognition of risk and protective factors for school failure, truancy, dropouts, bullying, school violence, student suicide, and other systemic problems; as members of school crisis teams, use data-based problem-solving and decision-making procedures, direct services, collaboration, and consultation for crisis prevention, preparedness, response, and recovery; deliver behavioral coaching, direct counseling, and indirect interventions by consulting for students experiencing mental health problems interfering with socialization and/or learning; develop, implement, and evaluate prevention and intervention programs that address risk and protective factors for serious learning and behavior problems; collaborate with students, school personnel, parents, and community resource providers to provide effective mental health support during and following crisis events or situations; promote resilience and wellness by collaborating with other healthcare professionals in delivering fundamental knowledge of health-enhancing behaviors for students, expediting environmental changes that enable good student health and adjustment, and accessing resources for addressing widely varied physical, mental, learning, and behavioral needs; and participate in implementing and evaluating programs to help make schools and communities safe and free of violence.

School and Systems Organization, Policy, and Practices

Schoolwide Practices to Promote Learning

ADDRESSING CONTEXTUAL VARIABLES

Scholarship increasingly demonstrates that interactions of individual student characteristics with environmental system features like the home, community, peer group, classroom, school, culture, etc. are responsible for student successes and difficulties in learning, emotional and social adjustment, and behavior. The roles of contextual influences on child development indicate the need for schools to design and implement educational services from an ecological orientation. Emphasizing ecological factors includes addressing classroom and school climates; facilitating home-school collaboration; and augmenting educational system capacities for providing universal interventions that effectively meet all children's academic, emotional, social, and behavioral needs. Such attention to contextual factors highlights a paradox in the nature of delivering educational and psychological services: because adults control children's contexts for development and learning, school psychologists must begin by directing their professional expertise and attention to adults in order to serve children effectively. Moreover, for optimal service to children from an ecological perspective, school psychologists and other educational professionals must deliver effective services to educational systems. This requires organizational consulting and systems skills. Beyond diagnosing and treating individual students, they must address district and school policies; school climate; learning environment; curriculum, and other systemic variables.

SCHOOL-BASED ORGANIZATIONAL CONSULTANTS

School-based organizational consultants intervene at the systems level to promote effective organizational functioning, which in turn helps students. For example, they may intervene with school districts or individual schools to improve school climate; school leadership; curriculum; instruction; team problem-solving; student academic performance; children's emotional and social development; interpersonal relationships; home-school interactions, etc. Theoretical experts frequently characterize organizational consultation as one type of approach within the context of multi-level, more general models of school-based consultation, or simply of consultation. System levels that these models focus on in their conception of consultation include individual students in client-centered consultation; teachers or other educators in consultee-centered case consultation; and schools or systems in organizational consultation. Multilevel consultation models are derived from ecological theories, e.g., Bronfenbrenner's ecological systems theory (1977), which views child development from the perspective of layers of environmental influences. Client-centered consultation involves environmentally-based interventions to change individual student learning, attitudes, or behavior. Consultee-centered consultation involves changing school systems, schools, parents, families, teachers, classrooms, etc.—the systems surrounding children. Organizational consultation focuses on systems, making it a part of all comprehensive consultation models.

URIE BRONFENBRENNER'S ECOLOGICAL SYSTEMS THEORY

According to Bronfenbrenner's theory, child development takes place via a series of transactions between the child and several environmental systems, which contain and/or affect the child and are themselves nested. The microsystem is Bronfenbrenner's name for contexts of the child's direct, immediate membership, e.g., the family, the neighborhood, and the classroom. The mesosystem is the system of interactions between/among different microsystems, e.g., the between general

52

education and special education teachers, school and family, family and friends, etc. The exosystem represents settings wherein the child is not a member/actively involved, but which still indirectly affect the child, e.g., the school curriculum committee or parents' workplaces. The macrosystem includes governments, laws, policies, and the larger cultural context influencing all lower-order systems. The chronosystem is the system of time, i.e., all life experiences including historical events, environmental events, and major life transitions. Each system is a layer, nested in the order of presentation here: The child is at the center; the microsystem surrounds the child; the mesosystem surrounds the microsystem; the exosystem surrounds the mesosystem; the macrosystem surrounds the exosystem; and the chronosystem is outside of the others.

THREE-TIERED, SCHOOLWIDE POSITIVE BEHAVIOR SUPPORT SYSTEMS

The three-tiered schoolwide positive behavior support systems widely used in American schools today provide for secondary and tertiary interventions, but strongly emphasize primary (Tier 1/universal) prevention. Preeminent theorists' work on prevention (Caplan—originator of primary, secondary, and tertiary prevention and intervention, 1964; Albee, 1988) demonstrates the significance of ecological theory for informing multi-tiered, preventive approaches to service delivery. The emphasis on interventions targeting contextual factors shows the connection between ecological theory and primary prevention. The "public health" approach characterizing three-tier models for preventing student mental health and learning problems additionally supports this connection. Organizational consultation's focus on the system enables achieving Tier 1 primary prevention goals. Collaborative strategies essential to organizational consultation include participants' active engagement and effective interpersonal communication skills. Stages of school-based organizational consultation are entry, including negotiating and agreeing to services; operational problem definition, based on multiple organization members' input; systemic needs assessment, based on data collection and analysis; intervention, developed collaboratively by consultants and organization members; and evaluation of intervention efficacy, acceptability, and integrity. Within the recursive process of organizational consultation, evaluation leads to modification of interventions as indicated.

ROLE OF ORGANIZATIONAL CONSULTATION IN STANDARDS-BASED EDUCATION

In recent decades, standards-based education has been an educational reform addressing student achievement through basing instruction and assessment on clearly defined academic content standards. It includes aligning curriculum, instruction, and assessment with state education board/department standards; supporting educators at classroom and systems levels by providing professional development; and implementing accountability systems using student performance indicators to punish or reward schools. One criticism is that standards-based education, by requiring minimal competency levels, forces teacher focus on average students at the expense of remedial and gifted students. Organizational consultation can help educators differentiate their instruction of core curriculum to support these students by leveraging professional development, a core element of standards-based education. It may also help extend standards-based education to encompass standards for social and emotional learning (SEL) as well as academic standards. Organizational consultants with child development, positive behavior support and intervention, applied behavior analysis, and other relevant content knowledge could help state and school district administrators develop SEL standards, which have already succeeded in some states (e.g., Illinois). Once state standards are established, they could help schools collaborate with parents and other community stakeholders; develop/select suitable SEL curricula; train staff in implementing curricula; and/or assess student SEL skills progress.

ROLE OF SCHOOL-BASED ORGANIZATIONAL CONSULTANTS IN RtI AND PBS MODELS

Response to Intervention (RtI) models typically provide preventive, primary intervention universally to students in Tier 1; targeted, secondary group interventions to at-risk students in Tier 2; and individualized, intensive, tertiary intervention to selected high-needs students in Tier 3. Ecological models of school-based organizational can help school districts and schools develop and implement support for educators via professional development in effective instructional and behavioral support delivery, screening, and progress monitoring, enabling preventive Tier 1 interventions' success by addressing both content and process issues. When information is lacking about how schools have modified RtI implementation to suit local settings; or if it has not been implemented with fidelity (as intended), it is impossible to conclude that a student is not responding to the curriculum. Organizational consultants can help districts/schools develop/identify treatment fidelity measures, and establish infrastructures that support educators in using the most effective methods of delivering curriculum. Like RtI, Positive Behavior Supports (PBS) involves three-tiered prevention and support, environmental factors, and data-based decision-making. Though PBS are effective for preventing behavior problems, many teachers also find conducting functional behavior analyses, teaching suitable replacement behaviors, etc. challenging. Organizational consultants can aid professional development of teacher PBS skills, and stakeholder (including school staff) buy-in for PBS implementation.

COMMUNITY AND SYSTEM RESOURCE MAPPING

Resource mapping has been used for many years, often by communities. Many different groups and organizations, including communities and school systems, use resource mapping as a system-building process for aligning their resources and policies with their systems' specific goals, strategies, and expected outcomes. Mapping programs, services, supports, and other resources can identify resources available to individual students in a given school or district, identify additional or new resources for maintaining specific existing initiatives or activities in a school/district, and/or identify resources for helping to establish and build the capacity for supporting more comprehensive service systems. Resource maps can afford comprehensive depictions of school/district vision, mission, goals, infrastructure, and projects. Resource mapping can help schools identify new resources; ensure all students have access to resources that they need; avoid duplicating resources and services; foster new relationships and partnerships; disseminate information across agencies that provide services to students; and encourage collaboration among stakeholders and agencies. Steps in the mapping process are:

1. Pre-mapping
2. Mapping
3. Taking action
4. Maintaining and evaluating mapping work.

Steps in resource mapping are:

1. Establishing consensus on map parameters by selecting a goal to map
2. Determining which kinds of resources on which to collect data—resources identified can include human resources; financial resources; in-kind resources; academic standards; technical standards; technical assistance; student services; family services; community services; supporting policies; agencies and organizations sharing common/similar goals and objectives, etc.
3. Developing data collection instruments
4. With help from stakeholders, collect data
5. Conduct an environmental or school scan

54

6. Synthesize, analyze, and interpret data collected
7. Communicate the findings
8. Develop products related to the goal, resources, findings, and priorities.

Mappers should prioritize resource-mapping goals according to the overall vision, and then map around each goal; and organize information to be responsive, comprehensive, and meaningful to stakeholders. Scanning the school/system/district for existing and potential resources includes analyzing internal and external issues likely to affect district/school/program resources. Mappers must determine specifically what assets the school/district has to help them meet their goals.

ELEMENTS TO INCLUDE WHEN IDENTIFYING RESOURCES

Regarding a particular school organization, program, initiative, or project, the mappers should select one of the goals they have identified to map; identify the key investors or stakeholders in the goal selected; and then detail/define each of these further. In identifying resources, first identify the purpose of the organization, program, initiative, or project; e.g., how legislation defines it. Then identify the source of funding for the organization, program, initiative, or project. Then identify service delivery, i.e., how funds are distributed in the school's state and the personnel who deliver services. The target population of students served should be identified (e.g., students with a specific category of disability; all students with IEPs; students in certain grades; students failing certain subjects; all students in a school or district, etc.), plus the number or percentage of students served according to the most recent available information. Next, identify the activities or services provided by the organization, program, initiative, or project (e.g., instruction, counseling, transportation, mentoring, etc.). Identify any agencies/organizations/businesses partnering with the school/district and the partnership's purpose. Identify the outcomes the organization/program/initiative/project is expected to achieve, and its strengths in meeting student needs. Identify other relevant information, e.g., planning cycles, decision-makers, etc.

CRITERIA FOR DATA COLLECTION AND ANALYSIS

The individual resource mappers must determine which criteria their data collection methods should meet. General criteria to guide mappers include:

- Credibility – the information should be relevant to the audience(s) identified.
- Practicality – the data should be collected without overly disrupting the usual school routines and processes.
- Timeliness – data should be obtained, analyzed, interpreted, and communicated to stakeholders in time to meet their needs.
- Accuracy – the information gathered should be trustworthy and relevant.
- Ease – the information collected should be easy for mappers to analyze.
- Objectivity – the data should be collected by personnel who are able to be objective.
- Clarity – the information gathered should be clear and comprehensible to multiple and varied audiences.
- Scope – the data obtained and used should answer questions being investigated without extraneous detail.
- Availability – information obtained and used should be existing data, hence easily accessible.
- Usefulness – information gathered should address stakeholders' current concerns.
- Balance – information should represent multiple values and perspectives related to the goal(s) and resources being mapped.
- Cost-effectiveness – the data collected should be worth the expense of collecting them.

STEPS IN ANALYZING DATA AND IN IDENTIFYING SERVICE DUPLICATION, OVERLAPS, AND GAPS

Four steps in analyzing resource mapping data collected for meaning are:

1. Reviewing the original purposes of collecting the data
2. Describing the information in tables or a narrative
3. Looking for patterns or trends, e.g., resources that overlap and gaps between/among resources, which may inform new ways of aligning existing resources to improve outcomes or indicate other resources untapped as yet
4. Assessing how comprehensive the information is in view of the goals identified.

If mappers identify any gaps in their data collection process through step (4), they may need to repeat data collection to obtain additional information targeting their goals. When analyzing resources to identify any overlaps and gaps, three steps in the process are:

1. List the same goal or desired outcome identified previously during the process of identifying the vision of the district, school, task force, committee, etc.
2. Review the resource map with respect for this goal, identifying services that duplicate each other, overlap, or are absent.
3. List the implications for the school/district's service delivery system; e.g., insufficient funding for duplicated or overlapping services, long wait lists for absent or insufficient services, etc.

HIGH-STAKES STANDARDIZED ACHIEVEMENT TESTS

Since the ESEA (Elementary and Secondary Education Act) or No Child Left Behind Act (2001), now the Every Student Succeeds Act (2015), mandated passing standardized tests for grade promotion and high school graduation, high-stakes testing has become the norm. Consequences such as repeating a grade or not getting a diploma, combined with the fact that students and parents often have inadequate understanding of standardized achievement tests, generate much anxiety. Parents and students must remember that achievement tests (and even IQ tests) are not absolute measures of student intelligence but of student test-taking ability and how well educators are teaching test-taking skills; and that these tests, designed to track academic progress, benefit students by informing teachers about what to help individual students with in classrooms. Some advantages of high-stakes testing include: They can help teachers base learning plans on student needs, enabling long-term student benefits. State-level testing data are typically available to the public, enabling parents to compare their school's performance to others' to make better-informed decisions about where and how to obtain their children's best education. Test-taking skills improve with time and practice; students benefit from learning how to handle pressure and develop strategies and skills to meet school and parental expectations.

DISADVANTAGES

Preparing for standardized achievement tests can detract time and attention from subject content that these tests do not assess, including subject areas that promote creativity; even experts concede this is true. Schools end up sacrificing the arts, sciences, history, social studies, and similar subjects to make more time for test preparation. As noted by Lynne Munson, President and Executive Director of the nonprofit educational advocacy group Common Core, Inc., although many schools have significantly cut down on these subjects to focus on language arts and math for standardized testing, these other subjects are actually included in the public school core curriculum mandated by the federal government. Therefore, she characterizes neglecting these other subjects as "...denying our students the complete education they deserve and the law demands." Also, the pressure on teachers exerted by high-stakes testing can stifle innovation and creativity. Teachers frequently

56

respond to government pressure by "teaching to the test," reducing their flexibility for customizing lesson plans for individual students or class groups. Reduced innovation and freedom can also cause teacher dissatisfaction and higher turnover. Furthermore, while constructive pressure motivates students to higher achievement, pressure for its own sake, unconnected to learning, suppresses learning and therefore, is counterproductive.

PROMOTION AND RETENTION IN AMERICAN PUBLIC SCHOOLS

Passing students to the next grade even when they have not met grade-level performance standards or academic requirements is called "social" promotion because educators frequently do it in what they believe is a student's best interests for social wellbeing, as well as psychological wellbeing. Despite this perception, research implies that achievement and opportunities in life are not enhanced by promoting unprepared students. Studies from the U.S. Department of Education show at the same time that retention of students, i.e., making them repeat a grade, frequently has adverse educational results, which include raising their probability of dropping out of school. State or district guidelines inform case-by-case decisions for promotion and retention in most U.S. states and school districts. When the American Federation of teachers surveyed large public school districts (1997), it found wide variations in how they use student attendance, performance, test results, teacher recommendations, and other factors to make decisions for retention and promotion. Education Week found (*Quality Counts*, 2004) that statewide test performance determined promotion to certain grades in nine states: Delaware, Florida, Georgia, Louisiana, Mississippi, Missouri, North Carolina, Texas, and Wisconsin.

Although educators and education researchers talk and write about social promotion in our schools and know that it exists, most discussion of this practice criticizes it. Therefore, school systems are reluctant to admit they promote/have promoted unqualified students. In the recent past (1997), the majority of teachers surveyed by the American Federation of Teachers reported having promoted unprepared students in the previous year. Though retention is also a complex issue, researchers have been able to measure its rates because school records document student retention, but do not show whether promotions were based on student performance or social reasons. The National Center for Education Statistics reported (1996) that of high school seniors, roughly 17% had been retained in at least one grade since kindergarten. Grades K-2 were the most often repeated. In another, longitudinal study (Heubert and Hauser, 1999) following 6- to 8-year-old students from the 1980s through the early 1990s, researchers discovered that by 12-14 years old, 31% of them—close to 1/3—were in grades inappropriate for their ages.

While researchers can quantify student retentions, they cannot differentiate social promotion vs. promotion for class/course grades, test scores, and other objective criteria. However, some experts reason social promotions probably exceed retentions, which are a last resort. Research finds neither retention nor social promotion effective to improve student performance. Excessive dropout rates, particularly for minority and low-income students and insufficient student skills and knowledge are outcomes of both practices, according to the U.S. Department of Education. A contributing factor may be that retention frequently entails grade repetition without changing instructional methods or academic content. Also, low-income and minority students are overrepresented by retention policies. Studies associate retention with adverse effects on student attitudes about school, attendance, personal adjustment in school, and achievement. However, public opinion is heavily against social promotion (>80% of teachers and employers, c. 75% of parents) instead of retention. Only 15% of teachers and 24% of parents find retention worse. A survey (Public Agenda, 2003) found 87% of parents would approve policies requiring passing a test for promotion, even if these caused retention. Alternatives include prevention and early intervention, intensive instruction, ongoing teacher professional development, and assessment to inform instruction and learning better.

EVIDENCE-BASED PRACTICE AND SCHOOL-WIDE POSITIVE BEHAVIOR SUPPORT

In efforts in education and mental health toward systems change and changes in current policy, one of the major areas of focus is to what extent U.S. states are making investments in practices and procedures that have the support of evidence obtained through rigorous research. Formal studies have found correlations between valuable outcomes for children and families and the use of evidence-based practices in school instructional and psychological services. School-Wide Positive Behavior Support (SWPBS) has become increasingly popular in recent years, with many state education departments and/or school districts adopting it as their system of choice for preventing and remediating learning and behavior problems. It owes much of its popularity to its emphasis on prevention, which is congruent with recent trends away from traditional reactive approaches. Consequently, educators and stakeholders in education have asked whether SWPBS is an evidence-based practice. The U.S. Department of Education's Office of Special Education Programs (OSEP) accordingly has provided (2009) evidence and citations of research supporting SWPBS status as evidence-based practice (Positive Behavioral Interventions & Supports, OSEP Technical Assistance Center). Criteria for evidence-based practices have additionally been proposed by the APA, SAMSA, What Works Clearinghouse, and Institute for Education Science.

Recommendations for defining evidence-based practices, based on quantitative research methods (Gersten et al); correlational studies (Thompson et al) and single-subject studies (Horner et al), summarized in a special section of *Exceptional Children* (Odom et al, 2005). According to the Office of Special Education Programs (OSEP) of the U.S. Department of Education, SWPBS uses a systems approach to establish behavioral, social, and cultural supports schools must provide for all students' academic and social success. In Tier 1, primary prevention universally supports all students. In Tier 2, secondary intervention targets identified groups of students at risk for learning/behavior problems. In Tier 3, tertiary intervention is intensive and individualized for students with higher educational/behavioral needs. Tier 1 core elements include: Defining and teaching behavioral expectations; implementing a system of rewards to reinforce desirable behaviors; applying consequences for undesirable behaviors along a continuum; and continuously collecting and using data to make related decisions. As of 2009 (PBIS, ED OSEP TAC), at least five studies documented SWPBS implementation fidelity; six randomized control trials evaluating SWPBS were recently completed, in process, or proposed; and many more evaluation studies with non-experimental designs using research quality measures found lower disciplinary referrals or higher academic performance.

In the systems approach of School-Wide Positive Behavior Support (SWPBS), three tiers represent primary, secondary, and tertiary prevention of academic and behavior problems. Tier 1 includes defining and teaching school behavioral expectations to all students; establishing systems of rewards for appropriate behaviors and consequences for inappropriate/problematic behaviors; and continuously collecting and utilizing data in decision-making. Tier 2 includes universal screening of all students for learning/behavior problems and associated risk factors; monitoring the progress of at-risk students; implementing a system to increase school/classroom predictability and structure; a system for augmenting adult feedback contingent on performance/behavior; a system connecting academic and behavioral achievement; a system enhancing home-school communication; and collecting and applying data in making decisions. As of 2009 (PBIS, ED OSEP TAC), at least two randomized control trials evaluating SWPBS Tier 2/secondary interventions were in process; at least 16 journal articles were published, plus one more submitted for publication, on specific secondary/Tier 2 interventions; and 13 refereed journal articles on secondary interventions, seven chapters/articles on dropout prevention, six publications on First Steps to Success, and four research summary articles on social skills training were published.

In Tier 1 primary prevention, SWPBS defines behavioral expectations and instructs all students in them. Schools establish systems to provide universal rewards and consequences for adaptive and maladaptive behaviors, respectively, to all students. In Tier 2, secondary measures include universal screening; at-risk student progress monitoring; systems to make schools/classrooms more structured and predictable, increase adult contingent feedback and home-school communication, and connect behavioral and academic outcomes. All three tiers require collecting and using data to make decisions, Tier 1 continuously. Tier 3 core components include Functional Behavior Analysis; comprehensive team assessment; connecting academic and behavioral supports; and interventions individualized according to assessment results, focused on preventing problematic conditions; teaching functionally equal replacement skills/behaviors and desired performance skills/behaviors; extinction strategies for undesired behaviors; enhancement strategies for contingently rewarding desired behaviors; and safety consequences as indicated. Most research into Tier 3/tertiary prevention has involved single-case designs evaluating specific intervention effects; however, studies are increasingly correlating these interventions to decreased behavior problems. As of 2009 (PBIS, ED OSEP TAC), 18 studies were published and one in press regarding tertiary interventions; one under review on SWPBS implementation and outcome; and one published, one in press on SWPBS fidelity and outcomes.

Although experts from professional psychological organizations, federal government educational and mental health services agencies all propose various criteria for evaluating whether practices such as SWPBS can be considered evidence-based practices, some general criteria have been offered by the U.S. Department of Education's Office of Special Education Services (OSEP)'s Technical Assistance Center. For example, claiming that any practice or procedure is evidence-based should be supported by an explicit description of the practice or procedure; clear definitions of who implements the practice or procedure, and in which settings; an identification of the population(s) expected to benefit from the practice; and a specification of what outcomes are expected. Authorities may review research using the practice/procedure in the context of these criteria. For documenting that a practice/procedure is evidence-based, one of the most rigorous standards is its support by at least two peer-reviewed research studies using randomized experimental control trials. For a practice/procedure to satisfy this standard, it must be defined operationally; formal fidelity and outcome measures must be conducted; and all these components must exist in a research design using randomized control group trials.

ORGANIZATION AND SYSTEMS THEORY
SCHOOL DISTRICT IMPROVEMENT PLAN BASED ON ORGANIZATIONAL AND SYSTEMS THEORIES

Organizational theory and systems theory are often applied by educators to inform efforts to understand and improve school organizations and systems. Identifying organizational systems in a school district that most affect school-level instruction and learning, and then working to achieve greater alignment and strength in those systems; ensuring the district's involvement in improvement plans for individual schools; and developing and implementing comprehensive, consistent accountability systems at the district level, are strategies for improving teaching, learning, and accountability. For example, some district-level activities designated by a state education department as parts of a district improvement plan include: Guiding improvement actions through identifying a few areas that take the highest priorities with stakeholders; identifying actions by personnel and outcomes for students as indices for each high-priority area targeted; guiding personnel's actions in each high-priority area by identifying a limited number of research-based strategies with high leverage; supporting implementation of the strategies identified through prioritizing how resources are utilized; and guiding decision-making and assessing progress by identifying measurable process results indicators or personnel actions.

Example of state education department's overall theory of action and operational theory of action: As one example, the Connecticut State Department of Education's (2010) overall action theory states that if the department helps a school district to fortify and align its organizational systems, especially systems most closely involved with the school-level instructional core, the learning of students in that district will improve observably and progressively. This state education department identifies such instructional core organizational systems having the most direct impact on school-level instruction and learning as: acquisition and support of human resources; curriculum; instruction; assessment; supervision and evaluation; professional development; school leadership; school culture; school climate; development of school improvement plans; and implementation of school improvement plans. It also identifies the district as playing a critical role in leading and designing school improvement agendas. This department's operational action theory states that if the department helps a school district to develop and effectively implement a coherent, comprehensive accountability system, school-level core systems most related to instruction and learning will become more aligned and much stronger, enabling continuous improvement and longitudinal maintenance of student achievement.

Based on organizational and systems theory, state education departments may conclude that their assisting school districts in improving their organizational systems—including developing and implementing/improving comprehensive accountability systems—will in turn improve school-level teaching and learning. In addition to implementing district improvement plans, some state education departments propose forming a data team for each school district. Some duties of district data teams include developing the district improvement plan; overseeing and monitoring its implementation; collecting, analyzing and interpreting data; applying data to evaluate and modify the plan; and overseeing and implementing the improvement cycle continuously. Similarly, some related duties of a school-level data team include developing a school improvement plan; and performing the same duties related to the school improvement plan as the district-level team does with its improvement plan. An instructional data team establishes student performance goals; collects and analyzes student/course/grade data to plan and improve instruction and assessment; supplies staff with a professional learning community; and implements improvement plan components. Classroom teachers collaborate with their school data teams in identifying and implementing effective instructional and assessment practices; and utilize their results to help the data team with continuing improvement activities.

RELATIONSHIP OF STUDENT LEARNING, SCHOOL IMPROVEMENT, AND SYSTEMIC SCHOOL REFORM

System-level school reform initiatives are centrally inspired by school improvement. This premise derives from two simple-sounding but deeply significant assumptions:

- Instruction must be improved on an equally wide scale as the scale on which educators want to improve learning; and
- Both instruction and learning are embedded in their organizational and social contexts, and thus, are profoundly influenced by them.

Research has shown how the school context affects student learning for the past several decades. Studies of effective schools in the 1980s; research into teacher learning and work in the 1990s; and investigations of high-performing school organizations and restructuring of schools in the late 1990s and thereafter have all provided evidence that improving schools is required for improving student learning. The consensus of all this literature identifies several factors critical to effective school organizations. Factors most frequently named include: A shared mission emphasizing teaching and learning; a strong professional community, founded on group responsibility for student learning and on collaboration; instructional leadership from principals (and/or others); sufficient human, fiscal, material, and instructional resources; accurate, timely student learning data; well-qualified instructional personnel; professional development opportunities; parent-teacher relational trust; and community support.

CHALLENGES TO IMPROVING SCHOOL ORGANIZATIONS AND TO REALIZATION OF STATE AND DISTRICT INITIATIVES

While plenty of research has identified some of the most important characteristics of successful school organizations, this knowledge does not necessarily include strategies that are effective for attaining this success. Some factors involved in identifying, selecting, and/or developing such effective strategies include the complex nature of schools; the enormous number of potential points for intervention; and the unpredictable nature of what the results of the interventions implemented will be. These factors have been identified by both systems theorists and researchers studying school reform. In addition, traditional school structures and norms are stubbornly entrenched, and it is difficult for new state and district policies even to extend to individual classroom practices, let alone influence them in any depth. These factors of resistance to change have been stressed by educational historians, institutional theorists, and implementation researchers. However, there is also evidence of exemplary improvement results in some schools, proving that true improvement is possible. Some main areas wherein school districts institute school improvement programs and policies include accountability, standards and assessments, data systems, and professional development.

Preventive and Responsive Services

VIOLENCE IN SCHOOLS

Among the many responsibilities of educators, one is to make and keep classroom environments safe and positive to promote growth and learning. Violence makes classrooms and schools unsafe, disrupting learning and even jeopardizing students and staff physically or emotionally. Conflicts in schools that can lead to violence include bullying and discrimination; however, actual violence and fighting in schools is even more serious. Although common perceptions tend to minimize public school violence, data from the National Center for Education Statistics show its prevalence; for example, from 1999-2000, 61% of public elementary schools, 87% of public middle schools, and 92% of public high schools had at least one violent incident. With funding from the U.S. Department of Education, the University of Nebraska-Lincoln has formed the Safe and Responsive Schools (SRS) project to develop resources that educators can incorporate into their schools for effectively preventing violence. Three strategies emphasized by this project's framework are:

- Establishing a positive school climate promoting interactions and alternatives to violence.
- Implementing a system for early identification of and intervention with students at risk for academic or behavioral problems.
- Developing effective responses to persistent, serious behavioral issues.

RISK FACTORS AND PROTECTIVE FACTORS AGAINST VIOLENCE

Risk factors are as follows:

- Individual – violent victimization history; ADHD; LDs; early aggression history; alcohol/tobacco/drug use; lower IQ; poor behavioral self-control; information-processing/social-cognitive skills deficits; emotional distress; emotional problems treatment history; antisocial attitudes/beliefs; family conflict and violence.
- Family – authoritarian parenting style; inconsistent/lax/harsh discipline; low parental involvement; low child emotional attachment to parents; low parental income; low parental education; parental criminality; parental substance abuse; family dysfunction; poor child supervision and monitoring.
- Social, peer – delinquent peer association; gang involvement; peer social rejection; lack of engagement in typical activities; poor academic performance; low school commitment; school failure.
- Community – reduced financial opportunities; low-income neighborhood; high transiency; family disruption; low community participation levels; neighborhood social disorganization.

Protective factors are as follows:

- Individual – Higher IQ; intolerance of deviance; high academic achievement/GPA; positive social orientation; superior social skills; realistic planning skills; religiosity.
- Family – connectedness; discussing problems with parents; perceived high parental expectations regarding school performance; frequent shared activities; consistent parental presence when awakening/returning from school/at supper/at bedtime; social activities; family/parent constructive coping models/strategies.
- Social, peer – prosocial, close, strong school relationships; school commitment; close non-deviant peer relationships; peer groups rejecting antisocial behavior; prosocial activities; school climates with clear behavioral rules, intensive supervision, teacher and parent engagement, and consistent negative reinforcement of aggression.

BULLYING

Bullying in school has adverse impacts on students' ability to learn, as well as threatening their physical and emotional safety. According to stopbullying.gov, a U.S. Department of Health and Human Services website, prevention is best. Prevention activities include:

- Assess the school's prevention and intervention procedures regarding violence, substance abuse, and other aspects of student behavior. Since many other behaviorally related school programs identify and address the same risk and protective factors as anti-bullying programs, educators can sometimes build on these or incorporate bullying prevention strategies into them.
- Assess school bullying frequency and location(s); adult and student intervention practices; and prevention effectiveness.
- Implement awareness campaigns to inform school members, parents, and community of prevention objectives and engage their participation: unified, community-wide stands against bullying are important. Form a school safety task force or committee to plan, implement, and evaluate the school bullying prevention program.
- Create and widely communicate/disseminate a mission statement, code of conduct, schoolwide rules, and reporting system establishing a climate making bullying unacceptable.

- Build a safe environment, using the student handbook, website, newsletters; staff, class, and parent meetings; and assemblies establishing a tolerant, accepting, respectful school culture. Reinforce inclusive, positive social interactions.

DISCRIMINATION IN SCHOOLS

Some experts speculate that bullying, other conflicts leading to violence, and actual outbreaks of violence in American schools may be connected to a cultural tendency toward xenophobia (meaning fear of the strange, alien, or foreign) causing intolerance of those who are different. Discrimination based on race, sexual orientation, religion, etc. is frequently classified as hate. The Southern Poverty Law Center's project Teaching Tolerance (Tolerance.org) published a guide entitled *Responding to Hate [and Bias] at School* providing the details of various strategies for appropriately addressing hate/bias/discrimination in schools, divided into three sections: before, during, and after crises triggered by bias incidents. Tolerance.org proposes educators must respond to overt intolerance with consistent, everyday actions. Through immediate intervention, educators promote positive communities rejecting hatred/bias; and model unbiased behavior. They should also demonstrate through discussion that hate/discrimination/bias incidents are unacceptable. Key concepts/principles include: Administrators and educators' prohibiting vandalism and hate graffiti; establishing environments making hate symbols and language unwelcome; vocal educator stands against hate literature, websites, e-mails, and music; educator vigilance for signs of student alienation; fearless educator confrontation of bigotry in colleagues; and active educator confrontation and discussion of national and community hate incidents.

SCHOOL CLIMATE ASSESSMENT

Whenever individuals interact in groups, the group dynamics and processes that develop constitute a sum larger than any of its parts, i.e., larger than what any single individual does. Peer-reviewed educational research studies have yielded consistent results showing the correlation of positive school climates with effective risk prevention, academic achievement, and the positive development of youth. School climate, i.e., the nature and quality of school life, is founded upon student, school staff, and parent experiences of school life; and reflective of organizational structures, values, goals, norms, instructional and learning practices, and interpersonal relationships. Positive school climates nurture the learning and development needed for students to establish satisfying, productive, and contributing lives in democratic society. Factors defining these climates include expectations, norms, and values supporting physical, emotional, and social safety; respect; engagement; educator, student, and family collaboration in developing, contributing to, and living a common school vision; educators' modeling and nurturing attitudes emphasizing the satisfaction and benefits of learning; and every member's contribution to care of the physical environment and school operations. The National School Climate Center and National School Climate Council identify safety, relationships, teaching and learning, and the external environment as main dimensions of school climate to assess.

CSH

The following are eight components of Coordinated School Health (CSH) as a means for schools to promote good health, according to the U.S. Centers for Disease Control and Prevention (CDC):

- Health Education teaches attitudes, knowledge, and skills for health literacy, health-enhancing behaviors and decisions, and promoting others' health. Comprehensive school health education includes nutrition, personal wellness, mental and emotional health, drug use/abuse, safety/injury prevention, sexual health, violence prevention, etc. and should address National Health Education Standards.

- Physical Education teaches lifelong physical activity skills through sequential, planned curriculum helping students meet national K-12 standards.
- Health Services include referral/access to primary healthcare services; communicable disease/other health problem prevention/control; emergency injury/illness care; optimal sanitation for safe school facilities and environments; and education and counseling to maintain/enhance individual, family, and community health.
- Nutrition Services enable health education and classroom nutrition learning experiences; reflect federal dietary guidelines; and are resources connecting to community nutritional services.
- Psychological/counseling and Social Services promote both student and school environment health.
- Safe, Healthy School Environment includes physical conditions, school culture, psychosocial climate, and aesthetics influencing wellbeing.
- Staff Health Promotion offers health-enhancing education, assessments, and activities, producing positive role models; increasing staff commitment to student health; reducing absenteeism and health insurance costs, and improving productivity.
- Family/Community Involvement—broad-based constituencies, coalitions, advisory councils—help school response more effectively enhance student health and wellbeing.

FACTORS RELATED TO ACADEMIC AND BEHAVIOR PROBLEMS DURING KINDERGARTEN AND FIRST GRADE

Among individual factors associated with cognitive and behavioral problems upon entering school, research (cf. Huffman, Mehlinger, and Kerivan, 2000) identifies low birth weight; neurodevelopmental delay; maternal medical and emotional problems during pregnancy; child medical problems; psychophysiological factors (e.g., slow complex reaction time, variable heart rate); cognitive deficits; difficult temperament; personality (high impulsivity, low anxiety, low reward dependence); early adjustment and behavior problems (hyperactivity, immaturity-dependency, externalizing, internalizing); age on entering school. Family risk factors include divorce, remarriage; low maternal education; parental substance abuse; maternal relationship problems history; parental psychopathology; poor parenting; maltreatment; insecure attachment; peer relationship difficulties. Daycare/school factors include non-maternal care; K-1 class sociodemographic characteristics, class organization, school facilities, teacher variables, social interactions; student-teacher relationships. Community risk factors include immigrant and minority status; lower SES. Protective factors include higher maternal IQ; easy temperament; higher child IQ; higher SES; positive family relationships; living with both parents; social support; internal locus of control; positive daycare experiences; more classroom friends upon entering school; preschool parental peer contact initiation; more preschool experience; and a positive relationship with the teacher.

FACTORS RELATED TO SCHOOL TRUANCY

Students develop self, interact socially, learn interpersonal skills, form peer groups, and express themselves in the primary context of school. Research shows school-related variables predict the probability of prosocial vs. delinquent behaviors like truancy. School environment and student experience in school are identified as related to truancy. Some researchers (Henry and Huizinga, 2007) identify school performance and involvement with delinquent peers as the strongest truancy predictor. A meta-analysis of over 100 studies found poor academic performance correlated with many delinquent behaviors' onset, frequency, and severity. Not only does delinquent peer association contribute to delinquency; once students begin offending, delinquent peer association intensifies and offense severity escalates. Better academic performance is a protective factor against adverse effects of delinquent peer association. Student perceptions of unsafe school environments, school gangs, and non-positive teacher practices also predict truancy. Experts identify strong school leadership, focus on teaching and learning, data-based problem identification and progress monitoring/information-rich environments; positive school culture; learning communities; continuous faculty and staff improvement efforts; continual professional development; parental involvement; community support; resource access; clear, strong attendance policies; timely parental contact about unexcused absence; meaningful incentives for parental responsibility regarding student attendance; and continuing truancy prevention initiatives as protective factors.

RESEARCH CONCLUSIONS ABOUT SCHOOL DROPOUTS

According to the National Dropout Prevention Center/Network (Hammond, Linton, Smink, and Drew, 2007), school dropouts are related to various individual, family, school, and community factors. Single factors cannot predict dropout risk accurately; combinations become more accurate. Dropouts are not homogeneous populations: depending on when risk factors emerge, combinations experienced, and their influences, researchers identify various subgroups. Risk factors have complex interactions; dropouts frequently cite reasons crossing multiple domains. Dropouts are often culminations of long disengagement processes, starting even before school entry, with risk factors longitudinally building and compounding. Risk factors: Learning disabilities; emotional disturbance; teen parenthood; excessive work hours; high-risk social behaviors; high-risk peer groups; high social activity outside school; low academic achievement; retention/being overage for grade; poor school attendance; low educational expectations; low effort; low school commitment; no extracurricular activities; school misbehavior; early aggression; low SES; low parental education; high family mobility; many siblings; parental separation/divorce; family disruption; low family educational expectations; sibling dropouts; low parental school contact; few/no conversations about school. Protective best practices in prevention programs include: developing life/social skills (communication/problem-solving/critical thinking/conflict resolution/peer resistance); many real-life practice opportunities and reinforcements; academic support (skills enhancement, tutoring, homework help); interactive normative education strategies; family strengthening; behavioral interventions.

SALIENT RISK FACTORS FOR YOUTH SUICIDE AND PROTECTIVE FACTORS AGAINST IT

According to the U.S. Centers for Disease Control and Prevention (CDC), individual, relational, community, and societal factors combined contribute to suicide risk—not necessarily causing, but correlating with suicide, including: family history of suicide, or child maltreatment; previous suicide attempt(s); history of mental disorders, especially clinical depression; alcohol and/or substance abuse history; hopeless feelings; aggressive or impulsive tendencies; religious and cultural beliefs aggrandizing suicide as a noble solution to some problems; local suicide epidemics; feeling socially isolated; obstacles preventing mental health treatment access; relational, social, financial, or work loss; physical illness; ease of access to means of committing suicide; and avoidance of seeking treatment due to stigma related to suicidal ideations, mental health and substance abuse disorders. Protective factors against suicidal thinking and behavior, while not as extensively or rigorously researched as risk factors, are still found equally important to research by the CDC, including: Easy access to various clinical interventions, and to support for seeking help; effective clinical care treating physical, mental, and substance abuse disorders; family and community connection and support; ongoing supportive medical and MH care relationships; problem-solving, conflict-resolution, and nonviolent dispute management skills; and religious and cultural beliefs discouraging suicide and supporting self-preservation instincts.

CRISIS PREVENTION AND PREPAREDNESS PLANS AND PROTOCOLS

Though highly publicized fatal school shootings/similar large-scale disasters occur rarely, schools and communities can sustain significant impacts from other, more frequent crises like violent acts/threats or accidental deaths. The National Association of School Psychologists (NASP) reports 78% of U.S. schools had one or more violent crimes during the 2005-2006 school year; 17%, one or more other serious violent incidents. About 6% of students aged 12-18 reported avoiding one or more school places/activities for fear of harm/attacks; nonfatal theft/violent crimes in schools victimized c. 1.5 million students aged 12-18. Student reactions to school crises can adversely affect their education, adjustment, and behavior. Crisis prevention, though required, is insufficient as it cannot prevent all crisis events; therefore, schools also need crisis preparedness plans to ensure effective resource deployment and meet all response and recovery needs. The typical simultaneous, multiple, non-routine demands of crises for immediate response dictate planning preparedness. Research supports this need by showing that school crises are not a matter of if, but when they will occur. In one survey (Adamson & Peacock, 2007), 93% of 228 school psychologists reported serious crises in their schools. Preparedness plans prevent unneeded trauma, panic, and chaos.

In addition to preventing and minimizing the damage to students, staff, schools, and surrounding communities that violent crises in schools can cause, another reason that schools need to establish crisis prevention and preparedness plans is a legal one. Litigation can ensue when schools fail to address crisis issues. Even though some experts have argued that local government immunity exempts schools from litigation, research studies still report very harmful effects to schools in terms of adverse public relations and the financial expense of defending lawsuits filed against them for failing to respond adequately to school crisis events. In contrast, schools that have crisis plans and teams established generate greater control and calmness, making them far better able to help school communities recover from crisis experiences. For instance, when a school identifies itself as having a crisis plan in place and having followed it, survivors are more likely to perceive after the crisis that it is manageable and that challenges related to it can be resolved. Schools with crisis plans can also more effectively decrease chaos levels during emergencies; identify individuals in need; and aid school communities in more quickly restoring normalcy.

FEDERAL, STATE, AND LOCAL LEGISLATION

Along with averting/minimizing school, student, staff, and community harm and avoiding legal repercussions, legislative initiatives motivate school crisis prevention and planning. For example, the Improving America's Schools Act (1994); Schools Safety Enhancement Act (1999); Goals 2000 Educate America Act; and School Anti-Violence Empowerment Act (2000) have funded crisis preparedness efforts. The No Child Left Behind Act (ESEA, 2001), now the Every Student Succeeds Act (2015), while mainly addressing academic accountability, also requires schools receiving federal funds demonstrate they have crisis plans (Title IV, Part A). Executive Order 13347, Individuals with Disabilities in Emergency Preparedness, signed in 2004 by President George W. Bush, requires public entities' emergency preparedness efforts to include people with disabilities (ED, 2006b). According to the National Education Association (NEA, 2007b), state and local regulations/laws also influence school district crisis prevention and preparedness. Some state laws require annual crisis response training, prevention programming, regular safety drills, and/or building-level/district-level crisis plans. The School Health Policy and Programs Study (SHPPS, 2007) reports 92% of states require school/district crisis plans. Law/regulation implementation and interpretation vary, though, as many federal/state laws lack specific definitions/guidelines. The Family Education Rights and Privacy Act (FERPA, 1974) lets schools disclose confidential student records without parent consent during safety and health emergencies.

GOALS OF ACTIVITIES

Developing school crisis teams and plans is the main goal of school crisis prevention and preparedness efforts. According to the U.S. Department of Education (ED, 2003), these plans and teams then enable developing protocols and procedures to decrease the probability of crisis event occurrence; for crises not preventable/prevented, ensure response readiness; minimize crisis impact and reestablish equilibrium immediately following crisis events by providing direction; help repair crisis damage, and restore baseline/pre-crisis functioning and operation. School crisis plans and teams supply guidance and leadership in each phase of a crisis (cf. Raphael and Newman, 2000; Valent, 2000). Additional goals identified by the National Association of School Psychologists (NASP)'s evidence-based PREPaRE (Prevent, Reaffirm, Evaluate, Provide and Respond, Examine) school crisis training curriculum model include having comprehensive plans and teams which address probable events with an "all hazards" approach; are collaboratively developed with community partners; are data- and information-based; are regularly practiced; receive continual review and updates; apply the National Incident Management System (NIMS)'s Incident Command System (ICS); and are customized to meet individual school needs.

BARRIERS

Research identifies crisis plan problems as one barrier to prevention and preparedness, specifically plans' lacking: comprehensiveness; regular practice; coordination with community emergency response agencies; discussion with students, staff, and families; attention to special-needs students' unique requirements; factual circumstances and data as bases; and/or regular updating and application. Many barriers originally identified persist after two decades. One is people's belief in the myth that crises will not occur in their school, interfering with planning and preparation. Another is "turf"/territorial issues, e.g., disagreements over who initiates/lead crisis prevention and preparedness initiatives; pays for supplies and training required; funds long-term support services; and, with multiple agency involvement, who is incident commander. These concerns illustrate the need for key stakeholder (school boards, administrators, community response agency staff) collaboration. School board and administrator leadership roles in crisis team and plan development promote collaboration, averting territorial disputes. School policies should reflect crisis prevention and preparedness aspects including design, updating, implementation; drill rehearsal; school board policy statement development; and incorporating crisis roles and responsibilities into job descriptions. Another barrier is resource limitations, e.g., time for fundraising, planning, and training; diminishing federal and state planning funds; and academic initiatives' taking economic precedence.

SCHOOL/DISTRICT EMERGENCY MANAGEMENT PLANS

According to the U.S. Department of Education (ED, 2007), school districts and/or schools should establish crisis response teams according to the Incident Command System (ICM) of the National Incident Management System (NIMS). They should establish meaningful collaborations with local government, law enforcement, emergency services, public health, mental health, public safety, and other community partners. In addition, they should establish memoranda of understanding among their crisis management teams and partners. School districts and/or schools should identify an "all hazards" approach to planning for emergency management. They should document their school board's approval of their crisis management plans. They should support the implementation of the NIMS, and otherwise demonstrate their integration and alignment with federal, state, local, and school district emergency management plans. Another general component that school district/school emergency management plans should include is specifications of the modifications and accommodations they will provide for individuals with disabilities and other special needs during emergencies. An additional general component is an included timeline for the maintenance and updating of all components of the emergency management plan.

EMERGENCY PREVENTION AND/OR MITIGATION

Prevention/mitigation components of school district/school emergency management plans identified by the U.S Department of Education (ED, 2007) include: supplying an assessment protocol, or basing the plan on one, that delineates an assessment schedule; personnel responsible for administering assessments; corrective actions; and/or support programs. Another component is assessing the buildings, region, and other environmental and physical safety and health risks. Assessing the emotional and social wellbeing of the students, faculty, and other staff is an additional preventative component. Assessment of the school culture and school climate are also components, because these can have positive or negative impacts on the occurrence, incidence, type, frequency, and severity of school emergency events depending whether or not/to what extent they promote safe environments, wellbeing, positive social interactions and relationships, open discussion, learning communities, motivation for teaching and learning, etc. Listing mitigation activities is another preventive component, as well as prioritizing continuing risks not subject to mitigation. Preparedness components include, among others, institutionalizing the NIMS ICS; assigning individual roles and responsibilities; defining crisis team and community partner duties identified in memoranda of understanding; integrating pre-negotiated contracts for potential emergency services like food, construction work, transportation, etc.

PREPAREDNESS

Among others, preparedness components include detailing steps to transfer command from school administrators to incident commanders during crises; supplying criteria for lockdown, shelter-in-place, evacuation, and/or other responses; listing the school's go-kit contents and emergency supplies, customized respectively for the classroom, cafeteria, gymnasium, auditorium, main office, restrooms, and other non-classroom school locations. Plans should include lists of available emergency medical and sanitation supplies; and floor plans, maps, utility cutoff locations, and other school facilities information. Emergency individual communication plans with students, faculty, staff, district administrators, first responders, parents, and media should be included. Plans should identify classroom-specific and schoolwide communication devices and instructions for their use in various emergencies. Plans and teams must ensure their communication equipment is interoperable with first responders' equipment. Plans for communicating emergency management procedures to parents, and family reunification plan and procedure guidelines are necessary components. Plans should specify transportation and traffic procedures to follow during and after emergencies. They should identify training the district/school will provide to crisis response teams, faculty, staff, students, and parents; include a schedule of emergency practice exercises and drills; and supply details of ongoing emergency management plan maintenance, revision, and enhancement activities.

EMERGENCY RESPONSE

According to the U.S. Department of Education (ED, 2007), school district and/or school emergency management plans should incorporate components related to response including: Designating a Public Information Officer (PIO) who will be responsible for communicating with the public and the media during emergency events or situations. Assigning an Incident Commander to manage the National Incident Management System (NIMS) Incident Command System (ICS)'s Command function is another response component of district and school emergency management plans. For the other four functions of the ICS – Logistics, Operations, Planning, and Finance-Administration – the district and/or school emergency management plan should also designate respective members of the emergency response team to be managers of each function. In addition, the school emergency management plan should assign a member of the crisis response team to take detailed notes about practice drills, specific events, and actions taken by school personnel during emergencies. The plan

should integrate the structure for conducting debriefings following emergencies. It should also define procedures for plan revision according to lessons learned from emergency experiences.

RECOVERY FROM EMERGENCIES

Emergency management plan recovery components include: a protocol for assessing damage to physical assets; strategies and procedures for structural and physical recovery; financial and logistical resources and protocols for recovery; decision-making procedures with respect to school closure; a Continuity of Operations Plan (COOP); criteria for reopening schools after closure; protocols for the activation of memoranda of understanding with mental health agencies; identification of types of support (for example, mental health interventions, extracurricular activities, etc.) available to students and staff who demonstrate post-traumatic stress disorder (PTSD) symptoms; strategies for follow-up services and ongoing interventions for mental and emotional recovery; provisions for obtaining parental consent to deliver mental health services to students; templates or samples of letters, e.g., for notifying families of student deaths, to inform school community members about emergency events; guidelines for temporary memorials, standing memorials, and anniversary observance; templates and protocols for the designated Public Information Officer (PIO) regarding ongoing parent, community, and media communication; guidelines for screening potential volunteers; and guidelines for accepting donations.

Legal, Ethical, and Professional Practice

Professional Foundations

NASP's Strategic Priorities for Advocacy

Among strategic priorities that National Association for School Psychologists (NASP) identifies are to advocate for children, youth, families, and schools by working to improve policies to meet the needs of the whole student more effectively; and improve professional advocacy by empowering school psychologists to meet high professional standards, reflect the full range of their expertise in their practice, and convey to important stakeholders the value of their work. The overall objectives for advocacy included in NASP's strategic plan are to increase or maintain the inclusion of school psychologists as service providers in federal, state, and local procedures, regulations, and legislation; increase the role of school psychologists in providing mental health services for children and adolescents; increase the role of school psychologists in crisis prevention, preparedness, response, intervention, and recovery; promote public awareness of and support for comprehensive school psychological services; increase public awareness of the importance and value for school psychologists of professional supervision; increase the numbers of school psychology graduate students, interns, and practicing school psychologists who have training in advocacy skills; and promote equity for all children and adolescents in access to mental health services and educational resources.

Advocacy Efforts

Federal Level

The Affordable Care Act (ACA's) Medicaid expansion; Children's Health Insurance Program (CHIP) renewal, projected to increase covered children from 7 million-11 million; and new School-Based Health Clinic funding are expected to increase school psychologists' services, and require their advocacy for their qualifications as providers. NASP-proposed federal advocacy includes: promoting adoption and use of ACA definitions of school psychologists, including state-licensed/certified; collaborating with Health and Human Services (HHS) in pressuring CMS to update their (1997) technical assistance guide to Medicaid and school health; promoting regulatory language adoption acknowledging the NCSP credential for school Medicaid service providers; continuing to monitor and communicate federal and state information related to school psychologist qualified provider eligibility; promoting regulatory language adoption acknowledging school psychologist state credentials/standards as sufficient for qualified provider eligibility; promoting federal regulation/statute use of "school psychologist"/"nationally certified school psychologist", etc. titles to prevent federal infringement on states' rights to set credentialing/licensure standards, and emphasizing profession standards; identification of and outreach to potential allies (e.g., American Association of School Administrators/AASA) to promote federal and state recognition of school psychologists as qualified providers; and increasing program and internship availability supporting license-eligible school psychologists following program completion.

State Level

In response to ACA provisions, NASP proposed federal and state actions to advocate for school psychologists. Proposed advocacy efforts for state governments include: promoting state regulatory adoption and use of ACA definitions incorporating specific references to school psychology/school psychologists, including those with state certification/licensure (e.g., "mental health service professional", "qualified health professional", "child and adolescent mental and behavioral health");

70

promoting acknowledgement of school psychologists as qualified providers by identifying and reaching out to the American Association of School Administrators (AASA) and other potential allies; promoting appropriate school psychologist licensure, including providing U.S. states a needs assessment and options flowchart (e.g., options to promote adopting state licenses like "Licensed Educational Psychologist" [California] or "School Psychologist Limited" [Virginia], promote NCSP acceptance as an eligible provider credential, promote doctoral-level school psychologists earning clinical licensure, and/or promote specialist-level school psychologists earning appropriate state licensure); promoting state regulatory and statutory adoption using "school psychologist/nationally certified school psychologist" titles; requesting state Attorney General rulings on Department of Regulatory Agency licensure-state education agency credential equivalency; and establishing a state directory/database of eligible school-based MH service providers, to link with ASPPB's national registry.

ONGOING PROFESSIONAL DEVELOPMENT

The National Association of School Psychologists (NASP) states that continuing professional development (CPD) is one of the responsibilities of every school psychologist. NASP also identifies one of its most important missions as facilitating such ongoing professional development. In order to fulfill this mission, NASP offers a number of different ways in which school psychologists can continue their educations and pursue the professional development and growth necessary to their effective practice of the profession. These include the NASP Online Learning Center, which offers live webcasts, webinars, workshops, videos, publications, on-demand continuing professional development, NASP Convention presentations, etc. in a variety of subject areas; NASP's annual convention, which members can attend; NASP summer conferences; the NASP Public Policy Institute, which provides training in government and professional relations; NASP's PREpARE curriculum of crisis prevention, preparedness, response, intervention, and recovery training; books, periodical articles, etc. for purchase at the online NASP Store to support self-study; the NASP Publications mobile app; NASP's Educators' Online Book Review; NASP approval of other CPD providers; and the NASP Speakers Bureau, wherefrom school psychologists can invite speakers to share their knowledge with them and their colleagues.

APA CONSIDERATIONS REGARDING LIFELONG LEARNING

The American Psychological Association (APA's) 2010 ninth annual Education Leadership Conference theme was Psychology and Lifelong Learning. APA Education Directorate executive director Cynthia Belar said that in psychology, more attention had been given to educational preparation than professional development and lifelong learning, even though the latter takes far longer than the former. Expanded technology and knowledge and greater accountability demands are increasing the importance of maintaining competence and lifelong learning in the health professions, prompting changes in policy, regulations, and credentialing at federal, state, program, and individual levels. The APA Code of Ethics requires psychologists to make continuing efforts to maintain and develop their professional competence. Psychology preparation programs are required to cultivate student commitment to lifelong learning for accreditation. Most U.S. States also require practitioners to pursue CE. However, the current approval system lacks any requirements for measures of actual learning or demonstration of transfer of learning to practice. Moreover, licensed psychologists surveyed apparently resist examination of their CE learning. Research supporting CE's utility in psychology has yet to develop. Belar said, "We need not just CE in evidence-based practice, but evidence-based CE."

CONTINUING EDUCATION

At the 2010 APA Education Leadership Conference, associate executive director of APA's Office of CE Greg Neimeyer distinguished continuing education (CE) vs. lifelong learning, explaining CE is

Mometrix

narrower, more utilitarian, and more formal. APA defines CE as allowing psychologists to stay abreast of emerging issues and technology, maintain and develop their competency to enhance their contributions to the profession, and improve their services through an ongoing process of formal learning activities. A CE goal is to combat the natural entropy process: over time, knowledge becomes obsolete; new developments reduce professional competence. State CE mandates are effective: of licensed professional psychologists surveyed in North America, Niemeyer found in states mandating CE, <2% avoided CE (= ≤5 hours annually); in states lacking mandates, nearly 20% avoided CE. Regardless, Neimeyer identified the "real question" as what difference CE makes. To find out, recommendations include emergent CE models; better measurement of CE learning; alternative models including cognitive apprenticeships (supervised, active tutorials); reciprocal teaching; problem-based learning; workplace audits and feedback; protocols; checklists; and practical, point-of-service learning. The Institute of Medicine identifies promising CE methods including case studies; simulations; needs assessments; small-group interactions; reflection opportunities; multimedia and multiple information exposures; and organized learning, rehearsal, and evaluation sequences.

BEST PRACTICE IN SUPERVISION AND HIERARCHY SCHOOL PSYCHOLOGICAL SUPERVISION

NASP considers "ongoing, positive, systematic, and collaborative administrative and clinical supervision from a qualified school psychological supervisor" as best practice. NASP's hierarchy of approved school psychological supervision includes the following: Supervisor qualifications include at least 3 years practical experience as a school psychologist; experience/training in school personnel supervision; and valid state school psychologist credentialing. Trainees should receive an average of two hours weekly in face-to-face supervision, and additional time should be allocated for reviewing their work products. Novice school psychology practitioners should be given at least an average of one hour a week of supervision and/or mentoring. Expert-level and other proficient school psychologists should be provided face-to-face supervision on an as-needed basis, and continue to be engaged in the process of supervision. It is necessary for school systems to allow sufficient time for school psychologists to participate in supervision and/or mentoring. To assure their effective professional practice and promote their skills development, novice and advanced-beginner school psychologists must have direct and frequent supervision. NASP also advises that every school system have a coordinated supervision plan that evaluates and is accountable for all school psychological services.

NASP advises that if some of the best practice options it has identified for supervision and/or mentoring are not available in a school psychologist's district, school systems lacking supervising school psychologists should assure opportunities for their school psychologists to obtain supervision outside of the district, including peer supervision networks; sharing supervisors between/among school districts or community agencies; and/or supervision online. In these cases, NASPE recommends (2011) that school district employers should provide these supervision opportunities with the same duration and frequency as it indicated for supervision within the district. School psychologists who are practicing in new districts, are still early in their careers, and others wanting additional supervisory support should pursue peer collaboration, especially with school psychologists having more practical experience than they do. They may also find opportunities to discuss specific situations with other school psychologists having similar experiences through local e-mail communities. Locating collaborative resources, professional guidance, and suggestions is also facilitated by NASP's Member Exchange online community, discussion board, and its other online communities for specific practice areas.

Copyright © Mometrix Media. You have been licensed one copy of this document for personal use only. Any other reproduction or redistribution is strictly prohibited. All rights reserved.

Ethical Principles of School Psychology

NATIONAL ASSOCIATION OF SCHOOL PSYCHOLOGISTS PRINCIPLES FOR PROFESSIONAL ETHICS

PRINCIPLE I

Principle I, Respecting the Dignity and Rights of All Persons, says school psychologists only conduct professional practices maintaining all others' dignity; show respect for individuals' autonomy, privacy, and self-determination rights, and commitment to fair, just treatment in their words and deeds. Principle I.1 is Autonomy and Self-Determination (Consent and Assent), respecting individual rights to participate in decisions affecting them. Standards I.1.1-I.1.5 cover parental participation, informed consent; and student decision-making participation and choice regarding psychological services. Principle I.2, Privacy and Confidentiality, requires school psychologists to respect individual privacy. Standards I.2.1-I.2.7 include respecting disclosure self-determination; minimizing privacy intrusions; informing students/clients of confidentiality boundaries; information release; respecting sexual orientation/gender identity privacy; and respecting privacy rights regarding sensitive health information. Principle I.3, Fairness and Justice, requires school psychologists to nurture safe, welcoming school climates without discrimination. Standards I.3.1-I.3.4 cover non-discrimination; diversity and individual difference factor awareness and knowledge; correcting discriminatory/unfair/legal rights-denying school practices; furthering safe, accepting, respectful school climate; and enabling equal opportunity for all students and families to access, participate in, and benefit from school programs and psychological services.

PRINCIPLE II

Principle II, Professional Competence and Responsibility, requires school psychologists to act for others' benefit by practicing within their competency limits, using scientific psychological and educational knowledge to aid others' informed choices, and taking responsibility for their activities. Principle II.1, Competence, requires only school psychologist practices for which they have qualifications and competence. Standards II.1.1-II.1.4 include recognizing their training and experience assets and limits; seeking consultation/supervision/referrals from/to others; diversity knowledge, understanding, and culturally competent services; personal problems and professional effectiveness; and ongoing professional development. Principle II.2, Accepting Responsibility for Actions, requires self-monitoring service effectiveness and self-correction. Standards II.2.1-II.2.4 include document accuracy; active recommendation and intervention monitoring, modification, and termination; appropriateness; and supervision. Principle II.3, Responsible Assessment and Intervention Practices, requires responsible professional practices in educational and psychological assessment and direct and indirect intervention meeting the highest standard. Standards II.3.1-II.3.11 cover current practice effects on student performance vs. disability categorizing/labeling; research-based assessment practices; multiple information sources; suspected disability assessment areas; assessment validity and fairness; interpreters; records use; results interpretation; research-based intervention, counseling, therapy, consultation, and other service methods; parental participation in designing interventions; and student participation. Principle II.4 involves responsible recordkeeping; II.5 addresses responsible materials use.

PRINCIPLE III

Principle III, Honesty and Integrity in Professional Relationships, requires school psychologists tell the truth, keep professional promises, cooperate fully with other disciplines to meet student and family needs, and avoid multiple relationships compromising professional efficacy. Principle III.1, Accurate Presentation of Professional Qualifications, includes Standard III.1.1 to represent one's credentials, education, training, experience, and competency levels accurately to others and correct

73

misconceptions; Standard III.1.2 prohibits using institutional/group/individual affiliations to imply false competency levels. Principle III.2 is Forthright Explanation of Professional Services, Roles and Priorities. Standards III.2.1-III.2.5 cover clearly explaining professional skills, duties, relationships, and services; integral service system membership efforts; communicating the priority of commitment to protecting student welfare and rights in services determination; averting conflicts of interest; and accurate representation of services, publications, and products. Principle III.3, Respecting Other Professionals, requires cooperation to serve students. Standards III.3.1-III.3.4 cover resource use, service coordination, referrals, and others' reports. Principle III.4, Multiple Relationships and Conflicts of Interest, includes Standards III.4.1-III.4.9, covering resolving these; personal interests; religious/personal beliefs/commitments; non-exploitation, non-harassment; business relationships; economic benefits; financial interests in services/products; referral non-remuneration; and dual-setting practitioners.

PRINCIPLE IV

Principle IV, Responsibility to Schools, Families, Communities, the Profession, and Society, requires school psychologists to promote healthy environments; proactively identify and work to reform school/systems-level social injustices; respect law; behave ethically; and mentor others and contribute to the school psychology knowledge base to advance professional excellence. Principle IV.1, Promoting Healthy School, Family, and Community Environments, includes Standard IV.1.1 regarding knowledge about service settings and collaboration with community services; and Standard IV.1.2 regarding promoting school/community service improvement and advocating for students and parents. Principle IV.2, Respect for Law and the Relationship of Law and Ethics, contains Standards IV.2.1-IV.2.3 including workplace legal requirements; Principles superseding law in stringency; ethical conflicts; and individual citizenship and professionalism. Principle IV.3, Maintaining Public Trust by Self-Monitoring and Peer Monitoring, requires responsibility for one's own and others' ethical conduct. Related Standards IV.3.1-IV.3.4 cover difficult situations and others' unethical practices. Principle IV.4, Contributing to the Profession by Mentoring, Teaching, and Supervision, includes Standards IV.4.1-IV.4.4 covering directing graduate education programs; practicum and internship supervision; hiring, training, and supervising professionals; faculty membership and graduate student field experience supervision. Principle IV.5, Contributing to the School Psychology Knowledge Base, includes Standards IV.5.1-IV.5.10, covering all ethical research practices.

STANDARDS FOR EDUCATIONAL AND PSYCHOLOGICAL TESTING

The American Educational Research Association (AERA), the American Psychological Association (APA), and the National Council on Measurement in Education (NCME) have jointly developed the *Standards for Educational and Psychological Testing* (2014 edition). According to the APA, the Testing Standards are the gold standard for guiding testing in the United States and many other nations. The three organizations have published these Testing Standards collaboratively since 1966. Part I of the Standards covers Foundations and includes testing validity; precision, reliability, and measurement errors; and fairness in testing. Part II covers Operations and includes the design and development of tests; scales, norms, scores, cut scores, and score linking; test administration and scoring, interpretation and reporting of test scores; supporting test documentation; the rights and responsibilities of those taking tests, and the rights and responsibilities of those using tests. Part III covers Testing Applications. This includes using tests for psychological assessment; for credentialing and workplace testing and evaluation; for educational assessment and testing; and for program evaluation, accountability, and policy studies.

The main purpose of the *Standards for Educational and Psychological Testing* is to supply educators and psychologists with criteria to evaluate testing practices and test instruments. The Standards apply to tests, assessments, inventories, scales, and a broad variety of other standardized instruments and procedures which sample the behaviors of individuals. In addition to standardized tests in multiple-choice question formats, the Standards also apply to tests consisting only of open-ended essay questions, simulations, hands-on assessments, and other formal assessments of performance. However, these Standards do not apply to observational forms, unstructured behavioral checklists, or other unstandardized questionnaires; teacher-made tests; teacher evaluations of classroom participation over a school term or year, or other subjective processes of decision-making. Test developers or test users' compliance with these Standards is not enforced by any mechanism. The Standards do not try to supply psychometric answers to legal or policy questions. They have, however, been cited in Supreme Court and other judicial rulings, including several major court decisions about employment testing (e.g., *Watson v. Fort Worth Bank & Trust,* 1988) and referenced in federal laws, including the Goals 2000: Educate America Act; and Title I of the Elementary and Secondary Education Act (ESEA), enhancing their authority.

HISTORICAL BACKGROUND

The American Psychological Association (APA) assigned a committee to prepare a document entitled *Technical Recommendations for Psychological Tests and Diagnostic Techniques*, which the APA published in 1954. In 1955, the National Education Association (NEA) published *Technical Recommendations for Achievement Tests*, prepared by a committee representing both the American Educational Research Association (AERA) and National Council for Measurement in Education (NCME, formerly National Council for Measurement Used in Education/NCMUE). A committee representing the AERA, APA, and NCME jointly prepared the *Standards for Educational and Psychological Tests and Manuals*, published by APA in 1966 to replace the two earlier documents. A committee also representing the AERA, APA, and NCME prepared the first edition of the *Standards for Educational and Psychological Testing,* published by APA in 1974. The same three organizations collaboratively revised the 1974 Standards; the APA published this revision in 1985. The 1985 edition was jointly revised again by a Joint Committee appointed by the same three organizations; this revision was published by the AERA in 1999. The new edition, prepared by a working Joint Committee selected by the Standards' working Management Committee, was published by AERA In 2014.

EVOLUTION

The *Standards of Educational and Psychological Testing*, 2014 edition, was preceded by two earlier documents of technical recommendations, for psychological tests and diagnostic techniques, published by the APA in 1954; and for achievement tests, published by the NEA in 1955. In 1966, the first edition of the *Standards of Educational and Psychological Testing* was published by the AERA, prepared by a committee of AERA, APA, and NCME (then NCMUE) representatives. Since then, these standards were revised four times: in 1974, 1985, 1999, and 2014, each time to reflect the advancements in educational and psychological testing since the publication of the previous edition. For example, significant developments in the testing field took place between 1999 and 2014, necessitating the revision and new edition of the standards. The 2014 edition devotes attention to five areas especially:

- Accountability issues related to using tests in formulating educational policy.
- Widening the concept of accessibility for all examinees to tests.
- More comprehensive representation of the role of tests in workplace settings.
- The increasing use of technology in testing.
- Improvements in the book's structure to communicate the standards better.

Ethical Use of Computer-Related Technology in Practice of School Psychology

Because computer technology has the potential to augment efficiency and effectiveness in their practices, school psychologists have an ethical obligation to explore the ways in which computers can expedite professional practice of school psychology. However, this responsibility is paralleled by an equally important duty to consider all professional practice and ethical implications carefully. The very same characteristics of computers that make them the most useful are also the characteristics that make them the most susceptible to violations of ethical codes. As the use of computer and related technologies becomes increasingly widespread, every practice setting using them experiences now conflicts emerging among personal values, principles of professional conduct, and professional ethical principles. Experts researching these issues recommend that school psychologists should use technology advances to enhance their practice rather than to replace traditional practices. In addition, they conclude that the responsibility still ultimately belongs with the individual school psychologist and cannot be transferred. In using computer-related technology, the same fundamental ethical principles apply as in any other professional discipline. As some members (cf. Pfohl, 2010) have observed, the NASPE code of ethics does not give school psychologists specific guidance regarding technology use. However, others (Jacob & Armistead, 2011) report that the NASP team revising its ethics code concluded this would be inappropriate. Their reason for this conclusion is that a code of ethics' purpose is to identify enforceable standards and aspirational principles to help school psychologists choose ethically sound options; but ethical codes are not ideal decision-making guides because they must apply to school psychologists' varied work settings, activities, and roles, and must also be sufficiently broad to offer practicable guidance as technology continues to progress. While these experts agree that specific guidelines for using technology in professional practice could benefit school psychologists, they find developing these to be outside of the NASP Ethics Committee's scope of responsibilities. They direct the responsibility and an invitation to draft such guidelines to NASP's Computer & Technological Applications Interest Group.

CASP Guidelines for Using Materials and Technology in Public Settings

The California Association of School Psychologists (CASP) is an example of a state professional organization that has published a code of ethics (revised 2007) including guidelines for the use of materials and technology (under III, Professional Practice – Public Settings). Its first six of 12 guidelines include: Maintaining security of psychological tests whose disclosure could invalidate their use; designing and implementing school-based research using sound research practices for choosing topics, methodology, and participant selection, data collection, analysis, and reporting procedures; communicating their graduate degrees and training levels clearly to research participants; conducting research complying with all legal procedures including informed consent, privacy, confidentiality, voluntary participation, harm/risk protection, results disclosure; respecting participant rights and wellbeing; not encouraging/promoting inappropriate use of digital reports/test analyses, e.g., representing them as their own writing, using digital scoring systems without test training; being fully responsible for technology services they use for diagnosis, consultation, or information management; applying the same ethical standards for interpreting, maintaining, and using technological data when utilizing data management services as for any other information; and before utilizing computer program results, ensuring their accuracy regarding all information generated. Guidelines 7-12 cover the following areas: School psychologists must not transmit student/client records electronically without guaranteeing confidentiality. For example, e-mails must either omit all personally identifying information or be encrypted; receiving fax machines must be operated by employees cleared to handle confidential files, and placed in secured locations. School psychologists acknowledge copyrights of published works/authors of non-published materials are protected by federal law; and obey copyright laws in their publications and presentations. They do not present/publish falsified/fabricated information. They publish corrections/errata/retractions of any errors discovered after presenting/publishing research/other information. They only publish information making original contributions to the professional literature, and do not publish the same findings in multiple publications or duplicate significant parts of their previous publications without copyright holder permission. When reviewing proposals, manuscripts, and other work submitted for publication/presentation, they respect author proprietary and confidentiality rights; limit materials use to review-related activities; and do not quote materials, duplicate or circulate copies of materials, or disclose author identity without permission.

Legal Issues Related to School Psychology

IDEA
HISTORY

Originally, Individuals with Disabilities Education Improvement Act (IDEA) was Public Law 94-142/the Education for All Handicapped Children Act (EHA), passed in 1975. Previously, only one in five students with disabilities received public educations. Many state laws excluded children with intellectual disabilities, emotional disturbances, blindness, or deafness. IDEA guarantees all children with disabilities qualifying under its definitions a free, appropriate public education (FAPE) in the least restrictive environment (LRE). This represented the federal government's mandate for students with disabilities to attend public schools receiving federal funding. Updated roughly every five years, IDEA originally applied to K-12 ages; in 1986, Part C was added, requiring early intervention services for infants and toddlers to identify disabilities, minimize impacts, develop Individualized Family Service Plans (IFSPs), and prepare children for K-12 education. The 1990 reauthorization changed the name to IDEA and required transition planning for students to employment, further education, community life, etc. The 1997 reauthorization required transition planning to begin by age 14. The 2004 reauthorization eliminated the "discrepancy model" of waiting until students performed significantly below grade level for special education eligibility, enabling schools to use Response to Intervention (RtI) to assess and address special needs sooner. IDEA requires Individualized Education Plans (IEPs) for all special education students.

PURPOSES OF 2004 REAUTHORIZATION

According to IDEA Section 601(d), the law's purposes are: (1A) To ensure the availability to all children with disabilities of a free, appropriate public education emphasizing special education and related services designed to meet their individual needs and prepare them for additional education, independent living, and employment; (1B) to assure the protection of the rights of children with disabilities and their parents; (1C) to help federal agencies, U.S. states, educational service agencies, and local educational agencies provide for educating all children who have disabilities; (2) to help U.S. states to implement statewide coordinated, comprehensive, interagency, and multidisciplinary systems for providing early intervention services to infants and toddlers with disabilities and their families; (3) to support system improvement efforts; coordinated employee education, training, and preparation; coordinated technical support, dissemination, and assistance; and media services and technology development to make sure that parents and educators have the means necessary for improving educational outcomes for children with disabilities; and (4) to evaluate efforts to educate children with disabilities and ensure the effectiveness of those efforts.

PARTS

The IDEA legislation is divided into Parts A through D. In Part A, the definitions of terms used in the IDEA regulations are provided. For example, the law defines the term "specific learning disability" as a disorder affecting one or more of the fundamental psychological processes that are involved in using or understanding spoken and written language, which may be manifested in deficits in the abilities for thinking, listening, speaking, reading, writing, spelling, or performing mathematical computations. This term includes minimal brain dysfunction, developmental aphasia, dyslexia, brain injury, perceptual disabilities, and similar conditions. Disorders that are not included in the definition of the term are learning difficulties that are mainly the results of intellectual disability; motor disabilities; emotional disturbance; economic, environmental, or cultural disadvantages; visual impairment, or hearing impairment. Part B of the IDEA regulations authorizes the federal government to provide funding to U.S. states for delivering services to children and youth with disabilities. This part includes the regulations and rules for U.S. state governments and school systems to follow to receive federal funding.

Part B of the IDEA legislation provides the regulations that U.S. state education departments and school systems must comply with to receive federal funds for delivering special education and related services to students with eligible disabilities. Included among the topics documented in Part B are the regulations and rules for the evaluation of children for disabilities; the determination of student eligibility for special education and related services; the advance notification and involvement of parents in their children's evaluation and placement; collaboration with parents in developing individualized education plans (IEPs) for their children; the provision of services to students with disabilities; the resolution of conflicts between parents and school systems; due process and other procedural safeguards available to parents of children with disabilities; the National Instructional Materials Accessibility Standard (NIMAS) provision of accessible text to students; and additional rules/regulations regarding special education service provision. Part C, the Early Intervention Program for Infants and Toddlers with Disabilities, includes home visits; family training; counseling; physical and occupational therapy; and speech-language services. Part D informs professionals and families of research and information including parent training and information (PTI) center operation; identifying best and promising practices; teacher education; technology development; and public information dissemination.

SECTION 504 OF THE REHABILITATION ACT OF 1973

Section 504 of the Rehabilitation Act of 1973 is a federal law to protect people with qualifying disabilities against discrimination on the basis of those disabilities. Its provisions against discrimination apply to organizations and employers receiving funding from any federal agency or department, including the U.S. Department of Health and Human Services (DHHS). Many human services programs, mental health centers, nursing homes, and hospitals are included among these employers and organizations. Section 504 prohibits employers or organizations from excluding individuals with disabilities from program services and benefits, and from denying them equal opportunities to receive these services and benefits. It also defines the rights it ensures to individuals with disabilities to have access to and participate in program services and benefits. Under Section 504, qualified individuals with disabilities protected against discrimination are defined as having physical or mental impairments that substantially limit one or more major life activities, including histories or perceptions of such impairments. Major life activities include breathing, seeing, hearing, speaking, walking, self-care, learning, manual tasks, and working.

Section 504 protects individuals with disabilities from discrimination. The definition under this law of disabilities is a physical or mental impairment that interferes significantly with major life activities, even with the assistance of aids, devices, or medications. Some examples of impairments that can significantly interfere with major life activities include blindness; visual impairment; Deafness; hearing impairment; heart disease; mental illness; alcoholism; drug addiction or substance abuse; diabetes; and AIDS. In order to receive education, training, or services, qualified individuals with disabilities must not only meet Section 504's definition of disabilities, but also meet its eligibility requirements. For employment purposes, qualified individuals with disabilities can perform the essential job functions for which they have been hired or have applied, with reasonable accommodation. This means that employers must take reasonable actions to accommodate an employee's disability unless doing so would create undue hardship for the employer. The U.S. Department of Health and Human Services (DHHS) Office for Civil Rights (OCR), which enforces Section 504, refers complaints of employment discrimination based on disability against single individuals to the U.S. Equal Employment Opportunity Commission (EEOC) to be processed.

ACTIONS PROHIBITED IN HEALTHCARE AND HUMAN SERVICES

The provisions of Section 504 of the Rehabilitation Act of 1973 prohibit discrimination against persons with disabilities on the basis of those disabilities. These prohibitions apply to the administrative responsibilities and activities of organizations that receive financial assistance from the federal government; and to the availability of services, accessibility to those services, the delivery of services, and to employment, from these organizations. Some examples of discriminatory actions prohibited under Section 504 include the following: Any organization receiving federal financial assistance is not allowed to deny any qualified individual an opportunity to participate in or benefit from federally funded services, programs, or other benefits on the basis of the individual's disability. These organizations are not allowed to deny opportunities for participation in, or access to services, programs, or benefits to qualified individuals on the basis of disability as a result of any physical barriers. They are not allowed to deny opportunities for hiring, training, promotion, fringe benefits, or other employment opportunities for which they are otherwise qualified or entitled to individuals on the basis of disability.

REQUIREMENTS AND ENFORCEMENT IN EDUCATION

The Office of Civil Rights (OCR) of the U.S. Department of Health and Human Services (DHHS) enforces Section 504 of the Rehabilitation Act in activities and programs that receive federal financial assistance from the U.S. Department of Education (ED). These include public school districts, state and local education agencies, and institutions of higher education. Like the regulations of the Individuals with Disabilities Education Act (IDEA), the regulations of Section 504 also require school districts to provide a free, appropriate public education (FAPE) to every qualified student with a disability, regardless of the severity or nature of the disability, who is within the jurisdiction of the school district. Section 504 defines a FAPE as providing regular education and/or special education and related services and aids that are designed to meet the individual educational needs of a student who has a disability with the same adequacy with which the school district meets the needs of students who do not have disabilities.

ADA

The Americans with Disabilities Act (ADA), which was passed in 1990 and became effective in 1992, prohibits state and local governments, employment agencies, private employers, and labor unions from discriminating against qualified individuals with disabilities in applying for jobs; hiring; promotion; job training; compensation; firing; and other privileges and conditions of employment. Qualification requires that the individual is able to perform the job with or without accommodations, which employers must provide unless these impose undue hardships. The ADA prohibits discrimination in employment (Title I) and also in public transportation (Title II), public accommodations (Title III), and telecommunications (Title IV). Title V covers miscellaneous provisions, including a prohibition against interpreting the ADA as applying to a standard lower than the standard provided under Section 504 of the Rehabilitation Act of 1973; and a provision prohibiting retaliation against people who refuse inadequate services or who file complaints of violations of ADA regulations. The ADA extends the provisions of Section 504 to include programs not receiving federal funding and the private sector.

REQUIREMENTS FOR STUDENTS TO CLAIM DISCRIMINATION

To claim discrimination based on disability under the ADA, students have the burden of proof that they were affected by adverse actions based on their disabilities. Historically, students with disabilities have typically been defeated when educational institution officials could demonstrate nondiscriminatory, valid reasons for taking such actions against them. Even when students make claims that they require accommodations to their disabilities to access education, the officials in educational institutions have to conduct inquiries into each individual student's circumstances before they make any decisions. To qualify for ADA protection, students must prove they have disabilities as the law defines them; are qualified otherwise; and need reasonable accommodations. Depending on how much a disability interferes with participating in major life activities, ADA protection of a student varies by the individual situation: an impairment can qualify as a disability for one student under certain conditions but not for another under other conditions. For example, a student with learning disabilities could need note-taking help for a lecture course, but not need any help with a course involving only hands-on learning.

When discrimination claims are filed against educational institutions on behalf of students with disabilities, if the students do not meet minimum admission or educational program maintenance requirements, the courts dismiss such claims. While the ADA requires institutions to provide reasonable accommodations to students with disabilities, the institutions are not required to lower admission standards or provide more than reasonable accommodations for admission. Following admission, students with disabilities may be required to meet usual academic progress standards and may be dismissed for failing to meet them. Though reasonable accommodations for academic access and achievement are required, institutions are not required to change their basic entry or program requirements for students with disabilities. For assessing whether program nature makes requirements essential, courts typically defer to educational officials' expertise. However, educational institution officials still bear the burden of proof to show a relationship between their requirements in employment education/preparation programs and the employment expectations of the applicable professions.

K-12 VS. POSTSECONDARY EDUCATION TESTING REGULATIONS FOR STUDENTS WITH DISABILITIES

An essential difference between laws regulating K-12 vs. postsecondary education for students with disabilities is that legislation like the Individuals with Disabilities Education Act (IDEA) and Section 504 of the Rehabilitation Act of 1973 require schools to provide both accommodations and modifications as needed to enable students with disabilities to access and participate in education. This includes testing as well as instruction. While accommodations change the manner in which instruction or assessment is administered without affecting the content, modifications alter the content of the curriculum delivered or assessment administered as well. However, the ADA requires higher education institutions to provide reasonable accommodations in test administration to qualified students with disabilities, but not to modify the actual content of tests for these students. A considerable amount of litigation has occurred over denials of student requests for testing accommodations based on disabilities. Testing accommodations are intended to enable effective assessment of student knowledge without disadvantaging students with disabilities, rather than give them unfair advantages over students without disabilities. However, even when accommodations do not confer unfair advantages, students may still have to show that the accommodations they request are related to their disabilities.

ESEA Legislation

President Lyndon B. Johnson urged that the United States "declare a national goal of full educational opportunity" for all students. Accordingly, he proposed a bill entitled the Elementary and Secondary Education Act (ESEA) to Congress. Once the House of Representatives and the Senate had both given majority votes in favor of this bill, President Johnson signed it into law in 1965. The ESEA was heralded as representing a new, major commitment on the part of the federal government to educating students in America with "quality and equality." In its original form, the ESEA had the purpose of making additional resources available to students who were at risk for school failure. For example, the law provided for federal grants to state educational agencies for improving quality in elementary and secondary education; new grants to school districts that served low-income students; federal grants to finance the purchase of school library books and classroom textbooks; the establishment of scholarships for low-income college students; and the establishment of special education centers.

Following the passage of the Elementary and Secondary Education Act (ESEA) by President L.B. Johnson in 1965, the federal government dedicated larger amounts of resources for education over the next 35 years. Yet state and local agencies are still largely responsible for educational decisions. Despite this decentralized approach, the federal government continued pursuing the commitment to provide increased resources for disadvantaged students. This attitude was informed by the knowledge that the United States was still not achieving Johnson's goal of "full educational opportunity" as a nation. Both political parties strongly supported reauthorizing the original ESEA; Congress passed a reauthorization in 2001 named the No Child Left Behind Act (NCLB), which President G.W. Bush signed in 2002. It established new measures to reveal achievement gaps, launching a significant national discussion on closing these. It importantly protected vulnerable students' civil rights by requiring school transparency and accountability for all students' achievement. However, its shortcomings included punishing failure more than rewarding success; giving states incentives for lower standards; disregarding progress and growth in favor of focus on absolute test scores; and dictating one-size-fits-all, pass/fail interventions.

Added Flexibility to NCLB Act

The 1965 ESEA, reauthorized as NCLB in 2001/2002, was due for congressional reauthorization in 2007 but did not receive it, despite acknowledgement by parents, teachers, school district leaders, and elected officials from both parties in federal and state governments of its necessity. The consensus among state and local educators and governments was strongly that progress was being prevented by outdated NCLB requirements. President Obama emphasized greater transparency, and his administration started allowing more flexibility in 2012 with some of NCLB's most objectionable regulations. States still had to identify achievement gaps transparently; but by showing their implementation, adoption, and/or planning of standards and assessments for career and college readiness, establishment of school accountability systems concentrating on schools with the widest achievement gaps and lowest performance, and district implementation of principal and teacher evaluation and support systems, they gained more flexibility in how they act relative to achievement gaps. By 2015, 43 states, the District of Columbia, and Puerto Rico have flexibility within/around NCLB. President Obama and U.S. Secretary of Education Arne Duncan indicated their commitment to reauthorizing ESEA/NCLB to protect historically underserved populations; give schools and educators resources needed for success; and ensure all youth's preparation for college and career success.

Planned Reauthorization of ESEA/NCLB Law

Some people discussing how to reauthorize ESEA to replace NCLB have opined that accountability requirements for states, school districts, and schools should be reduced, and states permitted to

81

reallocate funding from lower-income to higher-income districts. However, others strongly object, pointing out current all-time high rates of high school graduation and their improvement across all student groups, saying removing those NCLB provisions would reverse this national progress in closing achievement gaps. Secretary Duncan defined the Obama administration's vision for a new ESEA in January of 2015, including expanding high-quality preschool access; informing parents and teachers regularly of student progress; providing school administrators and teachers needed support and resources; encouraging district and school problem-solving innovations; investing equitably and strongly in high-poverty districts and schools; and ensuring action to provide greater support that students in the lowest-performing schools, students with disabilities, ELL students, racial minority students, and others need for achievement. Describing the current NCLB as "broken and...wildly out of date", Duncan called for a new law encouraging educator creativity and innovation more and suppressing these less, and realizing the vision of opportunity for success as the right of every child in the USA.

BUCKLEY AMENDMENT TO FERPA

The Family Educational Rights and Privacy Act (FERPA), i.e., § 513 of P.L. (Public Law) 93-380, The Education Amendments of 1974, enacted as new § 438, Protection of the Rights and Privacy of Parents and Students, of the General Education Provisions Act (GEPA), was signed by President Ford August 21, 1974, to be effective November 19, 1974. FERPA was not referred to Committee for consideration, but proposed and passed on the Senate floor as an amendment. Referring to N.Y. Senator James Buckley, its principal sponsor, it was popularly called the "Buckley Amendment." Four months later, Buckley and R.I. Senator Pell sponsored major amendments to FERPA enacted December 31, 1974, retroactive to the act's original November 19, 1974 effective date. Resolving concerns and ambiguities identified by institutions, students, and parents was the purpose of these Buckley-Pell amendments. For example, FERPA initially covered "any State or local educational agency, any institution of higher education, any community college, any school, agency offering a preschool program, or any other educational institution." Buckley-Pell amendments reworded this to "educational agency or institution", which they defined as "any public or private agency or institution which is the recipient of funds under any applicable program."

FERPA as initially enacted gave parents the right to review/examine their children's school records, which it defined as an extensive "laundry list" of specific items. The 1974 Buckley-Pell amendments, passed four months after FERPA and retroactive to its effective date, replaced this unwieldy yet not exhaustive list with the term "education records", and defined this term as "those records, files, documents, and other materials which contain information directly related to a student; and are maintained by an educational agency or institution or by a person acting for such agency or institution." The authors further excluded four categories of records:

- Records solely held by administrative, instructional, and supervisory personnel.
- Law enforcement records maintained only for law enforcement purposes, separately from education records, and unavailable to others unless law enforcement personnel have access to education records.*
- Records of personnel not in attendance.
- Records of psychologist, psychiatrist, or physician treatment.

The legislators expressed intentions that these amendments would not disrupt existing student and parent rights of confidentiality; and that the Education Department interpret treatment records narrowly, to exclude remedial education records that educational professionals created and/or maintained. *(This exception was amended in 1992.)

Congress provided for the following in some of the Buckley-Pell (1974) amendments to FERPA:

- Parental right to inspect/review children's educational records: These amendments clarified that with data/records involving multiple students, parents only have the right to inspect/review what relates to their children.
- Post-secondary student right to inspect/review records: These amendments excluded student access to parent financial records, and confidential recommendation letters entered into records through 1974.
- Parental right to challenge educational records content: The amendments reinforced this by requiring the Education Department to give parents an opportunity for a hearing when making funds available to an institution/agency; and granting parents the right to add written explanations about records content.
- Right to consent to educational records disclosure: The original enactment prohibited policy/practice of allowing release of/providing personally identifiable information without written parental consent. The Buckley-Pell amendments clarified this as "other than directory information", specifically defining directory information; and required public notice by educational institutions/agencies of any directory information, plus allowing reasonable time for parents to refuse its disclosure without their previous permission. These amendments also clarified that institutions/agencies determined which school officials with legitimate educational interests were excepted. They amended excepting local/state/federal "authorized representatives" from not accessing/collecting personally identifying information, to protecting and destroying it when no longer needed.

CHANGES RELATED TO PRIOR WRITTEN CONSENT, RECORDKEEPING, AND ED ADMINISTRATIVE REQUIREMENTS

The original FERPA excepted officials involved in student applications for or receipt of financial aid from its "Prior Written Consent" rule regarding educational records disclosure. In presenting the Buckley-Pell amendments, their authors stated this exception should permit disclosing Social Security numbers for student financial aid application/receipt. These amendments "grandfathered" in local and state authorities/officials as exceptions to the prior written consent requirement, allowing U.S. States to limit local/state official types or numbers beyond FERPA's minimum federal standard for records access and confidentiality. The authors explained this was to keep FERPA from superseding State authority.

Organizations researching for test development, validation, or administration; student aid program administration; and instructional improvement were accepted under specified conditions. Accrediting organizations; parents of dependent students; and appropriate emergency-related persons, if necessary for protecting safety/health, limited by regulations expected from the Secretary, were accepted. The amendments required recordkeeping by educational institutions/agencies of all access requests/access to student education records, specifying their legitimate interest (excluding school officials with legitimate educational interests). These amendments also added an administrative requirement prohibiting FERPA enforcement by any regional offices, except for conducting hearings.

PARC V. COMMONWEALTH OF PENNSYLVANIA

The Pennsylvania Association for Retarded Children (PARC), now known as the Arc of Pennsylvania, brought the suit of *PARC v. Commonwealth of Pennsylvania* (1972) in U.S. District Court against the Pennsylvania Commonwealth and State Board of Education, and the Secretaries of the Departments of Education and Public Welfare to advocate for access to public education for children with intellectual disabilities. Before this case, children with disabilities typically were denied free public educations other children were provided because school districts found the costs of appropriately educating children with disabilities prohibitive. In this decision, the court ruled because uneducated children would ultimately cause larger expenses by draining public funds, saving money on education was not a legitimate reason for excluding students with disabilities. The court also ruled such denial violated the Equal Protection Clause of the Fourteenth Amendment to the U.S. Constitution. This case was tried along with *Mills v. Board of Education of the District of Columbia* to include D.C., following the precedent of arguing *Bolling v. Sharpe* alongside of *Brown v. Topeka Board of Education* (1954) because the Equal Protection Clause does not apply to D.C., but the Fifth Amendment's Due Process guarantee does.

PARC v. Commonwealth of Pennsylvania (1972) was filed by the Pennsylvania Association for Retarded Children (PARC), an advocacy organization for children with intellectual disabilities. The PARC's complaint was against the practice of the Pennsylvania public school systems, common prior to 1972, of not admitting students with disabilities to avoid the additional expenses required for accommodating education to students with special needs. The court ruled this reasoning invalid based on the observation that costs to public funding to provide for the needs of uneducated individuals would become even higher than costs to public funding for school budgets. Some results of this case included the following: In its decision, the court included the establishment and enforcement of requirements for school systems to admit children with disabilities and provide them necessary services; and initiated the establishment of guidelines for student identification, placement, and reclassification for special services. Moreover, the court's decisions were part of a campaign that led to the Rehabilitation Act of 1973, the Americans with Disabilities Act (ADA) of 1990, and the Individuals with Disabilities Education Act (IDEA, formerly P.L. 94-142/Education for All Handicapped Children Act [EHA], 1975-2004).

In *PARC v. Commonwealth of Pennsylvania* (1972), the U.S. District Court enjoined the defendants from applying specific sections of the Public School Code (1949) to deny in any way, postpone, or terminate access to free, public education and training programs to any child with mental retardation; to deny maintenance and/or tuition to any individual with mental retardation, except under the same terms as those applied to other exceptional children, including those with brain damage in general; or to deny homebound instruction to any child with mental retardation solely because their disability was not short-term or because the child did not have any physical disability. Additionally, the court required the defendants to reevaluate the plaintiffs named immediately; and as soon as possible but no later than October 13, 1971, to provide each of them access to a free, public education and training program suitable for their learning abilities; and, as soon as possible but no later than September 1, 1972, to provide every individual with mental retardation, aged 6-21 years as of the order's date and thereafter, access to a free, public education and training program suitable for his/her learning abilities.

In addition to ordering that defendants must not deny/postpone/terminate any free, public education/training/associated tuition/tuition and maintenance to any child with mental retardation (MR); or deny homebound instruction to children with MR based on its being a long-term disability or on their lacking any physical disability, the court ruled that the defendants must reevaluate the plaintiffs named and provide them access to free, public education and training programs by a deadline six days after the order (by October 13, 1971, ordered October 7, 1971). It also ruled the defendants must provide access to free, public education and training programs appropriate to their learning abilities to every individual with MR aged 6-21 years on the date of the order and thereafter, by a deadline less than 11 months after the order (by September 1, 1972, ordered October 7, 1971). An additional court order was that wherever the defendants provided preschool education and training programs for children younger than 6 years, they must provide access to free, public preschool education and training programs to all children the same ages with MR. The court designated this case a class action for all Pennsylvania residents with MR aged below 21 years.

LAU V. NICHOLS

The school system in San Francisco, California was integrated pursuant to a federal court decree in 1971. In the San Francisco Unified School District, about 2,800 students of Chinese ancestry did not speak English. Of these 2,800 students, 1,000 students were provided with supplemental courses to instruct them in the English language; but the other 1,800 students did not receive any such additional instruction in English. On behalf of the students who were not given any English language instruction, attorneys filed a class action suit against the San Francisco Unified School District officials responsible for its operations. The suit alleged that these students were not given equal educational opportunities, and therefore, had been denied their Fourteenth Amendment rights to equal protection under the law. The District Court denied relief and when the plaintiffs' attorneys appealed, the Court of Appeals affirmed the denial based on the reasoning that factors separate from the schools, e.g., cultural, social, and economic background and the resulting disadvantages and advantages they afforded, accompanied each student to his/her educational career.

The complaint in *Lau v. Nichols* (1971) alleged that while some 1,000 Chinese students who attended public school in San Francisco, California and did not speak English were given supplemental English language instructions, another 1,800 such students did not receive any English language instruction and thus, could not access the schools' curriculum or teaching, which were all provided in the English language; and that this lack of access constituted a lack of equal educational opportunities and hence a violation of Fourteenth Amendment rights to equal protection under the law. When the District Court denied the petition and the Court of Appeals upheld this denial, ruling that individual student differences affecting their education came from sources apart from the schools; the plaintiffs' attorneys filed a petition to the U.S. Supreme Court for certiorari (review of a lower court's decision by a higher court). Because of the issue's public significance, the Supreme Court granted a writ of certiorari.

In Lau v. Nichols (1971), the District Court denied relief to the complainants' allegation that they were denied an education by not being provided with English language instruction in San Francisco public schools although they were children of Chinese immigrants and did not know English. The Court of Appeals upheld this decision, giving the rationale that students' languages, like their cultural, social, and economic backgrounds, were individual difference factors that were formed outside of the school system and therefore, were somehow not the schools' responsibility to address. However, when the plaintiffs' legal representatives filed a petition for certiorari (review by a higher court) with the U.S. Supreme Court, the Supreme Court granted it because it recognized the importance to the public of the concerns reflected by this case. The Supreme Court then identified the California Education Code's requirements that English be the basic language of instruction in all schools, that students aged 6-16 years receive full-time compulsory education, and that no student be permitted to graduate from 12th grade and receive a diploma without meeting English proficiency standards; and the California state policy of ensuring all students' English mastery.

After reviewing California state laws and policy, the U.S. Supreme Court decided in *Lau v. Nichols* (1971) that just because the schools provided all students with equal curriculum, books, facilities, and teachers, the California standards still did not enable equal treatment of all students. While the plaintiffs' attorneys originally cited the Fourteenth Amendment's Equal Protection Clause, the Supreme Court did not affirm their argument. Instead, it cited Section 601 of the Civil Rights Act of

1964 prohibiting discrimination in any activity or program receiving federal financial assistance on the basis of race, color, or national origin. In 1970, these guidelines for federally funded entities was expanded to include students with language deficiencies, and to require providing them with the tools to resolve those deficiencies. Since the San Francisco Unified School District (one of the defendants) received considerable federal financial assistance, it was required to ensure students were not denied equal educational opportunities on the bases of race, color, national origin, or language deficiency. Based on this legislation, the Supreme Court overturned the Court of Appeals judgment and remanded the case of *Lau v. Nichols* to be granted appropriate relief to the complainants.

HENDRICK HUDSON CENTRAL SCHOOL DISTRICT V. ROWLEY (1982)

Amy Rowley, a Deaf child, had excellent lip-reading skills and minimal residual hearing. The year before Amy entered Furnace Woods School in Peekskill, N.Y. in the Hendrick Hudson Central School District, her parents and school administrators agreed, to ascertain which supplemental services she would need, she would be placed in regular kindergarten. Several school administrators took a sign-language interpreting course; the principal's office had a teletype machine installed to facilitate communicating with Amy's Deaf parents. Following a trial period, they decided Amy should stay in the kindergarten class, but wearing an FM hearing aid to amplify teacher/student speech into a wireless receiver for some activities. A sign-language interpreter provided for a two-week trial reported Amy did not need interpreting then. Amy succeeded in kindergarten. Her first-grade IEP required regular classroom placement; continued hearing aid use; one hour daily Deaf education tutoring; and three hours weekly SLP therapy. Her parents agreed but additionally insisted on sign-language interpreting for all academic classes. School administrators found she did not need interpreting, based on the kindergarten interpreter trial and consultation with the district Committee on the Handicapped, which considered the parents' expert evidence; teacher testimony; others' testimony; and a Deaf education class visit.

A deaf child, Amy Rowley, had received certain supplemental services in regular kindergarten and first-grade classes, including a first-grade IEP. When the school denied additional sign-language interpreter services it found unnecessary, Amy's Deaf parents demanded an independent examiner hearing. The examiner concurred interpretation was unnecessary, as "Amy was achieving educationally, academically, and socially" without it. On appeal, the N.Y. Commissioner of Education affirmed this decision. Invoking the judicial review provision of the Education for All Handicapped Children Act (EHA, 1975), the Rowleys filed suit in the U.S. District Court for the Southern District of New York, alleging that denying Amy an interpreter denied her the free, appropriate public education (FAPE) the EHA guaranteed. The District Court observed that Amy was "remarkably well-adjusted", communicated well with teachers and classmates; was easily progressing from grade to grade; and performed better than her average classmate. However, it also noted she understood substantially less in class than if she were not deaf, and thus, was not performing academically as well/learning as much as she would with normal hearing. Based on this discrepancy between potential and achievement, the court decided Amy was not receiving FAPE, defined as equal opportunity to achieve her full potential.

At the time of this case, federal support for educating students with disabilities was still relatively new. Despite some U.S. State laws to enhance educational services to students with disabilities, a House of Representatives report observed millions of students with disabilities were entirely excluded from public education, or misplaced in regular education classes without services they would need to access instruction. Congress intended Education for All Handicapped Children Act (EHA) to make public education available to children with disabilities; however, it did not require/guarantee them any specific educational levels or outcomes once admitted. As noted in a

Senate report, both houses of Congress related EHA and its precursors to two previous federal court decisions: *PARC v. Commonwealth of Pennsylvania* (1972) and *Mills v. Board of Education of the District of Columbia* (1972). While both cases ruled that children with disabilities must have access to adequate public educations, and established principles and detailed procedures for individualizing educational programs, which informed EHA; neither these cases nor EHA required any specific educational levels/outcomes of U.S. States. Congress interpreted "appropriate education" as simply receiving some specialized educational services.

In its rationale that the EHA (1975) federal legislation was necessary, a House of Representatives report observed no previous congressional legislation had required a specific guarantee that all school districts would afford students with disabilities the constitutional (14th Amendment) equal protection right. In meeting this need to give students with disabilities the equal protection of a "basic floor of opportunity", EHA's history and provisions indicate Congress considered equal access to education sufficient for providing equal protection. Congressional motivation to advance equal educational opportunity was not interpreted as requiring U.S. States to conform to any real, specific educational standard. Therefore, when *Hudson Central School District v. Rowley* petitioned the Supreme Court to review District Court and Court of Appeals decisions in favor of the Rowleys' claim their child was denied an "appropriate education", the Supreme Court had to interpret this EHA provision, which the lower courts found EHA did not define "functionally" but left to the courts. The Supreme Court ruled the lower courts had found no school violation of EHA provisions; evidence established the school provided an "adequate" education; concluded the lower courts had "erred", and reversed their decisions.

IRVING INDEPENDENT SCHOOL DISTRICT V. TATRO (1984)

In this case, the Supreme Court identified the issue to decide in reviewing lower court decisions as whether or not the Education for All Handicapped Children Act (EHA, 1975) or Section 504 of the Rehabilitation Act of 1973 required a school district to perform clean intermittent catheterization (CIC) a student with a disability needed during school hours. Amber Tatro, an eight-year-old student, had the birth defect spina bifida, causing a neurogenic bladder preventing voluntary urination, requiring catheterization every 3-4 hours to prevent kidney damage. CIC requires a layperson less than an hour's training and can be performed in a few minutes. Amber's parents, teenage brother, and babysitter were qualified to administer CIC; Amber herself would soon be able to do so. The Irving Independent School District had agreed in 1979 to provide Amber, then 3½ years old, special education. Amber's IEP required early childhood development classes, physical therapy, and occupational therapy, but not CIC administration by school personnel. After seeking administrative remedies unsuccessfully, the Tatros brought action, seeking attorney fees, damages, and an injunction ordering the school to provide CIC.

The Supreme Court identified two separate issues in *Irving Independent School District v. Tatro* (1984): (1) Whether EHA regulations required the school system to provide student Amber Tatro with CIC (clean intermittent catheterization) services; and (2) whether Section 504 of the 1973 Rehabilitation Act obligated the school system to provide CIC services. When Amber's parents were not granted administrative remedies they sought, they filed suit for attorneys' fees, damages, and an injunction requiring the school perform CIC. They first invoked EHA because Texas public schools received federal funding, arguing that CIC is included under "related services" in the EHA definition of free, appropriate public education (FAPE). They also invoked Section 504 of the Rehabilitation Act of 1973, which prohibits exclusion from participation in, denial of benefits of, or discrimination under any federally funded program. In *Tatro v. Texas* (1979), the District Court denied the Tatros' request for a preliminary injunction, ruling CIC was not a "related service" under EHA because it did not meet a need originating from efforts to educate; and ruling Section 504 did not mandate establishing "governmental health care for people seeking to participate" in federally funded programs.

Suing the Irving Independent School District, the Tatros cited EHA and Section 504 of the Rehabilitation Act supporting their argument that the school should provide their daughter Amber with the clean intermittent catheterization (CIC) she needed during school days. The District Court denied their request, ruling CIC not a "related service" under EHA and Section 504's not requiring "setting up...governmental health care" to enable participation in federally funded programs. The Court of Appeals reversed these rulings in 1980, finding CIC *was* a "related service" under EHA because Amber could not attend classes or benefit from special education without CIC; and finding the school's denying CIC *did* exclude Amber from a federally funded educational program, violating Section 504. Answering the school's argument that EHA only allowed "medical services" for evaluative/diagnostic purposes, the District Court found CIC not a medical service under EHA because administering it did not require a doctor; deemed CIC a "related service" under EHA; ordered the school and State Board of Education to modify Amber's IEP to include CIC; awarded compensatory damages under EHA; affirmed the Tatros had proven Section 504 violation; and awarded attorneys' fees under Section 504.

The Supreme Court partly affirmed and partly reversed lower court decisions in this case. It affirmed the Court of Appeals decision that clean intermittent catheterization (CIC) services met the definition of a "supportive service" enabling a disabled student to benefit from special education by enabling Amber Tatro to stay onsite throughout the school day under EHA, citing *Board of Education of Hendrick Hudson Central School District v. Rowley* (1982), plus EHA provisions for analogous services like transportation enabling physical presence and EHA grant authorization to modify building/facilities/equipment for accessibility. The Supreme Court concurred with the Court of Appeals that CIC was not a medical service as the school claimed, and was a related service under EHA. EHA allowed only services required for students to benefit from special education, e.g., nothing that could be administered outside school hours; but in Amber's case, she required CIC every 3-4 hours, i.e., during school hours. Regulations excluded physician services but included nursing services; CIC did not even require a nurse. The Court observed the Tatros did not request the school provide CIC equipment, only services. It reversed attorney fee recovery under Section 504 because relief under EHA takes precedence.

OBERTI V. BOARD OF EDUCATION OF THE BOROUGH OF CLEMENTON (1993)

The Philadelphia Public Interest Law Center began representing the family of Rafael Oberti, a student with Down Syndrome. Rafael's parents sought his placement in a regular education classroom with needed special education supports. Clementon school district officials recommended segregated placement for Rafael before kindergarten, in another district more than an hour away from their home. The Obertis initially objected, then compromised with the school for limited periods of inclusion; however, this failed without required supports. Objecting to the district's repeated recommendation for segregated, out-of-district placement, the Obertis requested a due process hearing. They agreed to accept the district placement recommendation in exchange for promised district exploration of means for including Rafael in a regular education classroom. But they soon discovered Rafael had no contact with non-disabled students during school days, and the district was making no attempt to relocate his placement from the segregated class. They filed another due process complaint in 1991 requesting regular classroom placement in their neighborhood elementary school for Rafael.

In this case, the Obertis objected to school district recommendation to place their son Rafael in a segregated special education classroom outside the district and far from home. Even after compromising with the school district and reaching agreements, they found the district ignoring its responsibilities—first to provide supports required for Rafael to benefit from limited inclusion, then to seek means for inclusive education while Rafael remained segregated—and filed due process complaints. The Administrative Law Judge in the hearing agreed with the district that the segregated class constituted the IDEA-mandated Least Restrictive Environment for Rafael, concluding he was not ready for a regular education classroom, despite expert witness testimony to the contrary. The Obertis, wanting Rafael to learn social skills in a regular classroom that he could not acquire in the segregated class, appealed to the U.S. District Court for New Jersey. The 1992 trial heard new evidence from prominent special education authorities. Their expert testimony was that, with necessary resources and qualified teachers, Rafael could not only be integrated but would benefit greatly from regular education placement. The court found for the Obertis; the Court of Appeals upheld the ruling in 1993, setting a precedent.

The Clementon school district repeatedly recommended placing Rafael Oberti, who had Down syndrome, in a segregated special education classroom outside the district over an hour's drive from home, beginning before Rafael started kindergarten. Objecting to this placement and seeking Rafael's placement in a regular education classroom in their neighborhood elementary school, his parents compromised with the school district for limited inclusion, but this failed due to district failure to provide necessary supports. The Obertis requested due process hearings. When the district failed to honor its part of the agreement reached in the first hearing and the judge's decision in the second hearing sided with the school district, the Obertis appealed to U.S. District Court, which heard new expert witness testimony and found for the plaintiffs, affirmed by the Third Circuit Court of Appeals, which found schools must not segregate students with disabilities without considering "the whole range of supplemental aids and services" and making "efforts to modify the regular education program" to enable curriculum access. The court found that the district did not prove that Rafael could not be included in a regular classroom, given necessary services; and thus, the district had violated IDEA regulations.

The decisions of the U.S. District Court for New Jersey and the U.S. Court of Appeals for the Third Circuit, both finding for the plaintiffs in *Oberti v. Board of Education of the Borough of Clementon* (1993), not only enabled the Obertis to have their son Rafael, who had Down syndrome, placed in a regular education classroom in their neighborhood elementary school, where he could interact with non-disabled peers, learn normal social skills, and otherwise benefit more from education, instead of in a segregated special education classroom outside their school district and more than an hour's drive from their home; it moreover set a precedent for innumerable other families with special education students to seek and win relief under IDEA. It also established high standards, popularly dubbed "the Oberti test", for school districts to segregate special-needs students. However, limitations to this ruling's impact included insufficient family litigation resources; inadequate services and supports; and unqualified teachers. The class-action suit *Gaskin v. Commonwealth* (1994), filed by the Public Interest Law Center of Philadelphia, sought to remedy these limitations by enforcing school compliance with inclusive education and supports mandated by IDEA.

NEWPORT-MESA UNIFIED SCHOOL DISTRICT V. STATE OF CALIFORNIA DEPARTMENT OF EDUCATION

District Judge Taylor ordered that federal copyright law did not supersede the state statute requiring parents of special education students to be provided copies of test protocols, which fell within acceptable fair use under federal copyright law. Under California Education Code section 56504, defendant Jack Anthony requested copies of his son's test protocols before his scheduled IEP meeting. The school district refused to provide the copyrighted Woodcock-Johnson Test of Achievement III (WJ-III) protocol. Anthony filed a complaint with the California Department of

Education, which found the district violated section 56504 by not providing records within five days of the request; ordered the district to revise its student record request policies and procedures to comply with section 56504 and send the Department a copy of the new policy in 60 days; and denied a request for reconsideration of that compliance report. The district sued, claiming federal copyright law prohibited its supplying copies of copyrighted test forms. Invited by the Court, the publishers of the WISC-III and WJ-III intervened to claim copyright interest. The Court ruled on cross-motions for summary judgment after extensive conferences to develop a plan satisfying both special education and copyright interests failed.

This case represented a conflict between federal copyright law and the California Education Code. Under the latter, the school district must provide a parent of a special education student a copy of his child's copyrighted standardized test protocol or lose state funding; but doing so exposed it to copyright infringement liability under the former. Factors considered included: (1) The nature and purpose of test use, e.g., for nonprofit educational vs. commercial purposes. The parent's request was for evaluating special education needs and appropriate educational placement, not commercial gain, supporting fair use. Broadening understanding non-commercially, also the parent's purpose, supported fair use. Transformative use (adding something new) was another element: test protocols were transformative by including student responses. Public interest supported fair use: providing test copies effectively involved parents in their children's special education. (2) Nature of copyrighted work: Student responses made test protocols informational, supporting fair use. (3) Amount used: Portions of tests copied for parents were no more than required to see student responses and determine their proper evaluation/reasonable for assessing student educational needs, supporting fair use. (4) Market effect: No evidence of risk for widespread public access or adverse market effects was presented.

In this case, the Court found for the defendants; denied the plaintiff and plaintiffs-interveners' motion for summary judgment; and granted the defendants' motion for summary judgment. The Court also concluded that when parents of special education students requested copies of their children's test protocols under section 56504 of the California Education Code, the school's providing those protocols to parents would be a fair use under 17 U.S.C., § 107. It added that the school district could prevent the risk of improper use of test protocols by applying appropriate safeguards, e.g., requiring parents to review the original test protocols before requesting or acquiring copies; requiring written requests for copies of test protocols; requiring a confidentiality or nondisclosure agreement, or other reasonable precautions. In its conclusions, the Court additionally recommended that to protect California school districts against violating federal copyright law, and to prevent repeated fair use analyses every time a school district released any of its documents, the California legislature should update section 56504 to include applicable standards for both protecting disclosures for parents of special education students as it intended, and protecting legitimate concerns regarding copyrights.

LARRY P. V. RILES

In this class-action suit, plaintiffs Larry P., a black student and Lucille P., his guardian, represented the class of black children in California who had been or would in the future be incorrectly placed and kept in special classes for the "educable mentally retarded" (EMR). They challenged the placement process for EMR class placement, especially use of standardized individual IQ tests, which they claimed were racially and culturally biased; and therefore the defendants—the State of California, represented by Superintendent of Public Instruction Wilson Riles and members of the California State Board of Education; and the San Francisco Unified School District, represented by its Superintendent of Schools and Board of Education members—had discriminated against black students by using those tests' scores to determine placement. The plaintiffs alleged that misplacing black students in special classes doomed them to being stigmatized, not receiving adequate educations, and thus not developing skills needed to become successful, productive members of society. For example, while the general population of K-12 students in California at the time was only 10% black, the population of K-12 students enrolled in EMR classes in California at the time was 25%, indicating gross overrepresentation.

The Court found in favor of the plaintiffs' claims that the defendants had violated Title VI of the Civil Rights Act of 1964; 1973 Rehabilitation Act; Education for All Handicapped Children Act (EHA, 1975); and federal and state constitutional guarantees of equal protection under law. Another reason for the federal constitutional ruling was an "unlawful segregative intent." Informed by the history of California special education and IQ testing, the Court found the defendants' practices, though not necessarily intended to harm black students, did intend to place a greatly disproportionate number of black students in special EMR classes. The schools' use of racially and culturally biased, unvalidated placement criteria manifested this intention. Since it was impossible to support or permit assuming the black population had a higher incidence of mild MR and the intention the Court identified would only be congruent with such a wrong assumption, the Court stated it could not permit that intention, as racial discrimination was constitutionally prohibited. After the U.S. Department of Justice as *amicus curiae* found the defendants violated federal law; plaintiffs filed amended complains; and the court denied several motions for summary judgment and dismissal, trial became necessary.

In 1972 the court ordered defendant restraint from placing black students in EMR classes based primarily on IQ test scores if these caused racial imbalances in EMR class composition. Defendants appealed; the Circuit Court of Appeals affirmed the ruling in 1974. The court granted the plaintiffs' motion to modify the class and statewide preliminary injunction terms in 1974, including all black California students who were/might be classified MR based on IQ tests. Order provisions prohibited defendants from psychological evaluations of black California students using standardized IQ/individual ability tests not accounting for their cultural backgrounds and experiences; listing any individual IQ test not doing this as approved for California Education Code purposes; or placing black California students into EMR classes based on any test not doing this, effective since. Defendants voluntarily placed a statewide IQ testing moratorium for EMR placement, regardless of student race, in 1975. This case evolved from the San Francisco private class action with federal constitutional claims to statewide, with Department of Justice support, including many federal and state laws. 1977's amended plaintiff complaints added statutory bases, including the Civil Rights Act Title VI and Emergency School Aid Act; the state constitution and education code; and EHA.

LAWS GOVERNING RIGHTS TO PRIVACY, CONFIDENTIALITY OF RECORDS, AND INFORMED CONSENT

The Family Educational Rights and Privacy Act (FERPA), Individuals with Disabilities Education Act (IDEA), and Protection of Pupil Rights Amendment (PPRA) are some examples of statutory laws that protect the rights to privacy, records confidentiality, and informed consent of students and their families. Minor students have fewer privacy rights than adults. School assessment to determine student eligibility for special education services, or for educational professionals to obtain private information, requires reasonable grounds that such information is necessary. Parents have to be informed of the nature of any educational interventions; their risks, goals, costs, and benefits; and any alternative treatments available for their children. Before consenting to allow school assessment; give schools information; or accept school intervention plans, parents should be informed of their confidentiality rights. Regardless of whether students are given choices for participation/self-determination, for professionals to establish rapport and obtain student cooperation, they should always inform students of the nature and scope of any assessment/intervention plan. Parental informed consent should be (1) based upon complete information/explanation/knowledge; (2) delivered ensuring competency (without language barriers, etc.); and (3) not coerced, but voluntary.

LRE LAWS

Federal law requires local school districts to assure students with disabilities—including those in private/public/other institutions/care facilities—are educated with non-disabled students; and separate placement, special classes, or otherwise removing students with disabilities from regular education settings is only when the severity/nature of a student's disability prevents satisfactorily implementing regular education classes with supplementary services and aids. Also, since districts might exploit state special education funding methods by making specialized setting placements to receive more money, Congress requires state policy and procedure development to ensure any setting-based funding system criteria do not violate least restrictive environment (LRE) requirements. IEPs are federally required to include descriptions of how a student disability affects general education curriculum involvement and progress and related annual goal statements including short-term objectives/benchmarks; supplemental services and aids to provide the student; and program supports and modifications to enable general curriculum involvement, progress, and non-academic and extracurricular activity participation. Federal regulations require disabled student education in the same school as if non-disabled unless the IEP requires otherwise; and LRE selection considering any potential harm to the student or needed service quality. Federal special education laws and court decisions require integrated and prohibit segregated special education.

U.S. DEPARTMENT OF EDUCATION PRINCIPLES REGARDING STUDENT SECLUSION AND RESTRAINT

Make every effort to prevent seclusion/restraint need/use. Never restrict student movement with mechanical restraints/restrict movement/control behavior using medication/drugs (unless medically authorized). Only behavior imminently threatening serious physical harm to self/others, and other interventions' ineffectiveness, indicate seclusion/physical restraint; discontinue as soon as threats abate. Policies restricting seclusion/restraint apply to all, not only disabled, students. All behavioral interventions respect student rights to freedom from abuse and to treatment with dignity. Seclusion/restraint should never be for coercion, convenience, retaliation, punishment, or discipline. Seclusion/restraint never harms students/restricts breathing. Seclusion/restraint used repeatedly/multiply for the same student/by the same person/within the same classroom are reviewed; if indicated, current strategies addressing dangerous behavior revised; and positive behavioral strategies developed if not established. Behavioral strategies addressing behavior requiring seclusion/restraint address behavior's underlying reason/purpose/function. Regularly train teachers/staff in effective alternatives, and using safe seclusion/restraint only when required. Visually, continuously, carefully monitor every seclusion/restraint instance to ensure safety and appropriateness. Inform parents of federal, state, local laws and school policies regarding seclusion/restraint. Notify parents ASAP of seclusion/restraint. Regularly review and update seclusion/restraint policies as needed. Policies should require specific data collection enabling implementing these principles, and written documentation of seclusion/restraint incidents.

NEGLIGENT SUPERVISION LAWSUITS

When K-12 students are injured because a teacher, school psychologist, or other school personnel responsible for their supervision did not supervise them adequately, their parents may file lawsuits known as negligent supervision claims. Parents may file such claims when their children are injured because of the children's own behavior; or when other children in their school setting engage in dangerous or risky behavior and school personnel responsible for supervision are not available to intervene in the behavior. Claims against public school districts or city/municipality school systems, including negligent supervision claims, are subject to statutes of limitations with short durations in some U.S. States (e.g., New York) for filing. School psychologists, teachers, and school support staff have legal obligations not to leave students unattended and to prevent students from harming their classmates. One type of negligent supervision situation is a student's self-injury due to lack of supervision. Younger children especially tend to attempt ingesting/jumping on/climbing on/into harmful things. Another type of negligent supervision involves allowing a student to injure a classmate via throwing things, physical violence, etc. Self-inflicted vs. other-inflicted injury is immaterial when negligent supervision causes student injury.

CONFLICT OF INTEREST

The National Association of School Psychologists (NASP) policy on conflict of interest states that NASP greatly emphasizes ensuring that its members and the general public continue placing trust and confidence in NASP. This includes requiring any actions by its members be free of any conflict of interest, and in addition free "from even the appearance of impropriety". This policy further specifically prohibits any NASP Executive Council member; Delegate Assembly member; officer; committee member; or staff member from approving any activities or ventures, and/or participating in any decision-making process, that NASP sponsors or sanctions from which the individual might obtain any financial benefits. An additional provision of this policy is that before any such member recuses herself or himself from any such decision-making process because it constitutes a conflict of interest, the individual must disclose fully to NASP all and every financial benefit(s) s/he can expect to receive for the activity/venture, and must furnish NASP's President and Executive Director with complete copies of any related agreements, contracts, or other documents involving third parties.

CRIMINAL, JUVENILE, AND CIVIL LAW

School psychologists typically do not deal with criminal liability, except regarding child abuse. However, school psychologists with good intentions could unwittingly contribute to a minor's delinquency, which is illegal. While the juvenile law system is comparable to the criminal justice system, juveniles committing criminal acts are not guilty of crimes but "acts of juvenile delinquency". In juvenile court, youth are charged not with indictments or complaints like adults, but "informations." Juveniles have no right to trial by jury. Judges' findings of juvenile delinquency are not misdemeanors, felonies, or crimes, but determinations of status. Judges do not sentence juveniles, but enter dispositions focusing on their needs. Juvenile incarceration generally is limited to age 18. Regardless of age, juvenile cases can be transferred to adult court via discretionary/mandatory transfer. Civil law, including confidentiality and duty to warn, more often involves school psychologists, and does not involve incarceration except for immigration violations. Legal educator liability includes strict liability/intentional harmful behavior; intentional interference (e.g., assault, battery, defamation, intentional emotional distress, personal property trespass, false imprisonment); and negligence, the commonest. Elements determining negligence are duty of care (against reasonably foreseeable danger); standard of care (reasonable, prudent, circumstance/situation-specific care); proximate legal cause; and actual loss/injury.

Consultation and Collaboration

Consultation and Collaboration

RtI

Response to Intervention (RtI) is a variety of procedures for determining how students respond to specific instructional changes. IDEA regulations strongly support using RtI as part of the assessment procedures to identify students with Specific Learning Disabilities (SLDs). Also, IDEA prohibits past state practices of requiring school districts to consider IQ/achievement discrepancies as criteria for identifying SLDs. RtI is frequently incorporated into problem-solving models to help educators identify effective teaching strategies and evaluate their efficacy. Problem-solving models, typically having three (or more) tiers of intervention, address achievement and behavior problems by trying to ascertain the instructional/behavioral supports needed to solve these problems. Components include early intervention, school and general education classroom supports, ongoing student progress evaluation, and referral to special education evaluation when early supports are insufficient. Some districts determine SLDs by incorporating RtI procedures and non-traditional assessments into problem-solving models. RtI is part of comprehensive assessment. District-wide RtI and problem-solving models create greater need and opportunities for school psychologists in designing, implementing, and evaluating problem-solving and RtI approaches, as well as expanding their roles in assessment.

ROLES OF SCHOOL PSYCHOLOGISTS

SCHOOL TEAM COLLABORATION

School psychologists are frequently assigned school team leadership roles. School teams often view school psychologists, even those not appointed to lead, as leaders concerning mental health, assessment, school-agency and home-school collaboration, and similar issues. As special education team/IEP team and intervention assistance team members, school psychologists play crucial rules in implementing Response to Intervention (RtI) and problem-solving endeavors. These include: Consulting on an ongoing basis about individual student needs and implementation issues; collaborating to develop team procedures for referral, monitoring, and evaluation at each problem-solving program tier; developing specific RtI measurement procedures; developing interview and observation protocols, etc.; identifying team training needs; helping teams procure or providing training in applying progress-monitoring procedures to decision-making and other pertinent training; functioning as parent liaisons by helping parents understand new RtI/problem-solving school program models, how they affect their children, and promoting the integration of parental input into each intervention tier and evaluation; functioning as community agency/provider liaisons by providing in-services to familiarize them with new program models, and promoting (with parental consent) appropriate communication and involvement with them; and overseeing progress monitoring, and data integration into team decisions.

NEW SERVICE DELIVERY SYSTEM MODELS

Among school district professionals, school psychologist are among the best prepared to assist with new service delivery models in system design, development, implementation, and evaluation. Their roles include: Determining effective, relevant approaches for districts/states through identifying and analyzing RtI and problem-solving research literature; collaborating with administrators to identify key leaders and significant stakeholders to get their "buy-in" to promote system change; performing needs assessments to identify initial training needs, concerns, and potential problems; designing evidence-based models tailored to local resources and needs; planning and implementing

94

staff training in evidence-based interventions, student progress evaluation, and other training required for implementation; developing local academic achievement norms like curriculum-based measurement and other student progress measures; monitoring longitudinal norm validity and reliability; implementing and evaluating pilot projects; overseeing district-level implementation and continuing evaluation; communicating and consulting with parents, administrators, and school boards on an ongoing basis; identifying system-wide student need patterns (e.g., persistent basic phonics skills difficulties among kindergarteners); and collaborating with school district staff to identify intervention strategies that are evidence-based and appropriate.

MH CONSULTATION

Mental health (MH) consultation helps care/service professionals address psychological aspects of current and future work issues. The purpose is not to improve the consultee's sense of wellbeing, but to improve the consultee's job performance. According to Caplan's (1970) model, characteristics include these: The targeted work problem is in the mental health area. Consultation involves two professionals and layperson client(s). The consultee has no obligation to the consultant. The consultant has no administrative responsibility for the consultee's work. The consultant is external to the consultee's work. The basic consultee-consultant relationship is coordinate. Consultation involves a short series of interviews. Consultation is expected to continue indefinitely. The information involved is not predetermined. Goals of consultation are both improving the consultee's current coping with work difficulty, and increasing the consultee's ability for mastering similar future work problems. Consultation is only one of the mental health specialist's functions. Types of MH consultations include client-centered and consultee-centered case consultation; program-centered and consultee-centered administrative consultation; and school MH consultation. In schools, focus is strongly on primary prevention. Typology is school setting-specific. Service levels are I – student-focused; II – teacher-focused; III – system-focused. Common conflicts teachers encounter are with authority; dependency; hostility and anger; and identification.

BEHAVIORAL CONSULTATION

Behavioral consultation provides indirect problem-solving services. Behavioral consultation goals include changing client behavior; changing consultee behavior; and producing organizational changes. Its assumptions are: All behaviors are learned. Functional interactions are the focus. Assessment, intervention, and evaluation are connected and involve observable, quantifiable, measurable behaviors. Environmental antecedents are powerful change initiation points. Learners' learning histories differ. Systematic data collection is important. To modify an individual's behavior, one must also modify the behaviors of others the individual interacts with in the target environment. Verbal processes involved include specification, evaluation, inference, summarization, and validation. Elicitors and emitters of behaviors are consultant leads. Information that consultants obtain from consultees includes client behavior; behavior setting; environmental/background influences; special client characteristics; the nature of observations; plans; and additional data. The behavioral consultation process involves problem identification, problem analysis, plan implementation, and problem evaluation. Behavioral consultation is based in an empirical perspective on behavior; depends on behavioral technology and a structured interviewing process; emphasizes current influences on behaviors; and is frequently criticized as manipulative. One alternative to the behavioral consultation model is a model based on social learning theory, which combines some (but not all) principles of behaviorism with emphasis on the social contexts of learning.

IC MODEL

Instructional consultation (IC) is a stage-based, problem-solving early intervention process founded on consultee-centered principles of consultation. Its purpose is to improve teachers' abilities to address classroom issues with student academics and behaviors through data-based decision-making and evidence-based interventions. Since IC is based on ecological assumptions, problem-solving focuses on the "instructional triangle": modifiable student variables, instructional tasks, and instructional design. School psychologists and other educators assess variables from this instructional triangle to identify instructional matches promoting learning; identify whether gaps exist between current and expected student performance; and determine whether intervention for such gaps is required. If so, evidence-based interventions are implemented. Progress evaluation and decision-making about special education/other additional resources required are data-based. As instructional consultants, school psychologists must accept ecological assumptions underlying the IC model, and have collaborative problem-solving skills, including effective communication strategies and building working relationships with teachers; competence in instructional and behavioral assessment and intervention, including instructional and classroom management domains; and teamwork skills to work as IC Team members. In schools implementing IC teams, many school psychologists have been able to transition from limited psychometric roles in special education classification to roles with positive impacts on student and teacher development.

COMMUNICATION AND COLLABORATION SKILLS

Developing effective work relationships with teachers and accurately identifying classroom needs requires school psychologists' consultation skills. According to experts (Erchul and Martens, 2010), successful communication, consultation, and collaboration include:

- Problem-Solving Task – correctly identifying consultation reasons. Personal/emotional experiences can often cause adversarial teacher reactions; behavioral approaches to identifying issues by quantifying target behaviors and environments help minimize personal biases/emotional effects. Resulting teacher descriptions of issues in objective, actionable terms supporting effective interventions ensure optimal outcomes.
- Social Influence Task – In terms of individuals involved, and depending on included professionals' expertise, consultation transcends collaboration in multiple ways. Power/Influence affects how data are collected/exchanged/presented. The ratio of information elicited from teachers vs. information given by psychologists is described by "message control." According to research, psychologists should elicit far more information from teachers than they give during problem identification; but provide more information during intervention planning and implementation.
- Support and Development Task – (immediate and ongoing) – issues occurring at critical times accord them crisis status. After efforts to remediate classroom problems, most teachers reach consultations feeling frustrated, defeated, and powerless: psychologists must provide emotional support and affirmation. Repeated teamwork efforts and successes afford supportive consultant-partners, new perspectives, and better teaching methods.

ESTABLISHING POSITIVE COLLABORATIVE AND CONSULTATIVE RELATIONSHIPS WITH STAKEHOLDERS

The social nature of consultation requires the active engagement of all members. For effective collaboration, school psychologists must establish engaging, positive environments wherein all stakeholders including students, teachers, parents, and other professionals can participate. Doing so is informed by social psychology principles. For example, the fundamental attribution error ascribes others' behaviors to their disposition instead of the situation; avoiding this prevents judgments of others in consultative interactions. According to the elaboration likelihood model, either central communication—i.e., logical/cognitive arguments, or peripheral communication—i.e., perceived authority or mood—persuade people. Those convinced via central routes generally have deeper, longer-lasting beliefs; however, persuasion via peripheral routes is usually easier. The most effective change is likely a combination of the two. Experts advise school psychologists not to present themselves as consultation "experts," but true collaborators to establish environments conducive to change. They must communicate effectively with stakeholders not only face-to-face, but also in written communication. Effective spoken and written communication includes clarity, an engaging style, avoiding jargon; and probably most of all, using good listening skills.

REQUIREMENTS AS COMMUNITY FACILITATORS

For community facilitation, school psychologists must consult effectively from an ecological perspective by engaging with physical therapists, occupational therapists, speech-language pathologists, other specialists, social workers, counselors, and physicians. In diagnostic and treatment practices, they must address not only individual students, but also system-level factors to enhance school climate, leadership, home-school relationships; and create connections with community resources. An assumption guiding community facilitation is that other powerful, meaningful resources exist with equal status but different roles in the problem-solving process. The ultimate goal is school recognition that through networking with other community resources, they have the potential for solving their own problems. To fulfill the community facilitator role successfully, school psychologists must pursue community members' active engagement. Building rapport and trust with a variety of community resources and professionals can take months or years. Awareness of cultural issues relevant to families; the historical school-community relationship; and school openness to other resources and professionals are included in understanding the complex systemic and political factors operating in communities and schools. This understanding is part of the effective interpersonal communication that facilitates building strong community networks. For student and family wellbeing, school psychologists' community engagement efforts must be transparent.

COLLABORATIVE HOME-SCHOOL PARTNERSHIPS

According to the National Association of School Psychologists (NASP), school psychologists can do the following things to identify strategies for giving families and educators opportunities to establish and sustain partnerships, and to advocate for such partnerships: Acknowledge and promote the need for addressing issues across different contexts in which students live; implement evidence-based, systematic models for family interventions and school-family consultation; participate in and/or form school-based teams of educators, parents, and community members to assess needs, identify priorities, and plan and implement collaborative initiatives for enhancing students' educational outcomes; function as liaisons to support reciprocal communication and coordination of schools, homes, and communities; include families effectively in student assessment, planning, intervention, and progress monitoring to promote partnership between educators and families throughout the processes of screening, early intervention, and special education; provide families and educators with professional development opportunities regarding current research into the most effective collaboration processes, evidence-based academic, behavioral, and mental health interventions and programs, and regarding the positive effects of partnering; and support sustainable partnership practices through accountability and continuing monitoring.

SCHOOL-COMMUNITY COLLABORATION

According to one community facilitator and educational expert (O'Keefe, 2011), three things, among others, that can help to promote school-community collaborations are:

- Expanding the vision of the school to encompass the community. As other experts note, people contributing should not be educators only but include community members. Communities can create graffiti walls; play areas; brainstorming spaces; thought-provoking videos; ethical/philosophical challenges; quotations; trivia facts; questions; puzzles, "mind-bender" exercises, etc. In the community around a school, numerous opportunities for experiential learning exist. Asking the right questions and attracting the right people can help schools find ways of connecting core curriculum outside classrooms.
- Community walks by teachers, students, local business members—visiting senior homes, local businesses, etc. and conversing with them—enable outreach to all stakeholders in their own territory. Sharing passions, and dreams for better community-school partnerships; asking people how they can help, and what matters to them; and openly inviting reconnection will enable their making a difference.
- Making a community resource map visually represents skills, time, and materials people can offer and networks for raising community child and family needs awareness, facilitating collaboration and resource-sharing.

Beyond school, real-life experience, job experience, mentors, and peers contribute much of what we learn in childhood and adulthood. One way to promote school-community collaboration is to connect the real world to school core curriculum. Educators have all heard students ask how they will ever use certain content/lessons in their lives; students demand relevance in education. Teachers can design engaging, motivating learning experiences inside and outside classrooms. One expert (O'Keefe, 2011) recommends Chapter 4, "Asking the Experts", of the book *Fires in the Mind: What Kids Can Tell Us About Motivation and Mastery* (Cushman, 2010) for ideas. Project-based learning can involve community engagement. Teachers can match students with specific subject-matter experts, community organizations, and local businesses. A related source is *Reinventing Project-Based Learning: Your Field Guide to Real-World Projects in the Digital Age* (Krauss and Boss, 2015). Senior citizens in care facilities are often socially isolated; they can provide a wealth of knowledge and experience while benefiting from school outreach. Community design challenges are another strategy. Creating community gardens; redesigning classrooms; creating shared, open learning spaces; designing courses; modifying student decision-making participation are examples of school reinvention promoting local change. www.designthinkingforeducators.com offers a free toolkit.

COLLABORATION WITH COMMUNITY AGENCIES AND PROVIDERS TO PROMOTE STUDENT MENTAL HEALTH

In their roles that involve consultation and case management, school psychologists work to improve the coordination and effectiveness of school and community support for student mental health. They advocate for individual student needs both within their schools and outside them in the community. School psychologists help students' families to gain access to the community resources that are available and that they need. They are facilitators of the coordination among schools, parents, and community services. In addition to their advocacy efforts, school psychologists use interagency collaboration to further research evidence-based public policies and programs that will improve student academic and social outcomes. Some of the ways in which they do this is by establishing and sustaining collaborative relationships with community mental health services; developing crisis response systems that coordinate between the school and the community; advocating for and consulting with policymakers about legislation for mental health and education; pursuing funding for integrated school and community services; connecting mental health policies and programs to evidence-based practices; and providing in-service training for educators, parents, and community members.

MAKING STRONG PARTNERSHIPS BETWEEN SCHOOLS, COMMUNITIES, AND FAMILIES

Among the many services they deliver, school psychologists include in their jobs the functions that they perform to reinforce the connections and collaborations among schools, families, and community service agencies and providers, which in turn serve to improve student mental health, learning, performance, and thus, ultimately, education. For example, when students and their families are in need of services not provided by their school, school psychologists can help them to locate, access, and make connections with community service providers who do provide those services. They help families to locate the agencies and/or service providers most suited to address each student's and family's particular issues and needs. They help students' families find, apply for, and otherwise access funding for community services if they cannot afford them. They can also help families find free or affordable services among the agencies and providers available in the community. In addition, they assist students in making transitions between school and residential treatment programs, juvenile justice programs, or other community learning environments, which promotes community connections while helping students and families.

COMMUNITY SERVICE PROVIDERS AND AGENCIES IN CONSULTATION, INTERVENTION, AND PREVENTION

In the area of consultation, school psychologists often serve as liaisons between parents and community service providers and agencies. They also make working relationships among parents, teachers, and community service providers and agencies stronger through their efforts. They may recruit community providers as consultants in developing school programs. In the area of intervention, school psychologists not only provide psychological counseling themselves; but in addition, they can refer students and families to other providers in the community, both private practitioners and providers employed by community agencies. In districts, school systems, or individual schools where school psychologists are overextended and their schedules do not permit enough time for the counseling sessions needed, referral to other providers in the community can be a necessity. Also, many school psychologists have the wisdom to recognize when particular mental health disorders, family dysfunction, or other problems would benefit from expertise they may lack; they can refer students' families to community providers or agencies with practitioners having specialized expertise in the identified problem(s). In the area of prevention, school psychologists collaborate with community agencies and school personnel to provide services to enhance psychological and physical health.

Family-School Collaboration Services

PROMOTING FAMILY INVOLVEMENT IN SCHOOLS
OVERCOMING OBSTACLES

The U.S. Department of Education (ED, 1997) published an Idea Book of strategies effectively used by Title I programs in various local school districts and schools. For example, school personnel and families must have time to get acquainted with each other, plan how they intend to collaborate to augment student learning, and execute the plans they make. Families often experience time constraints, and schools frequently encounter resource limitations. Yet in successful district and school programs, participants find the resources and time to facilitate school-family partnership development by both educators and parents. Information, training, and skills for communicating with one another are also required to prevent mistrust and misconceptions between parents and school staff members. Every successful program reviewed by ED centrally featured initiatives for closing parent-school information gaps. Outreach activities including informational newsletters, handbooks, home visits; and workshops enable school employees and parents participating in effective programs to trust and work with each other toward student school success.

FORMING EFFECTIVE PARTNERSHIPS

The U.S. Department of Education (ED) has studied a number of schools that achieved successful partnerships involving families in their children's education. Based on the practices and experiences of these schools, ED has offered some guidelines for personnel in all schools to consider for encouraging parent and family involvement in their educational activities. In addition to tailoring their approach to whatever is already effective in their community and investing in staff development and training for families and school personnel, strategies include effective communication: even the very best school-family partnership plans will not succeed if the members are unable to communicate productively. Educators therefore need to plan strategies for accommodating the diverse cultural and linguistic needs of families and school staff members, in addition to their work schedules and lifestyles. Diversity and flexibility are essential guidelines: useful parental engagement has various forms, which may not necessarily entail their presence at school, meetings, workshops, etc. Parents' helping children learn is what is important; this can take place in homes and communities as well as schools.

EXPERT GUIDELINES

Based on the experiences of schools that have formed successful partnerships with families, the U.S. Department of Education (ED) has offered some guidelines to help other schools follow suit. Although partnership strategies necessarily vary among communities according to local resources, needs, and interests, a common characteristic shared among successful family involvement approaches is an emphasis on flexibility and innovation. Moreover, most successful schools studied by ED have implemented schoolwide programs, which enabled them to become even more flexible and innovative. One guideline is to build upon whatever is already working well: no "one size fits all" approach to partnering exists. Schools and families together should first identify student, family, and school staff strengths, needs, and interests; and then design strategies in response to those. Another guideline is to provide training and professional development to all school employees, parents, and family members, which is an essential investment in fortifying school-family partnership. Having the requisite knowledge and skills for collaboration with each other and the wider community enables them to support student learning together.

GUIDELINES RELATED TO MONEY, TIME, POWER IN NUMBERS, AND EVALUATION FOR SCHOOLS

School parent involvement initiatives need to make use of funding, technical and other assistance, support, and training from sources outside schools. For example, school districts; public agencies; community organizations; local universities and colleges; state education agencies; and Comprehensive Regional Assistance Centers sponsored by the U.S. Department of Education (ED) are some external funding sources. Many school programs include parent involvement activities financed by Title I program funds; however, some exemplary successful school programs have also sought support outside school for these activities, and by doing so have augmented their resources for involving parents in school and student pursuits. Experts from ED remind educators as a general guideline that "Change takes time": it takes ongoing effort to develop successful school-family partnerships. Moreover, resolving one problem frequently generates several new ones. Additionally, involving many stakeholders rather than only a few is necessary for successful partnerships. Family involvement projects must regularly evaluate their effects using multiple indices, e.g., of participation in and satisfaction with school activities by families, school staff, and communities; student educational progress measures; and school-family interaction quality measures.

STRATEGIES TO PROMOTE SCHOOL-FAMILY-COMMUNITY PARTNERSHIPS

No one individual or program can establish effective school-family partnerships; these require restructuring the schools so they support family engagement. Unlike traditional school practices and organization which frequently discourage family involvement, particularly in high schools, schools need to create more inviting, personal environments that welcome parents and recruit their support for their children's success. Regardless of specific actions individual schools take to develop school-family partnerships, personnel at the most successful schools are ready to revisit all their existing methods of operation and restructure their school organizations to be less hierarchical and more personal and accessible to parents. Family communication and participation in school activities can be impeded by differences in language, culture, and education between families and school personnel. Outreach to parents with less formal education; bilingual services to enable oral and written communications concerning student progress and school programs; and building trust between homes and schools to promote intercultural understanding are strategies for addressing these differences. Another strategy promoting partnerships that many Title I schools have used is tapping community and other external supports, e.g., partnering with healthcare and other community service agencies; universities and colleges; local businesses; and state and school district supports.

INTERAGENCY COLLABORATION

Interagency collaboration is a clearly defined, reciprocally beneficial relationship into which two or more agencies, organizations, or individuals enter to attain shared goals. It requires the members' commitment to defining their mutual goals and relationships; sharing responsibility and developing structure jointly; sharing accountability and authority for their success; and sharing resources and rewards. It is important to collaborate because most human services are crisis-oriented; and because many separate, rigidly classified programs and agencies usually administer human services. Each agency has its own respective categories reflecting the agency's specific focus, funding sources, guidelines, accountability requirements, and rules for funding expenditures. Also, agencies differing so markedly in their institutional mandates and professional orientation rarely view one another as allies. Moreover, funding is inadequate for the required prevention, support, and treatment services to have enduring impacts for youth needing to overcome years of neglect and multiple problems. Interagency collaboration is important for addressing all these factors, which are deficiencies in individual agencies but can be eliminated when multiple agencies collaborate.

When multiple agencies collaborate to deliver services to youth and families, they can pool their resources, which separately can often be insufficient; and coordinate services to the same clients, which would otherwise be separate, involving service gaps/duplications/overlaps; lack of communication; fragmentation; and inability to address the whole person's needs. Interagency collaboration enables additional elements essential to comprehensive service delivery. For example, when agencies coordinate/connect/combine services in recipient interests they share, families receive services within atmospheres of mutual respect, empowering them. Interagency collaboration builds trusting provider-family relationships, as well as service continuity. Collaboration among agencies emphasizes enhanced outcomes for families, children, and adolescents, founded on high yet realistic achievement expectations. To identify interagency collaboration as a solution to a community's lack of comprehensive, flexible, effective services, a service provider should ask whether the outcome desired is beyond the scope of his/her agency to accomplish alone; whether other agencies can help; whether they will want to help/what's in it for them; whether the time and effort of developing a collaborative relationship is worth it; and whether their agency is prepared to change its operations as needed to avail itself of collaborative help offered.

HISTORY IN AMERICA

The concept of service collaboration and integration has a long historical tradition in America. For example, in the late 1800s, social reformers of the Progressive Movement established settlement houses to help impoverished families. They formed collaborations among agencies and organizations to identify problems, assess needs, and offer families comprehensive services. More recently, various pieces of legislation have emphasized interagency collaboration. For example, the reauthorization of the Workforce Investment Act promotes collaboration among Workforce Investment Act (WIA) agencies and services; Temporary Assistance for Needy Families (TANF) agencies and services; and One-Stop employment services and agencies. The Rehabilitation Act requires interagency collaboration among vocational rehabilitation agencies and education agencies. And the Individuals with Disabilities Education Act (IDEA) dictates that by the time a student with disabilities reaches age 16, educators have developed a statement of relevant interagency connections and responsibilities. Interagency collaboration enables several elements essential to comprehensive service delivery, including a focus on the whole family; easy access to a broad range of preventive, support, and treatment services regardless of who provides these; and techniques for ensuring that families receive appropriate services, and services are adjusted accordingly as youth and family needs change.

GUIDELINES FOR PLANNING

Service providers seeking to form interagency collaborations need to identify common interests shared among the agencies they expect to collaborate. They need to ensure each agency involved will benefit from the collaborative process in some way. They must also consider that time and resources are required for prospective collaborating agencies to learn about each other and establish reciprocal trust. In addition, they must recognize that interagency is not an end in itself, but rather a means to an end—i.e., better coordination and delivery of more comprehensive services to the families and individuals who need them. Among a number of guidelines for planning collaborative efforts to be effective, one is a broad-based commitment to change, reflected in getting all key participants involved. For example, those participating should not be limited to professionals who have the power to negotiate change; they should also include children and other representatives from the families whose lives will receive the impact. Another guideline is for collaborative partners to select a realistic strategy that reflects resource availability, local needs; and the priorities of key policymakers, the public, and the service providers.

EFFECTIVELY PLANNING

In addition to getting all participants involved and choosing realistic strategies, guidelines for effective interagency collaborative planning include: recognizing shared clients; developing a shared vision; establishing communication processes allowing member disagreement; applying conflict resolution techniques to facilitate progress; establishing attainable goals and objectives, particularly at the outset, to create a sense of accomplishment and forward momentum for initiatives; extending commitment to change throughout all levels of each agency's organizational structure to build ownership at every level, incorporating enough time during in-service staff trainings for employees to express feelings about changes proposed and predict results of those changes; not letting technical difficulties, logistical dilemmas, or other red herrings interfere with developing a shared vision and become easy excuses for participants not truly committed to collaborating, since most such problems typically come from policies that can be changed or accommodated, or from misunderstandings; keeping "eyes on the prize" of improved family and

102

child futures, avoiding distraction by everyday operational difficulties and disagreements; institutionalizing change into their own organizational mandates and resources; and publicizing success to promote larger-scale comprehensive service funding and delivery.

Social and Academic Development and Interventions

Instruction at the Individual and Group Level

ELEMENTS IN COOPERATIVE LEARNING GROUPS AND PROJECTS

The following are essential elements in cooperative learning groups and projects:

- Positive interdependence: Students must believe they all "sink or swim together." Teachers must provide a group goal and clear task to promote this. Students realizing individual members' efforts benefit all others and themselves develop commitment to others' success.
- Individual and group accountability: No member rides on others' coattails; each is accountable for contributing his/her share. Groups must understand shared goals, and how to measure member efforts and group progress. Groups and members use individual performance assessment results to determine who needs more assignment support/help. Cooperative learning' purpose is stronger individual learners.
- Promotive/face-to-face interaction: Group members encourage/support/help and praise one another's learning efforts. Groups are both academic and personal support systems. Members connect new and prior learning; discuss concepts; teach classmates their knowledge; explain problem-solving orally. Mutual learning promotion uniquely enables certain significant interpersonal dynamics and cognitive activities, bringing personal commitment to mutual goals and each other.
- Interpersonal and small-group skills: Simultaneous taskwork and teamwork make cooperative learning more complex than individual/competitive learning. Teachers must instruct teamwork skills—decision-making, trust-building, communication, leadership, conflict management.
- Group processing: Members discuss their working relationships/interactions, goal achievement, effective/ineffective actions, and indicated changes; analysis enables continuous process improvement.

FLEXIBLE INSTRUCTIONAL GROUPING

Flexible grouping addresses individual student differences in learning rates and styles. Teachers can alternate whole-class, small-group, and individual learning activities:

- Teacher-led groups:
  - Whole-class/small-group activities: concept overviews; daily schedule/agenda outlining; sharing work; developing background knowledge; and presenting strategies. Teachers explain procedures; facilitate discussions; give explicit instruction; furnish instructional scaffolding; and affirm student diversity.
  - Individual activities: creating independent investigations; applying important concepts, skills, and strategies; written composition; and completing understandings. Teachers encourage individual student interests and guide individual student development.
- Student-led groups

- o Collaborative activities: organizing group projects, collaborating; applying important concepts and strategies; sharing group projects; discussing student evaluations of group success; and discussing various perspectives. Teachers describe student roles and interpersonal skills; encourage interaction; monitor group effectiveness; guide understanding; and affirm student diversity.
- o Performance-based activities: Organizing short-term groups; introducing new concepts; teaching specific skills and strategies. Teachers identify student needs and furnish scaffolding and explicit instruction.
- o Paired activities: Peer tutoring; peer writing review; helping partners; collaborating; partner presentation turns; Think-Pair-Share. Teachers identify student needs/interests; model instructional strategies; and guide understanding.

PROVEN STRATEGIES FOR DIFFERENTIATED INSTRUCTION AT PRE-K-8 GRADE LEVELS

The following are four proven strategies for differentiated instruction at Pre-K-8 grade levels, including some examples:

- Technology: Interactive websites offer many educational games at varied learning levels, e.g., math games on www.Multiplication.com and logical thinking brain-teasers from beginning to expert levels on www.ThinkFun.com. Streaming online videos facilitate differentiation. Teachers search, find lesson-related videos, add PowerPoint slides of matching activities; design different activities using the same video, e.g., of animals: (a.) creative writing; (b.) scientific description; (c.) a simpler level, e.g., drawing several animals from the video.
- Group Lessons: Teachers divide students by learning levels. For example, in a first-grade activity, one group uses manipulatives and receives teacher guidance; a second group uses manipulatives without teacher guidance; in a third group, paired students collaborate without manipulatives or teacher guidance. Other students choose independent work; if they solve the problem/complete the assignment, they circulate, helping classmates.
- Group discussions: Teachers write questions addressing each level of Bloom's Taxonomy, planning how to include every student and facilitate their success.
- Task centers/cards: Teachers create individual unit-based tasks for each Bloom's Taxonomy level, including within-level activities differentiated by student cognitive level (e.g., low-average, average-high). Color-coded task cards guide task-to-task movement, which students enjoy. They share their projects at the end of the unit.

INSTRUCTIONAL SCAFFOLDS

The following are a number of different instructional scaffolds, including examples and ways of using them to help students learn:

- Advance organizers: Venn diagrams illustrate comparison/contrast; flowcharts illustrate processes; organizational charts illustrate hierarchies; outlines show content; mnemonics aid recall' rubrics identify task expectations; statements place content/tasks in context.
- Cue cards: Vocabulary words for test preparation; problem-related formulas; concepts for defining; content-specific sentence-completion stems; discussion topics.
- Mind/concept maps: Completed; partial for student completion; or student-created, these depict relationships.
- Examples: Representative problems illustrating concepts/processes/relationships, etc.; real objects/specimens/samples.
- Explanations: Written task instructions; verbal process explanations; more detailed information aids student conceptualization and task progress.

- Handouts: Less-detailed content-related/content-related information, with space for student note-taking.
- Hints: Clues and suggestions facilitating student progress (e.g., "Find the verb's subject"; "Add water first, then acid"; "Press the Escape key"; "Put one foot in front of the other", etc.)
- Prompts: Physical – pointing, head-nodding, eye-blinking, foot/pencil-tapping; Verbal – words/phrases/statements/questions: "Stop"/"Go"/"It's right here"/"Tell me now"/"Why did the character do that?"/"Which icon on the toolbar do you press for inserting pictures?" etc.
- Question cards: Content-specific/task-specific questions.
- Question stems: Incomplete higher-order "What if...?" questions for student completion encourage deeper thought.
- Stories: Reciting stories motivate and inspire students, relating abstract and complex material to more familiar situations.
- Visual scaffolds: Pointing at objects; hand gestures illustrating shapes/movements/processes; charts, graphs, diagrams; highlighting text/illustrations/other visual information.

STUDY SKILLS STRATEGIES

Five key study skills strategies, including their component methods, strategies, rationales, or mechanisms, are discussed below:

- Reduce interference: Previously learned, similar material can confuse new material recall. Strategies: Overlearn. Make material meaningful through familiarity, mnemonic rhymes, finding patterns, and chunking. Minimize intervening mental activity (e.g., sleep). Avoid studying similar subjects concurrently/consecutively. Study different subjects in different rooms and separate sessions.
- Space out studying: Instead of cramming, spaced learning is better because: (a.) Attention and concentration are limited. (b.) Between-sessions breaks facilitate memory consolidation. (c.) Different environmental contexts aid memory.
- Whole and part learning: (a.) Study the whole, then give difficult parts extra study. (b.) Whole-Part-Whole: Study the whole quickly twice; study parts separately; then, review the whole. (c.) Progressive Parts: Study parts progressively and cumulatively, i.e., part 1; 2 + 1; 3 + 2 + 1, etc. The *serial position effect*: Initial and final items are easiest to remember, middle items hardest; the last few items are easier to recall than the first items. Rearrange item order; or if prohibited, study middle items.
- Recitation: Periodically pause and recite just-studied material without looking. If unable, reread/review/re-study. Flash cards and study partners help. Mechanisms: Active learning; feedback; concentration; test practice.
- Study system: e.g., SQ3R (Survey, Question, Read, Recite, Review).

METACOGNITIVE INSTRUCTIONAL STRATEGIES TO FACILITATE LEARNING HOW TO LEARN

Ten metacognitive instructional strategies that facilitate learning how to learn are explained below:

- During and after lessons, ask questions stimulating student reflection on their learning strategies and processes. Ask cooperative learning groups to reflect on their roles in team problem-solving.
- During and after learning activities, emphasize personal reflection; encourage students to analyze their own assumptions critically and how these might have influenced their learning.

- To promote independent learning and comprehension, ask students to produce and answer their own questions, which can be related to reaching their personal goals.
- As part of courses or instructional units, teach applicable metacognitive strategies directly.
- To promote learning autonomy, once they have acquired some content knowledge, encourage students to participate in challenging learning activities, requiring them to construct personal metacognitive strategies.
- Provide slightly more advanced peer mentors to share and demonstrate metacognitive strategies.
- Assign cooperative team problem-solving, enabling metacognitive strategy exchanges.
- Teach Think-Alouds. Students can self-correct/correct partners.
- Teach (spoken/written) self-explanation, enhancing comprehension.
- Provide students with opportunities to make mistakes while learning, stimulating reflection about error sources.

ASSISTIVE TECHNOLOGY FOR THE BLIND AND VISUALLY IMPAIRED

ASSISTIVE TECHNOLOGY FOR ADAPTING (ACCOMMODATING/MODIFYING) INSTRUCTION

There are a number of examples of assistive technology for adapting (accommodating/modifying) instruction for blind and visually impaired students. Low-vision devices like magnifiers assist viewing/completing near-vision tasks and telescopes aid distance vision tasks. Braillewriters are like typewriters that emboss Braille. Electronic braillewriters include keyboards, and often calculators/other added features. A slate and stylus—the slate holds paper in place, and the stylus enables punching it—offer a more portable way to hand-emboss Braille. Personal digital assistants (PDAs) enable electronic data organization and management, frequently integrating electronic note-takers. Braille note-takers are portable devices with Braille output, frequently integrated with other PDA features, which assist classroom reading and writing. Speech note-takers are portable devices with speech output, also frequently integrated with PDA features, to assist classroom reading and writing. Computers, particularly when they have specialized hardware and software installed, are excellent tools for information access, literacy activities and other learning activities for students with visual impairment. Refreshable Braille devices are integrated into or connected to a computer or note-taking device. They contain pins that can be lowered or raised for shaping Braille cells to represent Braille text. Text-to-speech/speech-access software enables computers to synthesize audible speech of text displayed visually on-screen. Braille translation software enables computers to translate print into Braille, and Braille into print.

Large computer monitors display larger images for low-vision students. Scanners enable converting print materials into different reading formats. Magnification software enlarges on-screen text. Special printers emboss Braille. Regular printers enable visually impaired students to provide sighted classmates and teachers with printed text. Tactile graphics makers, e.g., the Optacon (OPtical to Tactile CONverter, discontinued in the late 1990s to the dismay of many blind people), electromechanically convert printed text images into tactile vibrations whose shape is "read" using the fingertips. Computer word-processing software aids text composition and manipulation. E-mail assists visually impaired students in receiving and turning in assignments. Talking calculators assist numerical computations without requiring vision. Calculators with enlarged numbers on their keys assist low-vision students. Talking dictionaries electronically provide dictionary text speech access. Tape recorders enable preserving, listening to, and reviewing lectures, lessons, discussions, and meetings and reading books-on-tape. Portable digital players access digital audio recordings of books and other materials. Adapted keyboards, voice recognition, and other alternative access technologies enable students with physical disabilities to use computers. Augmentative and alternative communication (AAC) devices assist students with hearing/communication/physical limitations. Many adaptive devices are available for daily living activities, e.g., toys, games, writing aids, kitchen utensils, measuring tools, etc.

Many textbooks, workbooks, worksheets, and other instructional materials can be obtained in Braille form for students who cannot see print but know Braille. Tactile graphics enable visually impaired students to "see" illustrations, diagrams, maps, and other printed graphics by converting them to formats that they can access by touch. Audio recordings of actors, authors, and others reading books and other materials aloud, i.e., "books on tape," MP3 and other digital audio recordings, enable students who cannot read visually to listen to the same verbal content. With electronic access, students can access learning materials in electronic format using computers and/or electronic note-taking devices; for example, they can read textbooks in digital format or do research using online encyclopedias and other sources. A practice to assist sighted parents of blind students who read Braille is providing Braille textbooks to students, accompanied by print copies for their parents. Highlighting markers and tape help low-vision students spot important text portions. Large-print books/book portions enable low-vision students to read text/see images by enlarging them. Physical manipulative objects demonstrate math concepts and help students make tactile artworks.

The following are additional examples of adaptations (accommodations/modifications) to instruction for blind and visually impaired students:

- Hands-on experiences: Substitute or add real objects to pictures or text, e.g., actual coins to supplement coin photos in a book.
- Models: Instead of pictures of planets in the solar system, for example, provide tangible, three-dimensional models.
- Visual aid readability: Make chalkboard/whiteboard/overhead information more readable by giving the student individual copies.
- Clear directions: Use explicit language, e.g., "to the left/right", instead of "over here/there."
- Peer note-taking: Have a classmate take notes of material written on the overhead, chalkboard, or whiteboard and give the student a copy.
- Extra time: to read assignments, answer questions, respond during class discussions.
- Oral narration/description: of visually displayed material, e.g., artwork or sections of films or videos with no dialogue.
- Experiential learning: Provide direct experience with concepts which others see from a distance or in pictures; e.g., during a unit on farm animals, the student could visit an actual farm.
- Speaking/reading written/visual material aloud: As the teacher writes information on an overhead/board, s/he also speaks or reads it aloud; and/or describes the content of displayed pictures.

ACCOMMODATIONS AND MODIFICATIONS TO COMPLETE CLASSROOM ASSIGNMENTS AND HOMEWORK

There are many accommodations and modifications that can enable blind and visually impaired students to complete classroom assignments and homework. One accommodation that helps students with visual impairment to complete classwork and homework assignments is allowing extra time. Students with visual disabilities may use tools to read and write, and/or read and write at slower rates, requiring longer times for them to do the same work as sighted students. Teachers can allow descriptive responses in place of visual representations. For example, in a science class, an assignment could require looking at a cell under a microscope and making a drawing of it; a blind student could instead write a description of the cell. When demonstrating learning of science content is the objective, this would be an accommodation. However, if demonstrating drawing skills, as in an art class, were the objective, then substituting written description would be a modification. When an assignment involves making a drawing or diagram, teachers can assign blind students to construct a three-dimensional model instead of a two-dimensional image. When assignments involve copying problems or text (e.g., from the board to a notebook), teachers can provide worksheets where visually impaired students can write answers directly without copying the entire problem/text over again.

ADAPTATIONS TO ENVIRONMENT AND TESTING SITUATIONS FOR BLIND AND VISUALLY IMPAIRED

The following are some kinds of adaptations to the environment and to testing situations respectively that educators can offer to students with blindness or other visual impairments:

- Environment: Preferential seating allows students the best view of the board; minimizes glare by sitting away from light sources; or proximity to a power outlet for assistive technology devices. Flexible classroom movement enables low-vision students to move closer to demonstrations/other visual activities. Additional work/desk space accommodates students reading and writing Braille and/or using other assistive devices taking up more room. Braille books and other adaptive equipment require additional storage space/shelving. Brighter lighting helps some visually impaired students with reading/viewing; lower light helps others with photophobia (hypersensitivity to light).
- Testing: Students may need longer times to take tests due to slower reading and writing speeds and/or tools they use to read and write. Instead of writing answers, students may demonstrate knowledge/understanding by using concrete models and manipulatives. For students reading and writing contracted Braille's shortened forms, spelling tests using uncontracted Braille ensure they can read and write Standard English. Blind students can dictate answers to sighted "scribes." Enlarged text, refreshable Braille, or Braille hardcopies can provide visually impaired students with screen access to computer-administered tests.

SELF-REGULATED LEARNING
RESEARCH AND THEORETICAL BACKGROUND

Originally, behavioral research into self-control involved teaching individuals methods for decreasing disruptive, impulsive, or other dysfunctional behaviors. Behavioral researchers emphasize self-regulatory processes including self-monitoring—i.e., observing and recording one's own behaviors; self-instruction—i.e., applying and frequently verbalizing strategic steps or rules to complete tasks; self-evaluation—i.e., comparing some characteristics of one's own behaviors against established standards; self-correction—i.e., modifying one's behaviors that deviate from standards to match them more closely; and self-reinforcement—i.e., rewarding oneself with free time, points, or other desirable consequences for behaviors that meet or surpass standards. In education, the emphasis on self-regulated learning developed out of those research findings. One deficit of behavioral theories for educational application is that they consider only observable behaviors, excluding internal states such as beliefs, thoughts, emotions, etc.; thus, their explanations of learning are incomplete. Consequently, cognitive learning theories gained prevalence regarding learning. However, researchers then found learning was not completely explained by cognitive abilities and skills either. This implied that self-regulation, motivation, and other factors were involved. Thus, cognitive theories of self-regulated learning emerged.

COGNITIVE SELF-REGULATED LEARNING THEORIES

The following are three types of cognitive self-regulated learning theories that have been applied most to school learning and some principles of these theories:

- Information processing theory focuses on cognitive functions, e.g., attention to, perception, storage, and transformation of information. Some theorists propose four phases of self-regulated learning:
    - Defining the task—identifying the external/environmental task conditions (e.g., teacher directions) and internal/student cognitive conditions (e.g., motivation, past performance, and task self-efficacy).
    - Setting goals and planning how to attain them, including learning strategies the student will utilize.
    - Applying planned learning strategies.
    - Using metacognition to self-evaluate success; and, when needed, adapting plans and strategies accordingly.
- Social constructivist theory regarding self-regulation is exemplified by Vygotsky's developmental theory. Vygotsky emphasized the social system interaction of people and their cultural environments: adults teach children symbols, language, and other tools; by using these within the social system, children develop problem-solving, self-regulation, and other higher-order cognitive functions. Self-regulated learning includes memory, planning, synthesis, evaluation, etc.—coordinated processes, not operating independently of their context but reflecting cultural values. Vygotsky found language and the zone of proximal development (ZPD)—the distance between what learners can do independently and with assistance—primary self-regulation mechanisms.
- Bandura's Social Learning Theory proposes reciprocal interactions among cognitions, emotions, behaviors, and environmental conditions determine human behavior and learning.

ROLE OF PRIVATE SPEECH IN DEVELOPMENT

When children are very young, adults frequently direct their actions. As they develop speech and language skills, children develop a kind of speech that may strongly reflect the directive speech they have heard and responded to from significant adults. As young children work through performing various activities and tasks, they often talk aloud to themselves as they narrate and direct their own reasoning processes, decisions, and actions. Vygotsky termed this "private speech," i.e., speech not used for social communication but for directing one's own behaviors. Kopp identifies the transition from following others' commands to using one's own speech and other cognitive tools for planning, directing, and monitoring one's activities. As children learn from adults, they transition from having their behaviors regulated by others to regulating their behaviors themselves. From talking aloud, private speech is eventually internalized, becoming silent mental speech—i.e., thought. Children's development from responding to adult speech to using their own speech parallels their development from other-directed behaviors to self-directed behaviors. Self-direction equates to self-regulation.

DEVELOPMENTAL CHANGES IN STUDENTS

Researchers have discovered that from grade 5 to grade 8, students demonstrate increased use of planning, sequencing, and setting goals. Studies also show that while younger children study by rereading materials, older students study by taking notes and highlighting or underlining text more often as strategies. Another developmental difference is that younger children have less ability to monitor their comprehension of the text that the read; but older children have more ability for identifying inconsistencies in text, and when they do, they reread it to make sure they read it correctly the first time, or they read the larger surrounding passage to ascertain the context better, and/or take other actions to resolve the inconsistencies they have identified. Therefore, cognitive development and learning processes both enable improvements in self-regulatory processes including planning, setting goals, monitoring understanding, evaluating progress, and adjusting learning strategies accordingly. However, instruction is equally important, as students can be taught to become better at self-regulation.

GOAL-SETTING

Research shows greater self-regulation improves learning and achievement; and self-regulated learning skills can be taught, maintained, and generalized. Teaching goal-setting enhances self-regulated learning. Process goals reflect strategies/skills being learned; outcome goals reflect desired performance. For example, in algebra, learning to use the binomial theorem is a process goal; completing a problem set is an outcome goal. Researchers find self-regulated learning improves more through focusing student attention on process goals than outcome goals, particularly during early learning stages; however, shifting from process goals to outcome goals has benefits. For example, researchers taught high school students a writing revision strategy. Following the strategy's steps was a process goal, and the number of sentence words, an outcome goal. When researchers gave one group the process goal; one the outcome goal; and one to shift from the process goal to the outcome goal as their revision skills progressed, the third group showed more skill and self-efficacy (task-specific self-confidence) than the other two. Other researchers found that the highest use, maintenance, and generalization of a writing strategy were achieved by giving students a process goal to use the strategy plus feedback connecting strategy use to improved writing performance.

TEACHING THE PROCESS

Effective self-regulation correlates with improved learning and achievement. Self-regulation does not develop automatically; through cognitive development and learning combined, students develop self-regulatory proficiency. Though they may discover self-regulated learning strategies independently, students benefit from models and instruction that demonstrate and explain strategies. Self-regulation should not be taught separately, but together with academic subjects so students can apply them. While teachers typically evaluate student learning in schools, the cyclical self-regulation process of self-monitoring progress and adjusting tactics as necessary requires teachers to give students self-evaluation opportunities, as they may not self-evaluate automatically. Self-evaluation influences motivation and self-regulated learning. Simple self-monitoring for young children entails having them complete checklists or count finished items. Older students benefit from instruction in self-evaluating progress in reading comprehension, writing, and other areas difficult to assess. Students may not experience self-efficacy about enhancing their self-regulation, or be motivated to self-regulate without seeing the benefits. Giving them progress feedback connecting improved performance to using self-regulatory strategies can increase self-efficacy, motivation, and progress self-evaluation.

Issues Related to Academic Success and Failure

EBIs IN SCHOOL PSYCHOLOGY

Although most people envision clinical settings when thinking of mental health service delivery, the reality is that schools are the commonest settings for children; moreover, many children have no access to mental health services except in schools. Therefore, psychological and educational interventions and school psychologists implementing them are important to more and more children. Educational researchers increasingly emphasize evidence-based interventions (EBIs), supported by developments in psychology, education, psychiatry, and prevention science. However, new challenges to applying EBIs in practice have emerged. For instance, practitioners' and trainers' theoretical/philosophical beliefs may conflict with manual-based procedures/treatments. Four issues regarding EBI adoption and maintenance in practice are:

- As more educators seek evidence bases for their practices in research, consumers encounter challenges from the resulting variety.
- Because practical, administrative, and other obstacles in reality do not exist in research settings, integrating EBIs into practice is often not easy.
- Some psychologists are more influenced by clinical judgment than research supporting EBIs when designing, implementing, and evaluating their own interventions.
- Addressing training needs for adopting EBIs is complicated by many psychologist practitioners' and trainers' lacking training to implement EBIs in school practice, and the frequent involvement of teachers in school EBI implementation.

ADOPTION, IMPLEMENTATION, AND STRATEGIES

Clinical, counseling, and school psychology graduate preparation programs frequently characterize school psychologists as "scientist-practitioners." This view requires school psychologists to span the chasm between research and practice, an extremely challenging expectation. The essence of traditional problems around the scientist-practitioner model is reflected in the demands of adopting EBIs. The responsibility for meeting these demands in adopting and implementing EBIs is shared among researchers, trainers, and practitioners. This shared responsibility includes collaborating to assess how workable and effective EBIs are when integrated into training and practice settings; and recognizing the value of practitioner experience with EBIs, and of their contributions to the scientific knowledge base regarding EBI practices. Recommended strategies to promote evidence-based practice include: developing school psychology practice-research networks; expanding evidence-based practice methodology that accounts for implementing EBIs in practice as well as research; establishing guidelines for school psychologists' implementation and evaluation of EBIs in practice; providing professional development opportunities for researchers, trainers, and practitioners; and forming partnerships with other professionals who want to use EBIs more.

Regarding a strategy of developing better, more flexible guidelines for applying EBIs in school psychology, one main consideration is that the foci of such guidelines should include an understanding of fundamental principles of behavior change. A primary underlying assumption of the strategy for these guidelines is that certain features in common, which can be generalized past a specific application, are shared by all interventions. As an example, some researchers have approached identifying effective prevention programs' general principles through a "review-of-reviews" or meta-meta-analysis procedure. Others find that applications of constructs designed to explain variation among therapists look for empathy, relationship, or other commonly shared, generalizable psychotherapeutic techniques and procedures. As a result, fundamental principles of behavior change, and strategies for attaining it, must be taught to practitioners and integrated into guidelines for using EBIs in practice. For instance, transtheoretical analysis examines change separately from any specific models or theories, and could be applied across intervention approaches. In system-wide school reform, similar applications have been used in implementing a variety of service delivery models.

INSTRUMENTAL ORGANIZATIONS AND GROUPS

The Task Force on Evidence-Based Interventions in School Psychology at the University of Wisconsin at Madison; the American Psychological Association (APA)'s Divisions 12 and 53; the National Reading Panel; and the What Works Clearinghouse funded by the U.S. Department of Education are some examples of groups/organizations involved in the EBI movement. The aforementioned Task Force invited practicing school psychologists to join it for organizing evaluations in practice settings of EBIs and formed an Evidence-Based Practice Committee. It additionally proposed to serve as a clearinghouse for information on local, state, regional, and perhaps federal funding, and establish relationships with funding agencies; to develop an evaluation framework and competency-based training in EBIs, protocols for assessing interventions in school settings and other applications, and training in EBI efficacy research; additional evaluation of attitudes regarding EBP adoption, e.g., by adapting the Evidence-Based Practice Attitude Scale (EBPAs, Aarons) for school application; and to code interventions according to qualitative criteria to establish a basis for expanding the EBI contextual knowledge base, reinforce research-practice connections, and better contextually inform EBI adoption and use-related practitioner decisions.

GUIDELINES REGARDING INDICATIONS AND CONTRAINDICATIONS

School psychology practitioners and trainers can benefit from guidelines related to effective and ineffective applications of specific interventions identified as evidence-based. Literature reviews that apply meta-analysis techniques are the bases for most EBIs. Researchers have identified limitations and advantages of meta-analytic procedures as these have been applied. As an example, two significant limitations of any method for summarizing the existing body of research literature are biases against publishing negative results, and a common lack of attention to conducting replication research for reliability. Regardless of these limitations, researchers can still contribute to identifying the circumstances wherein a specific intervention might be subject to question, or even contraindicated, in practice by using meta-analysis. In a general example of this, decision-making regarding how feasible it would be to implement an EBI wherein training teachers and/or parents as intervention agents is required could be informed by meta-analytic studies of therapist training. Expert groups also identify and seek to provide data about minority populations, setting variables, and other factors related to intervention context as informing contraindications and indications for various individual EBIs.

EVALUATION

Experts have observed the model of school psychologist as scientist-practitioner. For consistency with this model, they recommend evaluating EBIs in their actual practice contexts. Regardless of the amounts of evidence accumulated in research studies that supports using a specific EBI, it still must be evaluated under real practice conditions in order for its use to be generalized effectively. Evaluation protocols are established during an EBI's development in some instances; these may even be included in its practice guidelines and/or practitioner manual. When this is not the case, experts recommend using protocols that have been developed for evaluating EBIs in clinical and school settings. For example, one protocol, entitled *Outcomes: Planning, Monitoring, Evaluating* (Stoiber & Kratochwill, 2002) can provide guidance to practitioners in selecting problems; designing interventions; implementing interventions; and evaluating intervention outcomes. The main publication containing this protocol, entitle *Outcomes: PME* includes an example of an intervention planning and monitoring training and practice protocol. This can help practitioners and researchers with conceiving of and performing outcome assessments to evaluate EBIs and their implementation.

FACTORS INFLUENCING STUDENT ACADEMIC PROGRESS

The academic progress of students involves a myriad of contributing factors, and a variety of theories recommend different methods for increasing children's academic success. Some factors affecting student success are beyond parental control; others are things that parents can change to give their children advantages for better early and continuing school progress. In general, family socioeconomic status; amounts of time parents spend with their children; types and quality of parenting practices; the quantity and quality of time children spend away from their parents; levels of physical and mental health; and the influences of relationships with peers are factors that can influence student performance in school. In addition, meeting children's nutritional needs; parental expectations; age-appropriate student reading levels; and well-trained teachers who know how to motivate students are influencing factors. Treating each child as an individual in home and child care settings is also considered a requisite for students' full school success.

When considering factors identified in research studies as instrumental for K-12 students to achieve academic success, it is important for their readers to remember that because of the statistical bases for identifying these factors, some children who are found to be at high risk for failing academically will go on to succeed academically despite the identification of those factors and risks. The media popularly highlight inspirational stories of individuals who have achieved extraordinary successes in education and in life through coping with and escaping from homelessness, poverty, abuse, violence, and other conditions that usually present high probabilities of failing and low probabilities of succeeding. These accomplishments are typically attained through relentless determination and perseverance. For some of these students, teachers supported and helped their aspirations; teachers are often their only resources in some situations. While such inspiring examples are certainly to be appreciated, students who succeed so well against all odds typically have exceptional self-motivating skills. Other students in similar circumstances can often be deprived of these abilities.

PARENTS

Among many factors identified as having influences on how students perform academically, the motivation and involvement of their parents is one of the factors associated most with determining student success. According to some experts, the consensus among research studies is that approximately 70-90% of students who earn A or B grades in school report that their parents encourage them to perform well in school. Such encouragement by itself can help children realize the importance of school. Parents who encourage their children to do well in school are more likely to help them with their homework; attend teacher meetings and conferences; and may sometimes volunteer at their children's schools. However, some research finds that around 49% of students who earn C or lower grades report that their parents do not give them such encouragement. In addition, schools themselves report consistently that when parents are actively involved in their children's education, those students are more likely to perform better in school and succeed academically.

SOCIOECONOMIC FACTORS

The approximately 19% of American children who live in impoverished households are in large part excluded from the statistical socioeconomic indicators for student academic success in school. In general, students from upper-income and middle-income families more often receive higher marks, whereas children from lower-income families are more likely to be retained in and repeat grades, particularly those from the lowest-income households. Getting lower marks school is often correlated with having single parents; being exposed to violence; abusive parenting; and other traumatic events in students' lives. However, with respect to single parents, who typically must work full-time or more (e.g., working longer than full-time hours and/or holding multiple jobs) to support their families, the factor which appears to influence children's academic success the most is how much time the single parent can find for spending with children. Many single parents have been found to achieve extraordinary results in balancing parenting, family, and employment demands. So single parenthood is one risk factor for academic failure that many exemplary parents and their children manage to defy.

EARLY CHILDHOOD CARE, EDUCATION, AND SCHOOL ATTENDANCE

One factor among many that influences the ways in which children progress in school is the kind of child care and education that they receive during their early childhoods. Child care centers and programs and early childhood education programs that employ designs, activities, and personnel that promote children's early physical, cognitive, adaptive, emotional, and social development are typically factors that contribute positively to children's subsequent academic success in K-12 school grades. On the other hand, overcrowded child care settings are less likely to provide young children with the skills they need to develop in order to perform well later in school; yet these are frequently the only choices for parents with limited finances. Head Start programs and early intervention preschools can help to prepare young children to succeed educationally. Students who attend school regularly tend to be more successful. Illnesses, other chronic conditions, family dysfunction, repeated relocations, etc. can result in frequent student absences from school, impeding their academic progress. Moreover, peer interactions, particularly those involving bullying, negatively affect both school attendance and academic progress. Thus educators and parents must both exercise vigilance and prompt intervention regarding abusive and/or bullying situations in schools.

NUTRITION

While nutrition has been recognized as essential to children's health and wellbeing; the federal government provides dietary guidelines for children's nutrition; and many other organizations advocate for better nutrition in schools, these efforts still seem to fall short of addressing the critical relationship of adequate nutritional quality for students to the quality of their ability to perform academically up to their potentials. Many students, even in primary and lower elementary grades, attend school without having eating anything for breakfast; or having eaten only sugar-laden cereals, pastries, or other processed products made from refined flour—or even candy. This is not only a socioeconomic effect, but also a cultural one when good nutrition is not appreciated or instilled by parents. Numerous research studies find students fed breakfast before taking standardized achievement tests perform better. Because standardized test scores do not typically determine student's school marks, parents and educators question why schools do not also provide daily breakfasts. Free/reduced-cost lunch programs can influence academics positively; but many advocates find these only include the poorest children and must be extended to improve school achievement and wellbeing for the majority of students who need them.

Primary, Secondary, and Tertiary Preventive Strategies

EFFECTIVE CLASSROOM MANAGEMENT

A mistake that many teachers make is assuming that discipline should only be used when necessary and that they may not need it immediately. This leads to the additional mistake of not having a good disciplinary plan in place at the beginning of the school year. Most students can very rapidly evaluate the conditions in different classrooms and determine what they will and will not be allowed to get away with by different teachers. Teachers who initially permit multiple class disruptions set a precedent, making it extremely difficult for them to initiate any improved discipline and classroom management techniques. In contrast, it is never hard for teachers who begin with strong discipline plans to become easier as the school year continues. Experienced

115

teachers say that although the saying "Never smile until Christmas" is exaggerated, it does contain some value. Another requisite educator behavior is fairness. Students have clear perceptions of fair and unfair actions. Teachers must treat all students equitably (rather than exempting the best students from punishment for wrongdoing, for example) to earn student respect. Students perceiving teachers as unfair are less motivated to follow their rules.

Classroom Disruptions and Confrontations

According to the experience of effective teachers, when classroom activities are disrupted by some students, two necessities are for the teacher to address them (1) immediately, not after they have continued for some time; and (2) in ways that interrupt the flow of classroom instruction as little as possible. For example, if a teacher is leading a whole-class discussion about a topic of study and several students are disrupting it by conversing among themselves about unrelated subjects, the teacher might reclaim their attention and participation by asking one of them a question related to the discussion. When a teacher interrupts the momentum of a lesson plan to address disruptions by students, s/he deprives all the other students who are motivated to learn of their valuable and limited classroom time. Whenever a student confronts a classmate or the teacher, there will always be a winner and loser in any confrontation. Although teachers must preserve classroom discipline and order, they should avoid confrontations and address disciplinary matters privately instead of making a student "lose face" with friends. Making an example of disciplining one student can make it impossible to teach that student anything thereafter.

High Expectations and Humor

Teacher expectations can easily become self-fulfilling prophecies in the classroom: positive expectations can produce positive behaviors, and negative expectations can produce negative behaviors. Teachers who approach each class with the expectation that their students will follow rules and behave well will have much better chances of achieving this result through effective classroom management procedures than teachers who begin with the expectation that students will behave disruptively. Teachers can reinforce their positive expectations by explicitly informing their students of these. For example, a teacher can begin a group instruction session by saying, "During this entire session, I expect you to raise your hand when you want to say something, and wait to be called on before you speak. Also, I expect you to respect your classmates' opinions, and listen to what every student has to say." When disruptive behavior creates a tense situation, getting everyone to laugh can sometimes diffuse tension and redirect the class to get back on task. However, sarcasm should not be confused with good humor: sarcastic teacher comments can damage relationships with students. Teachers must realize that what some find amusing, others find offensive; and use their best judgment.

Planning Lessons and Classes

When a teacher's lessons and classes leave unoccupied time open for students to go off task, do/discuss other things unrelated to and not incorporating identified topics of study, this establishes a precedent for students' perceptions about how the teacher regards his/her subject and academics in general. Teachers should plan lessons to prevent leftover downtime. The best way to do this is overplanning. When writing lesson plans, the teacher should include additional activities to provide for the event that delivering the main lesson content takes less time than anticipated. Having too much material to cover is not something to worry about; the teacher can use excess content and activities for other days or lessons and will never run out of material, as well as preventing unoccupied time. Planning mini-lessons also occupies short leftover time periods (e.g., 10 minutes—too short to begin a new activity, but too long to let students simply chat). 10 minutes downtime per 5-day week = one period weekly, one day quarterly, 30 classes yearly = six weeks lost annually.

SETTING CLASS RULES

Class rules should be limited in number: nobody, including students, can regularly follow 100 rules. A general ideal is 3-8 rules. Teachers must also make rules clear so students know what is acceptable and unacceptable. Moreover, teachers must ensure students clearly know in advance the consequences for breaking rules. Teachers should post class rules. Rules should be general enough to apply to varied situations, but not so general as to become meaningless; e.g., "Always respect everybody." Though this is a good principle, it is not a good rule for students because it does not tell them what they must do to demonstrate their compliance. Some examples include: "Arrive in class on time. This means being inside the room when the bell rings. Standing outside and rushing in after the bell starts ringing will be counted as tardy." "Stay in your assigned seat unless you have been given permission to get out of it. Throw away trash on your way out of the classroom at the end of the period." "No cheating. Students copying others' work, *and* those letting them copy it, will both get a zero and a phone call to parents."

STARTING EACH DAY

Although teachers should not ignore all prior rule infractions, a basic principle is starting every day afresh, expecting good student behavior. Even if the same student has disrupted class daily for a week, teachers should not assume repetition. This avoids self-fulfilling prophecy by treating a student differently through adverse expectations. For example, whenever a teacher called on a student with anger management and impulse control problems and a history of multiple suspensions and referrals, he gave flippant responses. He was also loud and disruptive. One day he was talking during her lesson. Without changing her tone, she invited him to join the discussion instead of having his own; he stood, knocked his chair over, and yelled curses. She made a disciplinary referral, resulting in week-long suspension. Upon his return, she met him, asking to talk for moment. Saying she wanted to start over, she gave him permission to step outside momentarily anytime he felt he would lose control. Thereafter he listened, participated, and even stopped other students from fighting once. He never exercised the privilege of momentarily leaving class. He wrote her an end-of-year thank-you note. This demonstrates the power of giving students some control.

SOCIAL SKILLS FOR STUDENTS

Social skills constitute learned behaviors, which students must have in order to interact successfully with others in home, school, work, and community environments. Social skills development can have salutary or adverse impacts on multiple and varied areas of students' lives; for example, their friendships; relationships; family dynamics and interactions; academic progress in school; social lives in school; leisure and recreational activities; and employment. Students whose social skills development is inadequate are found much more likely to be excluded by their peers; ignored; or bullied; and/or frustrated. In contrast, students who have developed competent social skills are more able to develop and sustain positive relationships and interactions with the peers and adults in their environments. A wide range of skills is included under the heading of social skills, which include abilities in the domains of conflict management skills; relationship skills with peers; classroom process and behavior skills; emotional self-expression and self-regulation skills; communication skills; decision-making and problem-solving skills; and community conduct skills.

CONFLICT MANAGEMENT AND RESOLUTION SKILLS

Conflicts arise sooner or later in virtually all human interactions. Therefore, for students to succeed academically, socially, and in their future or current employment, as well as to achieve fulfillment as independent individuals, they must learn effective skills for managing and resolving conflicts. Conflict management skills develop in early childhood. These are frequently informed by young children's abilities for reading nonverbal communication signals accompanying verbal social interactions, such as body language, facial expressions, volume and tone of voice, etc. Skills in specific and complex communication with widely varied audiences are also required for conflict management and resolution. Students with moderate or severe communication deficits typically need direct instruction to learn how to observe and accurately interpret nonverbal communication and use communication effectively to identify conflicts and identify and apply conflict management strategies. Direct instruction can include verbal prompts; visual prompts; authentic practice contexts; role-playing; and guided reflection. To promote student growth in conflict management and prepare students for school, workplace, and community situations requiring it, teachers, students, parents, and specialists can find a basic sequence and range of teachable skills in available curriculum guides, including goal areas and age/grade-leveled skill objectives.

PEER RELATIONSHIPS AND PROBLEM-SOLVING SKILLS

Social skills include domains of conflict management and resolution skills, classroom skills, emotional self-expression and self-regulation skills, conversation skills, community conduct skills, peer relationship skills and problem-solving skills. Among these, student skills in peer relationships and interactions are critical elements in the development of social skills. Research studies have repeatedly found social competency to be a variable that is critical to predicting future success in life. Studies have also found that being rejected by one's peers is frequently correlated with low self-esteem, impulsive behavior, hyperactivity, inattentiveness, aggression, and poor school performance. The skills that students develop and use in relationships with their peers enable them to participate in family activities; collaborate with groups or reams; and develop lifelong friendships. Another critical social skill essential to all social skills curricula is problem-solving ability. Students should know how to address problems occurring in school and the community. Moreover, they should know how to behave in ways enabling them to prevent potential or recurrent problems. Students with disabilities, and especially those with deficits in social skills, are often more likely to encounter problem situations and need to know how to resolve these.

CLASSROOM SKILLS AND COMMUNITY CONDUCT SKILLS

In inclusive classrooms, students require classroom skills to progress developmentally and academically. These vary from pencil-sharpening to making smooth transitions between classes by organizing materials properly. To have positive class experiences, students must understand school and teacher expectations; school and class rules; and school and class routines, and how these function inside their classrooms. For students with communication disorders or deficits, general education classroom teachers and special education teachers can collaborate in developing behavioral goals that will help them learn to function more independently in classrooms. These teachers can design such student goals to raise student social awareness and improve student academic achievement. Students with disabilities—particularly those with communication problems, who can experience social challenges—need community conduct skills as foundations. They frequently have difficulty noticing and/or understanding social cues in various settings, causing confusion, awkwardness, and embarrassment—which can reinforce inappropriate behaviors in some cases. The social skills curriculum should include community conduct skills, which can by taught via modeling, direct instruction, and role-playing. Teachers supply scaffolding, eventually fading it as students master skills and generalize these to actual community environments to achieve successful community interactions.

EMOTIONAL AWARENESS, SELF-EXPRESSION, AND SELF-REGULATION SKILLS

Emotional awareness, self-awareness, emotional self-expression and emotional self-regulation are complicated, abstract concepts—not to mention emotions themselves—which many growing students can find confusing, even overwhelming. Students with communication disorders/deficits

118

frequently have difficulty identifying, labeling, measuring, expressing, and controlling their feelings. Since emotions do not follow consistent, straightforward rules, definitions, or logic, students—especially those with communication needs—can have difficulty understanding and responding appropriately to them. Concrete, thoughtful instruction develops student comprehension and real-life application. Moreover, students with communication deficits often also have self-awareness deficits. This can be problematic for expressing their own unique qualities and needs and interacting with others. The more students develop self-awareness of personal strengths, needs, preferences, and skills for communicating these to others, the better social competency across settings they develop. Also, understanding the impacts of their behaviors on others is critical to acceptance and success in group interactions. Educators make abstract emotional concepts more concrete through modeling; structured learning; visual cues; incidental teaching; rehearsal, and similar instructional strategies, targeting goals and objectives they develop for developing emotional skills. They must also enable student generalization and internalization of skills by providing them with plenty of opportunities to practice these in varied situations.

CONVERSATIONAL SKILLS

During childhood, most typically developing children develop conversational skills naturally through observing and interacting with a broad variety of people in differing environments and situations. However, among children with communication deficits/disorders, many fall behind in this aspect and fail to develop adequate social skills for effective communication during conversations with adults and peers. Deficient conversational skills can be attributed to shyness, slowness to warm up, and other factors of temperament; behavioral issues; and significantly delayed development of receptive language, expressive language, and/or pragmatic language. Some characteristics of conversational skill deficits include being unable to make appropriate use of greetings; initiate conversations; maintain conversational topics; correctly ask questions and answer questions; display humor; and converse in popular peer jargon. Difficulties with observing and interpreting eye contact, facial expressions, gestures, posture, proxemics, movement, vocal clarity and tone, etc. are frequently additional issues, as understanding nonverbal communication is critical to appropriate social skills development. Educators can integrate opportunities to practice conversational skills into all parts of student educational programs. School districts often include goals and objectives promoting conversational skills for everyday functioning.

RISK FACTORS FOR LDs

In addition to family learning disability (LD) history, researchers find maternal smoking during pregnancy associated with lower birth weight, raising risk for LDs and other problems. Maternal alcohol use during pregnancy can cause malformation of developing neurons. Although drinking heavily while pregnant can cause fetal alcohol syndrome, any drinking while pregnant may cause later child developmental deficits in attention, learning, memory, and/or problem-solving skills. Crack cocaine and other hard drugs appear to change normal brain receptor development; current research implicates drug abuse as possibly damaging receptors, which receive sensory input and regulate physical responses to environmental stimuli. Some investigators think LDs and ADHD may involve receptor damage, associating LD difficulties understanding letters/phonemes with receptor deficits. Maternal immune system fetal rejection apparently causes new neuron dislocation to incorrect brain regions. Temporary oxygen loss during delivery can damage neurological functions, leading to LDs. Lead, cadmium, and other environmental toxins can disrupt new neurons and neural networks, which continue developing a year or more after birth. An NIH animal study found rats exposed to lead demonstrated learning difficulties lasting weeks beyond exposure. Chemotherapy/radiation treating cancer in early childhood, especially radiation targeting brain tumors, is increasingly associated with LDs.

RISK FACTORS FOR DEVELOPING MENTAL HEALTH PROBLEMS

According to the Mayo Clinic, one risk factor for mental illness is genetic: individuals with a parent(s), sibling(s), or other biological relative(s) who have mental illnesses are at increased risk of also developing mental disorders. *In utero* events, such as a mother's exposure while pregnant to environmental toxins; alcohol, tobacco, or other drugs; or viruses, can raise the baby's risk of later developing a mental disorder. After birth, children who are neglected or abused are at increased risk of developing mental health symptoms. Adolescents using illegal drugs are at higher risk of mental disorders. Divorce, a loved one's death, financial difficulties, and other life situations causing psychological stress are associated with higher risk for mental health problems. Having cancer or other serious chronic medical illnesses or conditions also contributes to the risk of developing mental health issues. Traumatic brain injuries causing neurological damage can result in mental disorders as well as many other neurological problems. Psychologically and emotionally traumatic experiences, e.g., being assaulted or enduring military combat, increase risks. Insufficient healthy relationships or friendships contribute to mental health risks. Prior mental illness puts an individual at higher risk of recurrence or another, different mental disorder.

LEA FOR LD INTERVENTION

The Language Experience Approach (LEA) focuses on constructing meaning in reading. Students gain even limited previous knowledge through their experiences, and it is meaningful to them. The LEA builds language experiences to develop literacy. Text uses uncontrolled, relevant vocabulary; specific student communication needs, direct experiences, and topics of interest. Its basis in student experiences affords natural scaffolding. Text taken from students' own words enables their comprehension and realization of written language's relevance. Vocabulary drawn from student speaking vocabulary enables acquiring sight words and natural grammatical and semantic structures rapidly. Typically used with groups, the LEA has consistently proven helpful for early literacy development and is frequently included in guided reading and other reading programs. A resource specialist (Ward, 2005) used the LEA with three students having severe LD: two learned to read at first-grade level with minimal support; read and write c. 60 words, including 50 high-frequency words, independently; and write 3-4 sentences with minor support. A student with severe autism and another with LD and autistic symptoms progressed from zero print awareness to reading within one school year. The student with severe autism read at grade level; the student with LD recognized c. 60 words and wrote 3-5 sentences.

STRATEGIES FOR LEARNING TO READ

One specialist (Ward, 2005) using LEA with LDs routinely identified and discussed learning themes; e.g., with students fascinated by trains, "train" book pictures; parents let children observe a local freight train, identifying its cars. Students drew pictures; the specialist wrote their utterances (including non-conventional language/writing). She brought motivational materials/objects for discussion to develop language (e.g., an animal pelt; they quickly learned words like *thick, long, hair, animal*); and made Friday fun activities (soccer-playing, kite-flying, bubble-blowing, Play-Doh) discussion and writing themes. She positively reinforced identifying recognized words during routine journal-reading. They saved retained recognized words in "word banks." A recognized Word Wall developed phonics and word use. Games used known words; varying activities prevented boredom. Correctly spoken and written sentences became game content to practice cloze procedures, syntax, and spelling. She increased vocabulary; reconstructed sentences using mostly student knowledge, making writing readable; taught unfamiliar word-solving, developing encoding and chunking strategies (e.g., *and, band, hand, land, sand*); modeled writing using lists, webs, charts, graphs; integrated journaling into daily routines; used student sounding-out attempts to teach word structure; held weekly spelling bees and Hangman games; and intensified literacy activities, increasing story-retelling opportunities, incorporating developed student oral narration skills into reading and writing.

MH SERVICES PROVIDED BY SCHOOL PSYCHOLOGISTS VS. COMMUNITY MENTAL HEALTH CENTERS

School MH services mainly focus on supporting education. Because schools' first mission is education, school MH services aim to eliminate/decrease obstacles to optimal student learning and achievement. These typically short-term services intend to promote healthy emotional and social development. School-wide positive behavior supports feature prominently among best practices. For targeted student groups, more individualized services involve individual counseling, group counseling, and/or skill training. School psychologists may conduct functional behavior analyses and develop positive behavior intervention plans for individual students. Schools typically refer individual psychiatric disorders; substance abuse; grief; and family problems requiring more intensive MH treatments to private clinicians/community MH centers, particularly psychiatric disorders requiring medication evaluations along with ongoing treatment. MH centers usually provide short-term individual/group therapy, but may also offer more comprehensive services like 24-hour crisis response; hospitalization evaluations; or day treatment. Schools follow Response to Intervention (RtI) models and school-wide positive behavior support systems; community MH agencies follow Systems of Care (SOC) models, which coordinate various agency/provider services. RtI and SOC share similar guiding principles and core values, emphasizing prevention; early intervention; evidence-based interventions; and child, family, and community involvement. SOC MH approaches can benefit students receiving intensive school services.

CASE REPRESENTATIVE OF SCHOOL-BASED INTERVENTION PROVIDED BY SCHOOL PSYCHOLOGIST

In a representative case, a classroom teacher referred a student for escalating, disruptive classroom behavior. From student interviewing and teacher consultation, the school psychologist identified organizational and study skills difficulties impeding student assignment completion. She taught the student to write assignments in a notebook to take home and other strategies for organizing assignments and improving study skills; and met with the parents, discussing how they could set up a good home study area, develop a consistent routine for doing homework, and otherwise support their child. As the student achieved better preparation for classroom participation, he demonstrated better behavior. This characterizes the typical problem-solving approach of school MH services to student referrals for emotional issues. Components of this approach include giving students and parents information about the issue; offering problem-solving options; implementing evidence-based interventions; and evaluating intervention results. Schools also use behavior management; social skills training; positive behavior supports; and parent training and counseling. School MH professional may collaborate with other agencies to arrange school-based and community-based counseling; coordinate community services; and arrange after-school tutoring, social skills instruction, etc. when more complex problems result from combined factors like environmental stressors, family changes, peer influences, etc.

School-Based Intervention Skills and Techniques

DIRECTIVE, NON-DIRECTIVE, AND MODERATELY DIRECTIVE COUNSELING TECHNIQUES

Directive counseling techniques confront clients directly and challenge them to take some specific action, e.g., completing homework. In non-directive techniques, the psychologist provides empathic client support. In moderately directive techniques, the psychologist balances a combination of helping the client take action (e.g., Active Scheduling*) and providing the client with support. The directive Individual Psychology technique of "Acting as if" uses role-play wherein clients act out how they would like to be in different hypothetical scenarios, and explore alternatives. The underlying principle is that desired behaviors become more natural with practice. In Carl Rogers' non-directive, Person-Centered counseling, the psychologist uses a complex of skills to clarify understanding, including active listening techniques of interacting with the client; affirming the client's expressions; rephrasing/restating client statements to invite elaboration, etc. In Behavior Therapy's moderately directive *Active Scheduling technique, the psychologist helps the client initiate activities promoting movement from inactivity to more vital, productive status. Itemizing strategies and choices involved in scheduling can also afford immediate positive impacts for the client aside from the activities initiated.

In a moderately directive (combining direction and support) technique from Albert Ellis's Rational-Emotive Behavior Therapy (REBT), the psychologist uses analogies or images to help the client view a problem from a different perspective. In a moderately directive technique from Behavior Therapy of assertion training, the psychologist helps clients confidently express their needs, thoughts, and feelings without muting or hiding them passively or forcing them and badgering others aggressively. This aids clients who have trouble saying "No" to others; cannot express frustration or anger; let others take advantage of them; have trouble expressing affection for others; and/or feel they have no right to express their feelings and thoughts. Assertion training involves a variety of techniques, including modeling, exposure, behavior rehearsal, and positive reinforcement. In a non-directive (empathic support without confrontation or direction) Individual Psychology technique, attending and listening allows the psychologist to ascertain the client's core feelings and thoughts through engaging the client using eye contact; being psychologically involved; and attending closely to the client's nonverbal as well as verbal communication.

A moderately directive (combining confrontation/direction with empathy/support) technique, called behavior modeling in Behaviorism and vicarious learning in Bandura's Social Learning Theory, has the client first observe a behavior modeled by the psychologist or another person; and then imitate the behavior modeled. Bandura first proved that people need not initially perform nor receive reinforcement for behaviors themselves, but could learn by observing others perform the behavior and receive reinforcement and then imitate the observed behavior to obtain similar rewards. The directive Individual Psychology technique of "catching oneself" is helpful for clients who are perfectionists; display obsessive-compulsive symptoms (obsessive thinking, compulsive doing); have eating disorders; and/or tend to catastrophize (expect the worst possible outcomes). The counselor teaches clients to "catch" themselves before performing dysfunctional behaviors, raising their awareness of irrational thoughts and/or self-destructive behaviors without condemning themselves; and to anticipate events and modify their behavior patterns accordingly. The directive technique of challenging, from Choice Theory, involves inviting the client to identify behaviors and thoughts that are self-defeating; harm others; or both, and change them.

From Albert Ellis's Rational-Emotive Behavior Therapy (REBT), the directive technique of the continuum line has substance abuse clients rate their feelings regarding their addictions on a scale of 1-100, i.e., 1 = they hate it; 100 = they love it. This helps the psychologist and client to understand where the client is in the treatment process; and offers middle-ground alternatives to clients who are thinking in terms of "black-and-white"/all-or-nothing. The directive technique from Cognitive Psychology of decatastrophizing involves the counselor's asking "What if" questions to help clients realize that they may have mentally blown their problems out of proportion. This decreases client anxiety, enabling client and counselor to engage in positive cooperation and collaboration. In the directive technique of encouragement from Individual Psychology, the counselor acknowledges, names, accepts, and praises the client's positive qualities, strengths, and progress. This offsets client discouragement, raises client self-confidence, and assists clients in setting realistic goals for themselves. Carl Rogers's non-directive Person-Centered Therapy technique of congruence requires the counselor to interact with the client using consistent, honest behaviors and language.

In the directive Gestalt therapy technique of exaggeration, the counselor asks the client to take a specific body movement, emotion, or thought that the client has just expressed and exaggerate it. By blowing the behavior, feeling, or idea out of proportion, the client is able to develop greater awareness of the defense mechanisms and emotions that s/he usually hides from himself or herself. In the directive Fruit Basket technique Taken from Albert Ellis's Rational-Emotive Behavior Therapy (REBT), the counselor shows the client a fruit basket that contains fruits in good condition and fruits that are rotten, spoiled, underripe, overripe, or otherwise in bad condition. This is used as an analogy to show the client that like the fruit basket, the client also contains a combination of good and bad components; and that although s/he has done some bad things and has some flaws, s/he also has virtues and is essentially a good person.

The counseling technique of language exercises is derived from Gestalt therapy and is directive— i.e., the counselor uses it to confront the client and direct the client to take some specific action. It involves the counselor's helping the client to examine his or her speech patterns. This enables the client to develop greater self-awareness; and by acknowledging the client's feelings, thoughts, and actions, encourages the client to take personal responsibility for what s/he feels, thinks, says, and does. Taken from Individual Psychology theory, the magic wand counseling technique is also a directive method. In it, the counselor tells the client to imagine that s/he has a magic want and can use it to bring about anything that s/he wishes. This technique enables the client to look past his or her current life situation and circumstances, in which many clients are often so mired that they cannot see beyond them; and to define what his or her true desires in life are.

INTERVENTION STRATEGIES FOR INSTRUCTING HIGH-FUNCTIONING STUDENTS WITH ASDS
IDENTIFYING STRATEGIES FOR SOCIAL SKILLS ACCORDING TO DEVELOPMENTAL LEVELS

Identifying appropriate intervention strategies for instructing high-functioning students with autism spectrum disorders (ASDs) in social skills according to developmental levels, certain procedures should be followed. After assessing needs, including differentiating skills deficits requiring direct instruction vs. performance deficits, in order to identify the appropriate strategy for intervention, school psychologists must evaluate service delivery models. Then they must examine various curricula, including those designated for specific age and/or grade levels; those designed to promote language and social skills development; and those that are designed to provide students with experience, understanding, and skills related to group dynamics to improve group interpersonal and social interactions. The school psychologist also needs to determine which format to select for implementing the intervention services. For example, s/he must decide whether a student should be in an inclusive group setting for intervention. S/he must also decide whether to involve multiple disciplines; and if so, which disciplines will be included on the multidisciplinary intervention team, e.g., a speech-language pathologist; an occupational therapist; an adapted physical education teacher; a counselor; the classroom teacher, etc.

GROUP INTERVENTION FOR SOCIAL SKILLS INSTRUCTION FOR HIGH-FUNCTIONING MIDDLE SCHOOL STUDENTS

For middle school students with Asperger syndrome and other high-functioning ASDs, one example of a group intervention involves a small group, led by the school psychologist in a small office setting. The format of this group involves reviewing previously learned skills; direct school psychologist instruction in new skills; role-plays and games helping students generalize acquired social skills to other settings/situations; frequent positive reinforcement to reward student accomplishments; and community outings to facilitate student generalization of learned skills. As an example of a specific lesson, students learn new social skills involving vocal tone and proxemics. First the psychologist reviews a previously learned introduction skill, asking whom they introduced themselves to/introduced; when; and what happened. Then s/he introduces a new skill involving tone of voice: they discuss what is appropriate; using just enough volume for others to hear; distinguishing Inside vs. Outside Voice; not speaking too rapidly for others to understand; and using a respectful, cheerful tone unless angry with somebody. They also work on standing at least one arm's length from others, not getting too close or far away.

Example School Psychologist Lesson: Students have previously learned about appropriate vocal tones and loudness. To apply these: As facilitator, the school psychologist models different tones of voice. Then s/he has students draw two cards, one from a set with situations and one from a set with manners of speech; and communicate a message to the rest of the group accordingly. The psychologist records student speech and replays it for students to evaluate their pace (too fast, too slow, or just right). Students have also previously learned about proxemics, i.e., maintaining appropriate distances from others. In the application lesson, the school psychologists leads students in role-playing different situations: When greeting others initially and saying goodbye when parting; when standing in line in public places or in school; while standing and sitting when riding the bus; when asking somebody for something; and when interrupting somebody to ask permission to do something or ask a question about what was just said.

Example School Psychologist's Lesson to Generalize Previously Acquired Social Skills: The school psychologist has previously instructed the students in small groups about using voice tones and loudness appropriate to settings/situations; and maintaining appropriate distances from others for settings/situations. To help them generalize these skills, the school psychologist deliberately stands far away, introduces background noise, or otherwise elicits the newly acquired skills with vocal loudness and tone by manipulating the environment to require students to use appropriate voices. The school psychologist prepares a "volume chart" that resembles a thermometer, assigning numbers to corresponding volume levels: 1 = zero volume; 2 = whispering; 3 = a normal conversational voice; 4 = an "outside" voice; and 5 = screaming. Students practice speaking, with the psychologist indicating their volume levels on the chart. The psychologist provides verbal praise and tokens for appropriate vocal tones or approximate/partial correctness. To help students generalize their learned skills for sitting/standing appropriate distances from others, the school psychologists has students extend an arm to visualize arm's length distance, and/or use a hula hoop to practice what personal space and social space look like.

INSTRUCTION AND SMALL GROUP LESSONS IN SOCIAL SKILLS FOR STUDENTS IN ELEMENTARY SCHOOL GRADES

For high-functioning ASD students in elementary grades, the school psychologist assigns groups of 2-4 students each, grouping them according to similar functioning levels and/or ages. The lesson sequence first reviews previous lessons; then introduces a new skill(s); then gives the students practice in performing the new skill; and then helps students generalize the newly acquired skill through activities and/or games. The process also includes plenty of positive reinforcement and regularly monitoring student progress. As an example of this general format in a specific lesson, the school psychologist instructs students in the social skills for giving and receiving compliments. First s/he reviews previous lessons with students wherein they learned how to use greetings, introduce themselves and others, and join and invite others to group activities. Then s/he introduces task-analyzed steps in giving compliments: (1) Look; (2) Use a friendly face; (3) Use a sincere voice; (4) Say what you like about the person; and receiving compliments: (1) Smile; (2) Make eye contact; (3) Say "Thank you." In an initial practice activity, the psychologist writes compliments on

Popsicle/craft sticks, places them in a jar, and has each student draw one and give another student the designated compliment.

Activities to Practice Newly Learned Social Skills for Giving and Receiving Compliments: In previous lessons, students learned giving/receiving compliments and practiced by drawing compliments from a jar provided by the school psychologist and giving selected compliments to other group members. Now the school psychologist provides additional practice activities in the form of role-playing, by writing different scenarios in various environmental contexts on cards. Students take turns drawing cards and acting out the scenarios. Students can play roles themselves, or use puppets. For example, school scenarios can include complimenting a friend on a new shirt, or on an achievement, e.g., making a difficult catch and/or basket in PE class, etc. Home scenarios can include Dad's helping figure out a new computer game, Mom's preparing a favorite dessert, etc. Community scenarios can include going bowling with a friend; meeting the soccer team's goalie after a winning game, etc. Generalization activities include having students write compliments and names of recipients outside the group on cards, encouraging them to give cards to recipients; challenging students to compliment their teacher at least once daily, giving bonus rewards if the teacher reports compliments to the psychologist; and having students practice, and then walk to the office and take turns complimenting school staff.

ABA

Applied behavior analysis (ABA) is the application of behavioral principles to increase or decrease targeted behaviors over time in everyday situations. It is a process of systematically applying interventions based on learning theory (behaviorist) principles, to achieve meaningful degrees of improvement in socially significant behaviors; and also to show that the interventions used are what caused the behavior to improve. ABA has helped students and others learn a variety of skills, including self-help, play, and language skills. It has also helped to reduce self-stimulatory behaviors, self-injurious behaviors, aggression, and other maladaptive behaviors. Any observable, measurable behavior can be increased or decreased through applying the principles of ABA. ABA practitioners are held responsible as members of this discipline for improving "socially significant" behaviors. These include gross and fine motor skills; skills for performing activities of daily living (ADLs) like toileting, dressing, eating, and personal self-care; household skills; communication skills; social skills; academic skills; literacy skills; work skills, etc.

PROGRESS MONITORING AND PROGRAM EVALUATION, SUFFICIENT AMOUNTS, AND PARENTAL ROLE

ABA uses data-driven decision-making (D3M) for determining individual student programs. It also uses objective data collected on student responses to interventions to ascertain whether students are progressing. If not, ABA requires reevaluating and changing programs to enable progress. While parents often ask about the best frequency and duration of ABA intervention, there is no one answer. Research indicates that intensive behavioral intervention for young children diagnosed with autism spectrum disorders (ASDs) should be at least 25 hours weekly for 12 months yearly. Lovaas's original ABA studies found around half of children participating attained typical development through an average of 40 hours weekly for two years minimum. Ideal numbers will differ for individual children. However, families should learn ABA principles and apply them throughout everyday activity contexts. Parents play vital roles in children's ABA programs; research shows measurable gains for children whose parents are actively engaged in the process. Parental knowledge of children informs and guides ABA programs; parents can continue/extend prompting and reinforcement throughout daily activities, promoting generalization; and parents can record and track data in home and community settings, facilitating functional behavior analysis and behavior antecedent/trigger identification.

CREDENTIALING

When seeking a practitioner qualified to provide ABA services, parents should look for a provider who holds certification in the Behavior Analyst profession. This formal credentialing process is coordinated by the Behavior Analyst Certification Board (BACB). This certification demonstrates to consumers that the professional has received specific training and supervision by certified, qualified Behavior Analysts; and has completed coursework specifically related to behavioral analysis and interventions. However, since ABA is a frequent method of choice for interventions with individuals who have autism spectrum disorders (ASDs), parents should also realize BCBA certification does not necessarily mean the professional has training and/or experience specifically with ASDs, or the skills required for achieving optimal treatment results. For this reason parents should always ask ABA providers about their training and experience specific to training and implementing ABA programs for individuals with ASDs. Also, BCBA certification is fairly new; but some ABA professionals without certification have many years of experience working actively in the profession. Parents should therefore request information about experience and qualifications of non-certified professionals if they are interested in working with them.

COMPONENTS OF EFFECTIVE ABA PROGRAM

The following components are among those meeting the criteria for effective research evidence-based interventions for children with autism spectrum disorders (ASDs), according to the National Autism Center's National Standards Report:

- Manipulation of antecedents – modifying environmental/situational events preceding a targeted behavior. Changing the antecedents is designed to make the targeted behavior's success more likely. Examples include contrived motivative operations; procedures of prompting and fading prompts; behavioral momentum; inter-trial intervals; and incorporating special interests.
- Behavioral treatment – programs designed to decrease maladaptive behaviors and increase functional alternative or replacement behaviors. Examples include chaining; discrete trial chaining; shaping; communication training; generalization training; mand (the ABA term for command) training; and reinforcement.
- Comprehensive intervention – in school, home, community and other varied settings, effective programs use 1:1 or other appropriately low student-teacher ratios; follow treatment manuals; give intensive (25+ hours/week) training; and include data-driven decision-making (D3M).
- Joint attention intervention – programs teaching children to initiate joint attention interactions and/or respond to others' social requests. Examples include following eye gaze; pointing at objects; and showing items or activities to others.

The following are four ABA program components that meet criteria for treating individuals with autism spectrum disorders (ASDs) and that are also effective with others:

- Modeling – Adults or peers demonstrate a target behavior, and the student is then asked to imitate it. Thus, the student must demonstrate having imitation skills as a prerequisite for participating in this intervention. To help a student acquire imitation skills when needed, ABA practitioners often combine modeling with prompting and reinforcement strategies.
- Naturalistic teaching strategies – To teach functional skills in the real-world natural environment, the practitioner uses interactions initiated by the child. To implement this intervention, the practitioner must provide a stimulating environment; model play behaviors; offer choices; encourage conversation; and reinforce/reward reasonable efforts.

- Peer training – The practitioner trains non-disabled age/grade peers of the student in strategies for interacting socially and in play with students having ASDs. Some examples of well-known, commonly used peer training programs include peer networks; buddy skills; Circle of Friends, etc.
- Pivotal response training – This is a program designed for targeting specific behaviors that are pivotal, i.e., they lead to improvement across a wide range of behaviors, e.g., motivation for social communication; self-initiation; self-management; and responsiveness to multiple cues, among others.

The following are three components of effective, evidence-based ABA programs for teaching behaviors to students with autism spectrum disorders (ASDs) and others needing intervention for learning social or other specific skills, decreasing maladaptive behaviors, and/or increasing adaptive behaviors:

- Schedules – This treatment procedure teaches the student to follow a pictorial or printed task list through a series of steps or activities in sequence for the purpose of completing a given activity. Task analysis breaks the activity down into its component steps, actions, or smaller activities to make the whole more manageable by enabling the student to perform or learn one part at a time, and continue to the next part until the entire schedule is completed.
- Self-management – In this intervention, the ABA practitioner teaches the student to record the target behavior's occurrence or non-occurrence, and to obtain reinforcement for performing this documentation. This teaches the student to regulate his or her own behavior.
- Story-based interventions – In this intervention, the stories are written descriptions of the conditions or situations in which specified behaviors are expected to take place. By teaching students who and what are involved in social interactions and when, where, and why they occur, story-based interventions improve student perspective-taking abilities. The best-known example is Social Stories by Carol Gray (2000, 2001, and 2010).

Child and Adolescent Psychopathology

DETECTING CHILDHOOD MENTAL ILLNESS

Once mental disorders have developed, they become regular features of a child's behavior, making them more difficult to treat. For this reason, recognizing mental illness symptoms in children as early as possible is important. However, it can be difficult for parents to determine whether a child or teen's behaviors are signs of a serious mental health issue or normal behavioral responses to ordinary environmental stressors. For instance, a child or teen might temporarily act out in reaction to being moved to a different school, or to having a new sibling in the family, etc. Some behaviors that can be warning signs of more serious mental health issues include these: The child or adolescent displays problems functioning in more than one setting, e.g., at home, at school, and with peers. The child/teen's usual appetite, eating patterns, and/or sleeping patterns change. The child/teen withdraws socially, or demonstrates or expresses fear of things s/he was not afraid of previously. The child regresses to behaviors typical of younger children, e.g., bedwetting, thumb-sucking, baby talk, etc. The child/teen appears tearful or sad. The child engages in self-injurious behaviors like head-banging, eye-gouging, or suddenly sustaining frequent injuries. The child or teen expresses recurring thoughts of death.

PSYCHOTHERAPY APPROACHES TO MENTAL HEALTH INTERVENTIONS FOR CHILDREN AND ADOLESCENTS

The following are several different types of psychotherapy approaches to mental health interventions for children and adolescents:

- Cognitive Behavior Therapy (CBT) examines distorted or confused thought patterns to help improve children/teens' anxiety, moods, and behavior. CBT therapists teach children that behavior is influenced by moods and feelings caused by thoughts. Children learn to identify harmful thinking patterns; therapists help them replace these with thoughts generating more appropriate feelings and behaviors. Specialized versions of CBT have been developed to help children with post-traumatic stress disorder. Studies find CBT effective for treating anxiety, depression, and various other conditions.
- Dialectical Behavior Therapy (DBT) can help older adolescents with Borderline Personality Disorder, self-injurious behaviors, or chronic suicidal ideations. Emphasizing examining one's responses to intense adverse emotions and taking responsibility for one's problems, it frequently combines individual and group sessions.
- Family Therapy provides education, support, and explores communication patterns to help families function more constructively. Sessions can include parents, siblings, and grandparents with children/adolescents. Couples therapy is a specific kind of family therapy for marital/relationship issues.
- Group Therapy involves one or more therapists leading multiple clients, improving social skills and/or augmenting understanding of mental illness using the power of peer interactions and group dynamics. It includes psychodynamic, substance abuse, social skills, parental support, multi-family, and other group therapies.

The following types of psychotherapy intervention approaches can be used with children and adolescents:

- Psychodynamic psychotherapy places emphasis on understanding motivations for and influences on a child's thinking, emotions, and behaviors. It can help to identify the child's typical responses to internal conflicts; defense mechanisms; and behavior patterns. Psychodynamic psychotherapy developed out of Freud's psychoanalytic theory and practice. Psychoanalysis is a more intensive, specialized form of psychodynamic psychotherapy, typically entailing several weekly sessions. The assumption that a child's feelings and behaviors will improve once internal struggles are revealed is the basis for psychodynamic therapies.
- Interpersonal therapy (IPT) is a brief treatment, compatible with many health insurance providers' coverage limits, that was developed and tested specifically for depression but is also effective and used for various other clinical diagnoses. It concentrates on how the client's emotional status is affected by interpersonal events, depicting individual problems in interpersonal terms and then addressing problematic relationships.
- Play Therapy helps younger children recognize, identify, and verbalize emotions using toys, puppets, dolls, blocks, drawings, and games. The therapist observes the child's use of play materials, identifying patterns or themes to inform an understanding of the child's issues. Children are able to understand and manage their feelings, conflicts, and behaviors better through combined play and talk.

SYMPTOMS OF LDS IN CHILDREN

Learning disabilities (LDs) include a diverse array of symptoms affecting child development and school achievement. While some of the following symptoms are demonstrated by all children at some point during their development, students with LDs demonstrate clusters of them, which do not go away as they get older. The symptoms observed most frequently in LDs are: A short attention span; a poor memory; difficulties with following directions; being unable to discriminate among or between letters, speech sounds, and/or numbers; poor reading and/or writing skills; poor physical coordination; problems with eye-hand coordination; problems with sequencing (letters, words, numbers, events, etc.); sensory difficulties; and disorganization. In addition, students with LDs may exhibit other characteristics, including: Variable/inconsistent day-to-day performance; frequent inappropriate responses; impulsivity, restlessness, distractibility; poor adjustment to change; difficulty attending, listening, remembering; meaning one thing but saying another; being difficult to discipline; difficulty telling left vs. right, telling time; letter reversals; incorrectly sequencing letters; problems sounding out words; immature/delayed speech development; and/or difficulty understanding words or concepts.

The following are common symptoms of four types of learning disabilities (LDs) related to reading, writing, math, and motor coordination:

- Dyslexia: Difficulties with: Phonics/letter-sound correspondences, spelling, word recognition; understanding others' speech; organizing spoken/written language; delayed speech development; word retrieval/self-expression; learning new read/heard vocabulary; learning other languages; learning rhymes and songs more slowly; understanding questions; following directions; recalling phone numbers/addresses/other numbers in correct order; telling left from right.
- Dysgraphia: Difficulties with: Writing/drawing; grammar; writing ideas down; rapid energy and interest loss while writing; writing thoughts down in logical order; saying words aloud while writing; omitting words from sentences or leaving them incomplete.
- Dyscalculia: Difficulties with: Understanding fractions, number lines, positive/negative numbers and other basic arithmetic concepts; math word problems; making change when exchanging money; messy writing of math problems; recognizing steps in math problems/other logical information sequences; understanding event time sequences; verbally describing mathematical processes.
- Dyspraxia: Difficulties with: Organizing belongings and self; breaking things; eye-hand coordination, e.g., coloring inside lines, puzzle assembly, precision cutting; poor sense of balance; sensitivity to loud noises/repeated noises like clocks ticking; sensitivity to touch, including clothing irritation.

RESEARCH EVIDENCE ON IMPACT OF MENTAL HEALTH PROBLEMS ON STUDENT EDUCATION

Some reports have observed that even though students with mental health issues find it impossible or very difficult to learn in school, student mental health has been disregarded by educational reform efforts. Research has also found that school failure to address student mental health problems encompasses more than academic issues. For example, a study by one educational expert (Spencer, 2013) examined data from case studies derived from the school records of students 12-16 years old who had received referrals to an area advocacy center over ongoing school failure, truancy, involvement in the juvenile justice system, or other involvement with the court system. She investigated what kinds of developmental and social factors were associated with risk for MH and behavior problems in early adolescence; and once students were identified as having mental health issues, what kinds of services they received. She found that in the state of Connecticut, more than 20% of children suffered with a substance abuse or MH problem annually, yet fewer than half of them received treatment.

Research has found that the warning signs of mental health (MH) problems can be manifested at preschool ages, but the majority of students do not receive treatment, even after their MH problems are identified. One way that this relationship is reflected is that children with MH issues demonstrate limited academic progress, beginning when they first enter school and continuing throughout the high school grades. Another finding is that school difficulties caused by student MH problems emerge at young ages. For example, the Yale Child Study Center conducted a national study showing that more children were expelled from preschools than from grades 1-12 because of MH difficulties. This study also showed that in the state of Connecticut, more than 10 students per 1,000 were expelled from state-funded preschools. This was one of the highest rates in the country. This Yale study also indicated that of students diagnosed with mental illness and behavioral health issues by the time they were in middle school, more than 70% had displayed warning signs of these problems by the time they were in the second grade.

According to national research conducted by the Yale Child Study Center, among children who received diagnoses of MH and behavioral health issues by the time they were in middle school, nearly 20% of them had suffered from exposure to trauma, social risk factors, health issues, developmental issues, and other warning signs of MH problems before they were in kindergarten. In addition, 25% of the children studied had records containing documentation of traumatic experiences. However, according to the Connecticut nonprofit agency the Center for Children's Advocacy, which offers legal support to victims of child abuse and neglect, the educational records of children referred to this Center showed that their behavioral and mental health problems were not identified until they had reached the middle school grades. Researchers found that in a study sample, every adolescent had documented significant MH and/or behavioral health problems. More than half were at risk of or had had juvenile justice intervention, court involvement, or court referral for families having service needs.

CONNECTIONS BETWEEN EARLY WARNING SIGNS IN CHILDREN AND MH DIAGNOSES DURING ADOLESCENCE

Among adolescents studied who were identified with significant MH and/or behavioral health problems, a very high proportion (82%) had exhibited disruptive behavior; explosive behavior; incidents of aggression; and being suspended from school multiple times. Of these students, 25% were identified with symptoms of depression; 20% were diagnosed with anxiety disorders; 17% were diagnosed with post-traumatic stress disorder; 16% had demonstrated self-injurious and suicidal behaviors; and 17% had been hospitalized in psychiatric facilities, some of these for extended durations or for multiple times. In addition, 12% of these students' records included reports of physical, sexual, or emotional child abuse. One university dean, educational consultant, and researcher who studied the impact of overlooking early MH warning signs in young children on their later educational status (Spencer, 2013) recommended that students with early MH risk factors should be screened and identified earlier, and that better methods of screening and identification should be used, to change the fact that even though many children demonstrate early MH warning signs in early childhood, most are not identified with MH problems for another 10 years or more.

SOCIAL FACTORS THAT CAN IMPACT MENTAL HEALTH OF CHILDREN AND ADOLESCENTS

When their education is interrupted, as by frequent family relocation, legal problems, chronic illnesses or conditions, and other causes, this interruption has an adverse impact on children's mental health status. Being orphaned or separated from their parents also poses mental health risks, as does having their parent(s) imprisoned. Being homeless affects children's mental health. Being placed in foster care is another social factor that can have adverse impact on mental health. Being exposed to child abuse, domestic violence, and other traumatic experiences can also influence children's mental health negatively. Some actions that one educational expert (Spencer, 2013) has recommended after studying the effects on students of not being identified with MH warning signs at early ages include: Making improvements to how many young children are referred to mental health and special education early intervention services; improving how various service providers collaborate with one another; increasing and enhancing parental and community education regarding MH risk factors and available support; and providing better training and requiring greater accountability for school personnel and other service providers to make MH identifications and referrals for younger children.

PSYCHOPHARMACOLOGY

According to the American Society of Clinical Psychopharmacology (ASCP), psychopharmacology is the study of how drugs are used to treat mental disorders. It is a complex discipline, which requires practitioners to stay up to date with frequent new advances through continual study. The principles of pharmacokinetics, i.e., the effects that the body can have on various psychoactive medications; and pharmacodynamics, i.e., the effects that various psychoactive medications can have on the body, that are clinically relevant are among the knowledge that is required of psychopharmacologists. Included in this knowledge are understanding the process of protein binding, which determines how available to a patient's body a medication is; the factor of half-life, which determines how long a drug remains present within the body; the characteristics of polymorphic genes, i.e., genes that differ greatly among individuals and hence affect how their bodies interact with medications and vice versa; and drug-drug interactions, i.e., the ways that different medications affect each other.

AREAS OF KNOWLEDGE

Because psychotropic medications are prescribed for treating mental disorders, psychopharmacologists, psychiatrists, psychologists including school psychologists, and other mental health personnel must understand not only basic psychopharmacology, but also basic neuroscience, clinical medicine, differential diagnosis of mental disorders, and different treatment options for mental disorders. In addition, psychopharmacologists must have the same skills for developing and using therapeutic relationships with patients that are required of psychologists, counselors, and others who conduct psychotherapy. In its general meaning, any physician who prescribes psychoactive medication to patients as part of their treatment is considered a psychopharmacologist. Psychiatrists have even greater psychopharmacological expertise and knowledge than physicians who have completed residencies, who already have high levels of psychopharmacological knowledge and expertise. In its more specific meaning, a psychopharmacologist can be a physician with training advanced psychopharmacology and specializing in the field. This specialty requires passing the American Society of Clinical Psychopharmacology (ASCP)'s Examination in Advanced Psychopharmacology every 5 years.

PHARMACOLOGICAL CONCEPTS RELATED TO HOW PSYCHOTROPIC MEDICATIONS WORK IN THE BRAIN

The site of action is the place in the body where a medication exercises its therapeutic effects. The mechanism of action is the way in which the medication accomplishes those effects. Biologically, most psychotropic drugs affect people by influencing the ways in which the brain's neurons (nerve cells) communicate with one another. Cellular membranes have specific protein structures that regulate how substances and signals flow into and out of the cells. This regulation controls how electrical impulses travel along neurons, and are transmitted between neurons at synapses, the spaces between neurons where they exchange chemical neurotransmitters. One cell releases a neurotransmitter; receptors on another cell receive it. Scientists know of or suspect around 40 neurotransmitters in the brain, including acetylcholine; dopamine; serotonin; norepinephrine;

gamma aminobutyric acid (GABA); and several different amino acids. Acetylcholine is associated with the transmission of brain impulses enabling cognitive processes like remembering, thinking, reasoning, etc. The primary mechanism in Alzheimer's disease is acetylcholine neuron death. Acetylcholine receptors are present in the brain; the spinal cord; the autonomic nervous system's ganglia; and at the end organs of the autonomic nervous system's parasympathetic branch.

ANTIDEPRESSANTS

By chemical structure and mechanism of action, antidepressants include tricyclics and tetracyclics (TCAs); monoamine oxidase inhibitors (MAOIs); and serotonin-specific reuptake inhibitors (SSRIs). Some tricyclics/tetracyclics are Elavil (amitriptyline); Anafranil (clomipramine); Tofranil (imipramine); Pamelor (nortriptyline); Norpramine (desipramine) Sinequan (doxepin); Vivactil (protriptyline hydrochloride), etc. SSRIs are effective for alleviating depression, bipolar I disorder, dysthymic disorder, panic disorder, obsessive-compulsive disorder, borderline personality disorder, and eating disorders and other disorders. Prozac (fluoxetine) has become the most widely prescribed antidepressant because it has the least toxic effect on the heart and fewer other adverse side-effects than others. Other popular SSRIs include Paxil (paroxetine), Zoloft (sertraline), and Luvox (fluvoxamine). Anxiolytic/antianxiety drugs/tranquilizers are also prescribed for depression, social phobia, panic disorder, bipolar disorder, and substance abuse withdrawal symptoms. Benzodiazepines have mostly replaced barbiturates as they have less potential for abuse and a higher therapeutic index. Anxiolytics include Xanax (alprazolam); Atenolol (tenormin, a beta blocker also used for heart disease); BuSpar (buspirone, which is neither a benzodiazepine nor a barbiturate and has no risk of abuse); Librium (chlordiazepoxide); Klonopin (clonazepam) and Catapres (clonidine).

ANTIPSYCHOTIC DRUGS

Formerly called major tranquilizers or neuroleptics, antipsychotic medications consist mostly of drugs in the dopamine blocker class. They are prescribed for schizophrenia, schizoaffective disorder, schizophreniform disorder, delusional disorder, major depressive disorder with psychotic features, manic episodes, brief psychotic disorder, and other psychotic mental illnesses (those involving loss of contact with reality) that are idiopathic, i.e., they have no known cause. They are also widely used to treat severe agitation and aggressive or violent behavior; movement disorders, anxiety disorders, and psychoses with organic etiologies. Some examples are Haldol (haloperidol); Thorazine (chlorpromazine); Stelazine (trifluoperazine); Mellaril (thioridazine); Serentil (mesoridazine); Loxitane (loxapine); Prolixin (fluphenazine); Risperdal (risperidone); and Navane (thiothixene). Common side-effects include tardive dyskinesia—involuntary movements from long-term use; extrapyramidal syndrome (EPS), which can occur immediately, including tremors, akathisia, dystonia, parkinsonism, neuroleptic malignant syndrome, which is life-threatening; and other movement disorders. There are other medications to treat these side-effects—e.g., anticonvulsants, anticholinergics, anti-parkinsonism drugs, and others—but unfortunately, these also have their own side-effects.

Diversity in Development and Learning

COMPETENCIES REQUIRED TO ADDRESS DIVERSITY AMONG DEVELOPMENT AND LEARNING

In order to serve today's increasingly diverse populations of public school students, school psychologists must have preparation and expertise pertaining to the psychology of individual differences; and must apply their knowledge for developing and implementing interventions on the basis of the student, family, or system's individual characteristics. They must have both information about and sensitivity to diverse linguistic, cultural, racial, ethnic, socioeconomic, biological, and gender-related backgrounds; and personal individual disabilities and abilities; and be able to apply this information and awareness across a wide variety of strategies for promoting student learning and development. For example, school psychologists can identify individual students' specific learning needs and develop instructional strategies whereby schools can meet these needs. They assess sensorimotor skills, cognitive skills, emotional functioning, social functioning, and academic performance. They diagnose a complete range among educational and psychological strengths and needs relative to education. They also cultivate sensitivity within the school community to diversity-related matters; and promote schools' integrating all groups' diverse strengths and talents into their educational programs.

COMPETENCY, KNOWLEDGE, ETHICS, AND SUPPORT SERVICES

According to the APA and NASP, daily school psychology practice will increasingly incorporate the theme of cross-cultural competency into all of its facets. Many state education departments identify human diversity as one area in which school psychologists are required to demonstrate foundational knowledge. Ethical principles commonly shared by ethical codes of conduct for school psychologists include respect for human dignity, which itself includes non-discrimination and fairness in interacting with all individuals. School psychology is included among student support services in public schools. State education departments require student support services specialists, which include school psychologists, to have knowledge about diversity issues that influence students and schools, e.g., cultural, communication, health, and emotional issues; and skills to serve students and families effectively by considering and responding to these issues. Identifying risk factors for learning difficulties and designing and implementing applicable interventions in a timely manner are important for enhancing student performance. So are identifying student talents and strengths; and helping students develop post-secondary plans applying these assets.

U.S. PUBLIC SCHOOL STUDENT DIVERSITY AND ASSOCIATED SCHOOL FAILURE RISKS

As an example of rapidly increasing diversity, the U.S. Department of Education reports (Aud et al, 2013) from 2000 through 2010, the demographic composition of public school populations in America shifted from 61% to 52% white and from 16% to 23% Hispanic; and the proportions of ELL students rose during this period. These researchers expected these trends to continue for at least the next 10 years. Research literature indicates increased risk of school failure for some groups of culturally and linguistically diverse (CLD) students. Racial/ethnic minority students are more likely to be overrepresented in special education identification. ELL students receive the lowest scores in academic achievement and are at the highest risk of dropping out among all students in public schools. Lower academic achievement is also consistently associated with lower family socioeconomic status. Long-term implications of these adverse impacts of student diversity on school achievement include lower educational attainment levels, and hence lower rates of employment and lower annual earnings as adults, for African-American and Hispanic students than for white peers.

REPRESENTATION OF CLD STUDENTS IN SCHOOL PSYCHOLOGY RESEARCH LITERATURE

The APA and NASP's professional guidelines reflect their acknowledgement of the significance of diversity factors, particularly the historical risk of school failure for certain groups of culturally and linguistically diverse (CLD) students and the USA's increasing demographic diversity. Researchers additionally observe that studies omitting CLD samples can cause incorrect generalization of results and inappropriate interventions for some student groups, indicating the need for better research methodologies. Despite realizing the need to incorporate diversity issues into research methods and practices, researchers and personnel who issue professional guidelines have not kept up with the speed of demographic changes occurring in American students, and hence in school psychologists' needs. Literature reviews from 1975-2013 found only a minority of school psychology journal articles represented CLD student groups; and of these, the majority concentrated on assessment, with only a minority addressing intervention. Some authors suggested multiple reasons for the dearth of diversity in school psychology research; e.g., practicing school psychologists most likely to encounter diversity issues in everyday practice typically do not submit manuscripts for publication; many researchers may not be interested in the topic of diversity; and scholars from racial/ethnic minorities more likely to contribute to this research are underrepresented in academia.

CULTURAL BROKERS

The NASP defines cultural brokers as representatives of specific language or ethnic groups who function as liaisons between schools and students' parents. They may also communicate comparisons and contrasts among cultures in functioning as intermediaries to bridge cultural gaps. By addressing student cultural needs, cultural brokers also enhance school psychologists' sensitivity to the diversity needs of students and families. According to the National Center for Cultural Competence, as adopted by the NASP, four distinct roles that cultural brokers can fulfill effectively in school settings are as liaisons; as cultural guides; as mediators; and as catalysts for change in education. As liaisons, cultural brokers communicate with students, parents, and educational providers in school systems to build better connections between schools and student families. Cultural brokers have knowledge in two main areas: (1) their community's or cultural groups' educational beliefs, values, and practices; and (2) the educational system and how to navigate it effectively on behalf of students and their families.

FUNCTIONS

The NASP has adopted four functions of cultural brokers identified by the National Center for Cultural Competence: liaisons, cultural guides, mediators, and catalysts for change. In their capacity as cultural guides, cultural brokers can offer guidance to school systems in the process of incorporating values, principles, and best practices that are linguistically and culturally competent. In doing so, they apply the principles of recognizing, responding to, and using the cross-cultural nuances of verbal and nonverbal communication effectively. Cultural brokers are knowledgeable not only about the community's needs and strengths, but also about the school environment's structures and functions. Having acquired the trust and respect of the community is a critical requirement for cultural brokers. When schools employ community members as cultural brokers, they acknowledge the existence of this expertise in their communities. In serving as cultural guides, cultural brokers can offer guidance to schools and their stakeholder partners for implementing educational diversity initiatives; and help to develop educational materials that will enable students and parents to learn more about the educational system and its functions.

MEDIATOR ROLE

According to the National Center for Cultural Competence, cultural brokers can serve four discrete roles in school settings: as cultural liaisons, cultural guides, mediators, and catalysts for change. The NASP has also adopted these roles. In the mediator role, cultural brokers can address the inherent and/or historical mistrust of educational institutions that many culturally, racially, and ethnically diverse populations often experience. Economic inequality, social inequality; and historical influences including war, internment, racism, and discrimination have engendered many minority groups' suspicion of offers for assistance; majority group blame of and hostility toward them; and limited access to the resources they need. Cultural brokers further greater utilization of educational services by minority communities when they serve as mediators. For them to deliver such services effectively, they need two elements to be in place: (1) being able to establish and sustain trust with these communities; and (2) being able to dedicate enough time for developing meaningful relationships between service providers and students and their parents.

CATALYSTS FOR CHANGE

By establishing inclusive, collaborative environments for students, parents, and educators, cultural brokers can launch school transformation, making them agents of change. They also serve as models and mentors in changing behavior, which can dismantle institutional obstacles like prejudice, discrimination, and bias in educational systems. They can help to change interpersonal and intergroup relationships. Cultural brokers can identify values which shape and direct a culture's perspectives and behaviors. Thus they support school crisis prevention and response plans by assessing and understanding their own cultural value systems and identities; and by ensuring organized crisis responses that cumulatively reflect a culturally diverse population's needs through involving neighborhood groups, civic associations, social clubs, faith-based organizations, interfaith groups, volunteer organizations, mutual aid societies, nonprofit advocacy groups, and social service and healthcare providers in crisis preparedness and management. Cultural brokers, by clearly comprehending traditional community educational beliefs, practices, and changes caused via acculturation, advocate for students to assure culturally competent, effective educational practices. NASP experts recommend that school psychologists practicing in diverse school settings incorporate some of these cultural brokerage skills into their work.

CULTURAL BIAS

EDUCATIONAL ASSESSMENT, SCHOOL INSTRUCTIONAL MATERIALS, AND SUBJECTS

Historical research findings of cultural bias in education include the work of Russian psychologists and theorists Lev Vygotsky (1896-1934) and Alexander Luria (1902-1977), both of whom investigated and discovered inherent cultural bias in how assessors judged problem-solving strategies in young children. They both found that when testing Russian children from impoverished families, evaluators from mainstream Russian culture rated the children's responses as incorrect on cognitive items—frequently reflecting the evaluators' cultural frame of reference rather than the children's cognitive abilities. They identified criteria for correct responses that were both biased against culturally alternative methods of knowing, reasoning, and problem-solving; and biased toward methods preferred by the mainstream culture. Ongoing cultural bias in student performance evaluations has been identified in 21st-century studies. APA and other researchers also note that majority culture/race members contribute most academic materials in America; and such materials typically emphasize majority group superiority. For instance, most American history textbooks for elementary and secondary schools underrepresent or misrepresent Native American and African experiences in the USA, while romanticizing European experiences in the USA; and additionally marginalize minority groups' traditions and achievements. Studies also identify European/American ideological biases in English, natural sciences, and other academic subjects.

DIFFERING INSTRUCTIONAL METHODS AND DIFFERING CULTURAL PERCEPTIONS

One example of cultural bias observed by multiple researchers (2000-2006) is that American classrooms emphasize separate student seating; independent student work; working on single tasks; working quietly; and interacting only with the teacher in controlled environments. These all reflect mainstream cultural bias: many ethnic minority students' cultures emphasize sitting together; working interdependently/cooperatively/collaboratively; working on multiple activities simultaneously; and more vocal/verbal social interactions through working communally. Another example of cultural bias is explicitly demonstrated in a study (Perry and Delpit, 1998) wherein students shown a picture of a man wearing a suit and carrying a briefcase were asked where he was going. White children said he was going to work, which was scored as correct; but many African-American children said he was going to church, which was scored as incorrect. This reflected

135

cultural bias in that many African-American men had jobs requiring uniforms, scrubs, or other non-suit garments, and only wore suits/carried briefcases to church. Later studies (cf. Baker, 2005) confirm such biases toward mainstream cultural values and against alternative yet equivalent cultural value systems.

RECOMMENDATIONS TO REDUCE CLASSROOM CULTURAL BIAS AND PROVIDE CULTURALLY RESPONSIVE INSTRUCTION

To make classrooms culturally responsive, researchers advise teachers and administrators to examine their own biases about appropriate vs. inappropriate classroom behavior. They find teachers benefit from using self-reflection to understand their own instructional biases before incorporating diverse students' cultural belief systems and values into their teaching. An integral part of the reflective process is understanding how inherent biases in favor of mainstream culture can influence the classroom learning activities teachers offer and allow; the types of instruction they practice; and how they assess student progress. APA research (2003) indicates teachers must increase their self-awareness as cultural beings and recognize their own biases toward specific cultural values. Self-reflection promotes developing positive attitudes toward culturally/ethnically diverse student values and learning styles. Such positive attitudes enable educators to align their curricula and classroom activities with culturally diverse values and behaviors. Researchers find teacher willingness to establish culturally responsive classrooms significantly influenced by teacher attitudes toward diverse cultural values. Some also find a first step for creating culturally responsive learning environments and reducing cultural bias in instruction is self-reflection about culturally based instructional beliefs and practices.

BENEFITS OF CULTURALLY CONGRUENT TEACHING PRACTICES

Some experts find "teacher caring," i.e., teacher practices promoting strong interpersonal teacher-student bonding, facilitates interacting with culturally and ethnically diverse students. Multiple studies find caring teachers, rather than demonstrating biases against student minority cultural values, find ways of incorporating these values throughout their classroom practices. Researchers find "warm demander" teaching styles combining affection with authority and mutual respect (akin to Baumrind's Authoritative and Shaffer's Warm Controlling parenting styles) improve diverse student experiences, especially among low-income African-American students as they reflect parent-child dynamics these students typically experience outside of school, creating cultural continuity. Studies also show diverse student performance is improved through building lessons and activities on their cultural values. This allows students to continue their cultures' learning preferences and behaviors instead of abandoning and replacing them. Through culturally responsive practices, teachers learn about alternative, non-mainstream learning activities and instructional strategies which benefit diverse student performance, expanding teacher understanding of what is most effective for these students while also decreasing cultural bias in instruction.

SOCIAL JUSTICE IN EDUCATION

In a "Call to Service" lecture at Harvard (2010), U.S. Secretary of Education Arne Duncan said, "We need to make education our national mission....Education reform is a daily fight for social justice. The battle for a quality education is about so much more than education. It is a daily fight for social justice." In inviting students to become teachers, he added, "Please join us in that fight." Characterizing education as a civil rights issue, Duncan asked Congress to reauthorize the Elementary and Secondary Education Act (ESEA, aka No Child Left Behind/NCLB), and also to implement the significant changes in education that the President's Blueprint for Reform proposed. In addition, he called for continuing the national investment in either transforming or closing underperforming schools; and employing high-quality classroom teachers and school leaders, particularly those with the most underserved student populations. Duncan advocates applying rigorous academic standards for every student that will enable fulfilling careers and/or higher education.

According to an expert teacher (Mullenholz, ED.gov, 2011), just as social justice entails preserving core values of solidarity and equality while protecting human dignity; conversely, as a nation, not providing our students quality education basically undermines their human dignity. Placing students in failing schools/to underperforming teachers/principals fails to prepare them for higher education, limiting the choices they can make in life. This expert describes U.S. Secretary of Education Arne Duncan's call for reauthorizing the Elementary and Secondary Education Act (ESEA, aka No Child Left Behind/NCLB) as identifying the main reason for such reauthorization: not as a top-down legislative issue or a partisan political issue, but an issue of reaffirming the human dignity of American students and their civil rights. The author equates the American dream that Dr. Martin Luther King, Jr. spoke of in his historic "I Have a Dream" speech to the dream of American students. This author finds the ESEA/NCLB and educational system are both "broken"; letting this continue continues denying children's fundamental rights, eroding student dreams and futures, and further deteriorating the nation and economy; and fixing the law is "a social justice issue."

EDUCATIONAL FAIRNESS/EQUITY AND ECONOMIC EQUITY AND STUDENT ACHIEVEMENT OUTCOMES

On the smaller classroom/school level, fairness and equity involve calling on every student; giving every student a chance to speak; designing tests many students, not just one, can pass; organizing libraries so books are available to many, not just one student, etc. On a larger international scale, the PISA (Program for International Student Assessment) finds that countries which address social inequities achieve better student learning outcomes, whereas countries which disregard social inequalities either fall in the assessment's ranks or stay at the same rank. The USA ranked in the middle of the PISA list.

One expert (Carey, in Downes, 2011) attributes this to the highly developed economies and stable democratic governments of educational competitors like Canada, Finland, Japan, New Zealand, and Norway; and moreover to their *not* "...destabilizing their...regions...miring UN troops in internecine warfare or letting large segments of their populations starve." PISA authors observed that national wealth or poverty did not determine educational rankings, but rather social division of wealth. National attitudes that "we're all in this together" promote educational equity and by extension, better learning outcomes. The contrasting "us vs. them" attitude represented by the growing economic inequality in America apparently is reflected in our educational inequality.

DEMOCRATIC PRINCIPLES OF EMPOWERMENT FOR EDUCATIONAL ENTITIES

According to one expert (Downes, 2011), among democratic principles for ensuring a stable network, four elements for empowering individual entities in the educational networks are:

- Autonomy – every entity within the educational system should use its own internal principles, criteria, and mechanisms to govern its own activities, enabling judgment and resistance capacities. Maximizing autonomy enables learners to be guided and guide themselves by their own values, purposes, goals, or objectives.
- Diversity – Every entity comprises many different entities with their own inputs, connections, and unique perspectives, assuring more reliable, multidimensional perceptions and variety in perspectives. Maximizing diversity in educational resources nurtures unique viewpoints, creativity, and valuable contributions to society based on personal experiences and insights.

- Openness – system-wide freely-flowing content; input and output; and entities freely flowing into and out of relationships indicate openness, which enables network perception; fluid connections enable adaptation and learning. Educational systems and resources structured to maximize openness enable people to enter and leave systems freely, and ideas and objects to flow freely within systems.
- Interactivity – not propagating but creating knowledge: member interactions enable network adaptation and growth. Society/community immersion produces learning; cumulative whole-society/community interactions produce society/community knowledge.

GACE Practice Test

1. Which of these is correct about characteristics of the interview process?
   a. Establishing a relationship with the respondent will only interfere
   b. Most often the interview questions are standardized for uniformity
   c. Good interviewers focus only on information, not on social factors
   d. Rapport will create the trust needed to share personal information

2. What is true about observational measures used by psychologists?
   a. Observations focus only on the processes of behavior
   b. Observations focus only on the products of behavior
   c. Observations conducted must be by direct observation
   d. Observations can be all of these; no one answer is sufficient

3. At the beginning of the school year, for a new student with no previous assessments or school records which of these would be least indicated for problem identification?
   a. Complete IQ testing
   b. Portfolio assessments
   c. Personality inventory
   d. Tests for social skills

4. The Activity-Based Assessment Inventory, or ABA Inventory, is not designed to explore which area of a student's life?
   a. Family
   b. Friends
   c. Grades
   d. Games

5. What is true regarding the Child Behavior Checklist (CBCL)?
   a. The information it collects is reported by a child's parents
   b. It assesses behavior problems but not social competencies
   c. It is a self-report measure, so interviewers are not allowed
   d. Its items are not standardized and they can be individualized

6. For which teachers would the History/Transition Information Profile be most useful?
   a. "Step-up" teachers who follow their students from one grade to the next
   b. Teachers of mixed-age classes with the same students for several years
   c. Teachers with a class of all new students who have past school records
   d. Teachers with a class of all new students with no earlier school records

7. Which of the following people developed the first working intelligence test?
   a. Alfred Binet
   b. Lewis Terman
   c. David Wechsler
   d. Raymond Cattell

8. Of the following tests, which is not a standardized achievement test?

    a. The ITBS
    b. The CTBS
    c. The SAT
    d. The TAT

9. In the Wechsler Intelligence Scale for Children (WISC), which of the following subtests evaluates short-term memory?

    a. Vocabulary
    b. Digit Span
    c. Block Design
    d. Symbol Search

10. What is not a type of executive function that students must use to succeed in school?

    a. Being able to retrieve previously learned information
    b. Being able to organize a report, essay, or project parts
    c. Being able to assign appropriate priority to each item
    d. Being able to follow specific, step-by-step directions

11. Research finds that which of these is most effective for developing phonemic awareness?

    a. Oral language teaching only
    b. Print language teaching only
    c. Both oral and print teaching
    d. None of these is found most effective

12. Which of the following tests is not designed for assessing children's social skills?

    a. SSRS
    b. SIB-R
    c. Vineland
    d. Peabody

13. What is the most accurate statement relative to assessment of students?

    a. It is important to assess both intellectual ability and adaptive behavior
    b. It is more important to assess adaptive behavior than intellectual ability
    c. It is more important to assess intellectual ability than adaptive behavior
    d. Either may be assessed, but both are not needed as they usually match

14. A typical elementary school student is most often in which of Erikson's psychosocial stages of development?

    a. Trust vs. Mistrust
    b. Autonomy vs. Shame and Doubt
    c. Initiative vs. Guilt
    d. Industry vs. Inferiority

15. For conducting a functional behavior assessment, which of these should be done first?

    a. Collect information on possible functions of the behavior
    b. Collect information to assess and describe the behavior
    c. Collect information to refine definition of the behavior
    d. Collect information to verify how serious the behavior is

16. Of the following personality theorists, who did not propose a personality type theory?

a. Hippocrates
b. Galen
c. William Sheldon
d. Gordon Allport

17. Which of these is not one of McCrae and Costa's "Big Five" personality traits?

a. Neuroticism
b. Psychoticism
c. Agreeableness
d. Conscientiousness

18. What is the correct chronological order of Freud's five stages of psychosexual development?

a. Latency, Oral, Anal, Phallic, Genital
b. Phallic, Oral, Anal, Genital, Latency
c. Oral, Anal, Phallic, Latency, Genital
d. Anal, Oral, Genital, Phallic, Latency

19. According to some researchers (Herman et al 1992, O'Malley & Valdez Pierce, 1996), all performance-based assessments have certain characteristics. Which of these is not included in performance-based assessment?

a. Norm-referenced tests
b. Process plus product
c. An integrative quality
d. Authenticity of design

20. Which of the following is not an advantage of curriculum-based assessment?

a. The scoring is objective
b. Validity and reliability
c. Practical to administer
d. No need to give often

21. According to Piaget's theory of cognitive development, when assessing a developmentally normal four-year-old, which of these tasks would be most appropriate?

a. Liquid conservation
b. Object permanence
c. Pretend play games
d. Oral logic questions

22. According to the Standards for Educational and Psychological Testing (AERA, APA, & NCME, 1999), what is not one of the most important criteria for high technical quality of assessments?

a. Validity
b. Reliability
c. Lack of bias
d. All of these

23. Which of the following is not one of the categories of evidence that can be used to verify test validity?

    a. How much the content of the assessment aligns with standards
    b. How much consistency exists among different raters of the test
    c. How the assessment is related to other measures of proficiency
    d. How much accurate results are ensured in the response process

24. Test reliability is compromised by error in an assessment instrument. Which of these is not a main source of error in testing?

    a. Factors in the test that is given
    b. Factors in students being tested
    c. Factors in the scoring of the test
    d. These are all main error sources

25. Test results can be less accurate and/or less valid when bias is present. Two common sources of bias are race or ethnicity and cultural differences. Which of these is not another source of bias in testing?

    a. Gender
    b. Disability
    c. Language
    d. They all are

26. Which of these is not a meaning included in the term ipsative (assessment, measurement, or scoring)?

    a. These are all meanings included among definitions of the term "ipsative"
    b. Comparing a student's current score to the same student's previous score
    c. Comparing scoring of different subtests within the same test instrument
    d. Comparing a student's scores on different scales, equating score variance

27. Joseph Renzulli (2005) has proposed that IQ score alone is insufficient to define giftedness. In his "three-ring conception of giftedness," all except which of the following is included?

    a. Ability
    b. Creativity
    c. Versatility
    d. Task commitment

28. Using standardized IQ tests, these students had the following results: Johnny's score was below 20. Jill's score was 102. Jackie's score was 67. Albert's score was 123. Gail's score was 154. Based on these scores, which of these statements is not correct?

    a. Johnny has profound intellectual disabilities
    b. Jackie has moderate intellectual disabilities
    c. Jill's intelligence is considered average
    d. Albert's IQ is considered above average

29. Which of these is not a measure of central tendency in statistics?

a. Range
b. Mean
c. Mode
d. Median

30. What is not an accurate statement regarding correlations?

a. A correlation coefficient of 0 means there is no consistent relationship between two variables
b. A strong negative correlation means if scores are high on one variable, they are low on the other
c. A strong positive correlation means if scores are high on one variable, they are high on the other
d. A perfect positive correlation between two variables means that one will always cause the other

31. Which of the following is not a characteristic of descriptive statistics?

a. Measures of central tendency
b. Statistical significance
c. Measures of variability
d. Correlation coefficients

32. In experimental research, which of the following is manipulated by the researcher(s)?

a. An independent variable
b. A dependent variable
c. A confounding variable
d. None of these variables

33. If you had identified a group of children placed in an early intervention program as preschoolers and you wanted to see whether the salutary effects of the program, as measured at the end of the year, were maintained in these children five years later, what type of research design would you be most likely to use?

a. Cross-sectional design
b. Cross-sequential design
c. Longitudinal design
d. Any of these designs

34. Steele (1973) identified six types or categories of approaches in program evaluation. Two are evaluation as input into decision-making and evaluation processes models. Which of the following is not one of the other four?

a. Kinds of data and activities
b. Evaluation of program parts
c. Results: objectives attainment
d. These are all identified types

35. What is not true about quantitative and qualitative research methods when used in program evaluation?

    a. Quantitative methods make it easier to generalize the research findings
    b. Quantitative methods make it easier to summarize and compare groups
    c. Qualitative methods make it easier to go into greater depth and detail
    d. Quantitative methods and qualitative methods are mutually exclusive

36. Learning certain social skills is a requisite to the success of cooperative learning groups. One of these is leadership. Which of the following is not one of others?

    a. Decision-making
    b. Problem-solving
    c. Trust-building
    d. Communication

37. According to researchers in educational psychology, cooperative learning requires five conditions to be productive. One condition is that social skills are taught (#36 above). Which of the following is not one of the other four conditions?

    a. Positive interdependence in the group
    b. Face-to-face interaction in the group
    c. Individual and group accountability
    d. Fostering competition of members

38. Which is most correct about Vygotsky's concept of scaffolding?

    a. It is given as needed and gradually withdrawn as competency grows
    b. It is support given to children in advance of their learning new things
    c. It is a structure built to support children who cannot stand up or walk
    d. It is a type of assistance provided to learners throughout their lifespan

39. What is an example of Vygotsky's zone of proximal development?

    a. An adult teacher assigns children exercises just beyond their ability
    b. Two or three children on the same academic level help one another
    c. A child who is slightly more advanced helps another child to learn
    d. Children using various approaches to a task combine their findings

40. The Individuals with Disabilities Education Act (IDEA) mandates that if assistive technology (AT) devices or services are needed for a student with disabilities to access a free and appropriate public education (FAPE), they must be provided. The Office of Special Education and Rehabilitative Services (OSERS) has clarified the law on a number of points. Which of the following does not correctly describe one of these points?

    a. AT must be supplied to the student's family at no cost by the school district
    b. AT's necessity to assure a FAPE must be determined on a case-by-case basis
    c. The student's IEP must show the kind of AT and extent of support services
    d. If the student's IEP specifies AT is needed, it is for school but not home use

41. Three students are starting the same new class at the beginning of the school year. On the first day before class, Pat says, "I want to get the highest grade of anybody in this class." Chris says, "I just don't want to flunk out of this class." Mia says, "I want to learn all there is to know about this class." Which of the following statements is not correct about these students?

    a. Pat and Mia have performance-approach goals
    b. Chris evidences a performance-avoidance goal
    c. Pat demonstrates a performance-approach goal
    d. Mia's goal orientation is that of a mastery goal

42. Classmates are discussing their scores on a recent test. Courtney says, "I'm glad I studied so hard for this test; that's why I got such a high grade." Britney says, "I got a high grade too, but I didn't study hard; I was just lucky." Bert says, "It's my own fault I got a low grade; I stayed up too late playing games with my friends and didn't review before the test." Ernie says, "My grade stinks! It's not fair; the teacher hates me and I can't win." According to Julian Rotter (1966), which statement is accurate regarding locus of control in these students?

    a. Courtney demonstrates external locus of control
    b. Britney demonstrates an internal locus of control
    c. Courtney and Bert have internal loci of control
    d. Courtney and Ernie have external loci of control

43. In studying achievement motivation, David McClelland has labeled the need for achievement as n Ach. Which of the following is not true about some of his findings?

    a. Sons with high n Ach scores tended to surpass their fathers' job status
    b. Individuals with high n Ach scores will work harder to achieve goals
    c. Individuals with high n Ach scores will give up difficult tasks earlier
    d. Individuals with high n Ach scores require more efficiency/less effort

44. In a 1975 longitudinal study of over 26,000 children (Broman et al), which factor(s) was/were found most predictive of a child's IQ score at age 4?

    a. The IQ test scores of both of the child's parents
    b. The IQ test score of the child's mother only
    c. The educational level of the child's mother
    d. Socioeconomic status and mother's education

45. Manuel's parents are Latino immigrants to the U.S. Born in the U.S., and Manuel enters school speaking fluent English. His teacher gives him a negative evaluation because he never volunteers to answer questions or speaks up in class. What is the most likely explanation for this based on the information given?

    a. Manuel is uncomfortable with speaking English
    b. The teacher is prejudiced against Latino students
    c. Manuel is shy, socially inept, and afraid to speak
    d. Manuel is not as intelligent as the other students

46. The High School and Beyond survey (Gamoran & Mare, 1989) studied the effects of academic tracking in high school. Which of these is not true about the study's findings?
  a. Placement in the college track improved achievement in mathematics
  b. Placement in the college track raised chances of high school graduation
  c. Tracking reduced achievement differences in students of different SES
  d. Tracking reduced the differences in achievement between boys and girls

47. Which of the following is not true about English Language Learners (ELLs) in American schools?
  a. From 1986-2006 ELL population grew 14 times more than general school population
  b. The ELL population in America as a group speaks more than 400 different languages
  c. Projections are that by 2015, 30% of school-age children in the USA will be ELLs
  d. Of the ELL population in America, 50 percent speak Spanish as their first language

48. In providing Positive Behavioral Support in the classroom, which of these is not a preventive strategy for the physical classroom environment?
  a. Keeping areas with high traffic free of congestion
  b. Keeping furniture setups constant once arranged
  c. Being sure the teacher can easily see the students
  d. Keeping often-used materials and supplies handy

49. Positive behavioral support in the classroom dictates that the teacher's communication of expectations to students should have all but which of these qualities?
  a. They should be as thorough and detailed as possible
  b. They should be few in number, such as three to five
  c. They should be stated in positive, not negative terms
  d. They should be concisely stated in simple sentences

50. Dan Olweus' famous Bullying Prevention Program has components at four levels. Which of the following is not one of these levels?
  a. School-level components
  b. Individual-level components
  c. Classroom-level components
  d. School system-level components

51. Of the following, which educational level was the Olweus Bullying Prevention Program not specifically researched and designed for, but has also used the program for bullying?
  a. Elementary school
  b. Middle school
  c. Junior high school
  d. High school

52. In recent years, school safety has become an increasingly important issue. Educators point to which of the following as factors contributing to the need for school safety?
  a. More students from dysfunctional families
  b. More students from impoverished families
  c. More students with parents who are teens
  d. More students from all of these categories

53. In implementing a safe-school plan, which of these would not be a goal for school administrators?

    a. Providing leadership in developing, monitoring, and evaluating the plan
    b. Setting up a program of constant tracking and reporting of school crime
    c. Being models of pro-social behavior as well as teaching school subjects
    d. Assuring safe traffic to, from, and within schools by environment design

54. A school safety council should include all except which of these as representatives?

    a. Members of the school's staff
    b. Students attending the school
    c. Some of the students' parents
    d. All of these should be included

55. Which of the following is not correct regarding applied behavior analysis (ABA)?

    a. ABA is not known to be as effective in classroom learning as it is with autism
    b. ABA is often the preferred treatment for behavior problems related to intellectual disabilities
    c. ABA has produced very significant results with autism spectrum disorders
    d. ABA has been quite successful in working with people with brain injuries

56. Of the following, which is not an appropriate activity for a school counselor?

    a. Helping individual students plan their academic programs
    b. Conducting clinical therapy 1:1 with individual students
    c. Group counseling with small and large groups of students
    d. Counseling students who have problems with discipline

57. With regard to developmentally appropriate practices, what is not true about early childhood education and special education?

    a. Both fields stress the importance of individualized intervention and programs
    b. Assessment of children's progress must be multidimensional and naturalistic
    c. Learning must be personally relevant for children with and without disabilities
    d. Federal law dictates that each of these fields has separate, exclusive programs

58. Those teaching conflict resolution to children advocate four things they need to do. Which of the following is not one of these things?

    a. Understand
    b. Don't make things worse
    c. Take charge
    d. Work together

59. According to the Crisis Management Institute's training for crisis management planning, which is not a level at which crisis planning takes place?

    a. Building
    b. Classroom
    c. District
    d. Team

60. Which of these instruments would not be used to assess school climate?

a. All of these would be used as school climate assessment instruments
b. Education, Training, Research Character Education Survey (2000)
c. Tribes Assessment Questionnaire (1996)
d. CASE-1987

61. Of the following diagnoses that a student might have, which would not be found in the DSM-5?

a. Cystic fibrosis
b. Schizophrenia with childhood onset
c. Antisocial personality disorder
d. Speech Sound Disorder

62. With the DSM-5 incorporating so many changes in its structure, Jack feels confused about how to use it for assigning diagnoses required for treatment plans. What is the MOST effective way for him to gain expertise in the new DSM?

a. Ask colleagues for advice on his paperwork.
b. Read the DSM-5 cover to cover.
c. Attend a professional seminar on using the updated DSM in practice.
d. Put off his paperwork until he is more comfortable with the new format.

63. What change in the DSM-5 better aligns it with global healthcare organizations?

a. It refined the Global Assessment of Functioning (GAF).
b. It added the World Health Organization's Disability Assessment Schedule to Section III.
c. It replaced Axis IV with psychosocial context.
d. It eliminated the GAF.

64. Which of the following is least likely to be a sign of substance abuse in a student?

a. The student's grades suddenly fall dramatically
b. The student tells you all about personal problems
c. The student is uncharacteristically truant/absent
d. The student has lost interest in favorite subjects

65. For which of these would it not be appropriate for the school to request a behavioral consultation?

a. A student diagnosed with autism spectrum disorder
b. A student who has a diagnosis of a bipolar disorder
c. Any of these if behavior problems are serious enough
d. Students with attention deficit/hyperactivity disorder

66. In the best early childhood programs, what is not true about the roles of mental health consultants?

    a. Mental health consultants in early childhood programs do not as a rule conduct direct therapeutic interventions with the children enrolled in the programs

    b. Mental health consultants in early childhood programs inform, teach, and support teachers and administrators on behavior and developmental delays

    c. Mental health consultants in early childhood programs consult with teachers or teams to resolve problems with an individual child and/or child's family

    d. Mental health consultants in early childhood programs may coach parents to interact more effectively with their children when they are in their home

67. According to the University of Maryland's laboratory for instructional consultation teams, which of these is the goal of IC teams as opposed to an objective of IC teams?

    a. To establish a support network, with a trained IC team, in every building

    b. To improve teacher skills and use of best practices in testing and teaching

    c. To develop norms school-wide for working together and solving problems

    d. To enhance, improve, and increase the performance of students and staff

68. According to the Indiana School Boards Association, which of these statements is not correct regarding school board policy?

    a. School board policies should determine a definite course of action for schools

    b. School board policies should tell administrators what they are supposed to do

    c. School board policies should tell administrators how to do what they should do

    d. School board policies, in some cases, have been determined by certain legislation

69. Which of these brain structures is most associated with the formation of explicit memory?

    a. The hypothalamus

    b. The hippocampus

    c. The cerebellum

    d. The amygdala

70. A student returns to school following a head injury. You find that this student now displays new problems with making up her mind, planning her activities, and setting goals for herself. Which lobe of the student's brain is most likely to be damaged?

    a. Frontal

    b. Parietal

    c. Temporal

    d. Occipital

71. Which of the following is not true about findings of research into schizophrenia?

    a. The risk of schizophrenia for children whose parents both have it is 46 times greater than in the general population

    b. The probability for identical twins both having schizophrenia is about three times higher than for fraternal twins

    c. Neither emotional reactivity nor environmental stressors were found to affect schizophrenia symptoms

    d. Brain imaging has shown that many people with schizophrenia have larger brain ventricles than normal brains

72. Research into schizophrenia has found that which of the following environmental factors is/are associated with higher rates of the illness?

    a. Living in urban environments
    b. Having economic difficulties
    c. Migration to another country
    d. Research identifies all of these

73. You are told that a student suffers from Wernicke's aphasia. You would expect this student to:

    a. Have difficulty understanding what you say
    b. Have difficulty expressing himself verbally
    c. Have difficulty hearing things that you say
    d. Have difficulty with spelling and grammar

74 Which of these is not a common characteristic of autism spectrum disorders?

    a. Repetitive and ritualistic behaviors
    b. Difficulty with social interactions
    c. Not understanding others' feelings
    d. Having a very short attention span

75. With reference to Pavlov's classical conditioning experiments, which of the following is correct?

    a. The food was a conditioned stimulus
    b. The food was an unconditioned stimulus
    c. The tone was an unconditioned stimulus
    d. Salivation was always an unconditioned response

76. What is not true about classical conditioning and operant conditioning?

    a. Classical conditioning was developed earlier in time than operant conditioning
    b. Operant conditioning involves voluntary behaviors; classical, involuntary ones
    c. Classically conditioned and operant responses are elicited by particular stimuli
    d. Operant conditioning can change a behavior by manipulating its consequences

77. Who of the following researchers has/have viewed adolescence as a period of great turbulence?

    a. G. Stanley Hall
    b. Margaret Mead
    c. Ruth Benedict
    d. Jeffrey Arnett

78. Charlie's teacher yells at him in school. He goes home and yells at his little sister. Which of Freud's ego defense mechanisms does this illustrate?

    a. Projection
    b. Displacement
    c. Regression
    d. Sublimation

79. **Whose personality theory is not a cognitive theory?**
    a. Albert Bandura
    b. Walter Mischel
    c. Nancy Cantor
    d. Carl Rogers

80. **Social psychologist C. Daniel Batson (1994) has proposed four motivations for pro-social behavior, such as the behavior of people (not government agencies) who went out of their way to help victims of such natural disasters as 2005's Hurricane Katrina in the United States, the 2008 earthquake in Sichuan, China, and the 2010 earthquake in Haiti. Which of the following is not one of the motives defined by Batson?**
    a. Altruism
    b. Egoism
    c. Collectivism
    d. Socialism

81. **Different theorists of intelligence have proposed one or more factors of intelligence. Which pair defined, respectively, the most reductionist and the most expansionist views of intelligence?**
    a. Spearman; Gardner
    b. Cattell; Sternberg
    c. Gardner; Sternberg
    d. Spearman; Cattell

82. **Of the following theorists of language development, who is not known for subscribing to the idea of linguistic relativity?**
    a. Edward Sapir
    b. Benjamin Whorf
    c. Roger Brown
    d. Noam Chomsky

83. **Which of these is a limitation of self-reporting measures in testing?**
    a. Speech and language deficits
    b. Some psychological disorders
    c. The issue of reporting validity
    d. These all represent limitations

84. **Who of the following pioneers in the field of psychology was known for making extensive use of naturalistic observation in doing research?**
    a. Sigmund Freud
    b. B. F. Skinner
    c. Jean Piaget
    d. All of these

85. You are told that a new student in your school has Broca's aphasia. You would expect this student to:
   a. Have trouble understanding what you say
   b. Have trouble expressing herself in words
   c. Have trouble understanding what she sees
   d. Have trouble with her motor coordination

86. Which kind of test validity relates to how thoroughly a test measures the complete range of the domain being tested?
   a. Content validity
   b. Criterion validity
   c. Predictive validity
   d. Construct validity

87. In formal assessment, split-half reliability:
   a. Is measured using parallel test forms
   b. Is an indicator of test-retest reliability
   c. Is one measure of internal consistency
   d. Is described accurately by all of these

88. In the 1970s, researchers examined items on an IQ test after black children with lower socioeconomic status got lower scores than white children with higher socioeconomic status. On an item about the logical relationships of objects, the question stem asked what the word "cup" went with, and the choices were "saucer" (the correct choice), "table," "fork," or "chair." While most higher-SES white children chose "saucer," many lower-SES black children chose "table." The researchers concluded that this was due to:
   a. Cognitive impairment caused by poverty
   b. A lack of proper vocabulary development
   c. An inherent racial disparity in intelligence
   d. An unfair cultural bias in the testing items

89. The Principles for Professional Ethics of the NASP's Professional Conduct Manual for School Psychology lists six general principles under the General heading of the Professional Competency section. One of these is that school psychologists know and apply the Principles in their practices. Which of the following is not one of the others?
   a. Recognizing the strengths and limitations of their training and experience
   b. Not informing their clients of the details of their education and experience
   c. Not using their affiliations to mislead clients about their competence levels
   d. Pursuing continuing professional development to stay current in their field

90. The American Psychological Association (APA)'s ethical principles give guidelines for the use of intentional deception in research, as in some studies it would bias the results to inform participants of everything in advance. One guideline is that participants should not be misled as to the probability of physical or emotional distress the study could cause. Which of the following are additional APA guidelines regarding deception?
   a. The research must be important enough to science and education to justify deception
   b. Researchers must show that no procedures just as effective, using no deception, exist
   c. Participants must have the deception explained to them after the study has concluded
   d. All of these statements represent additional APA guidelines with regard to deception

91. Stanley Milgram's (1965) classic experiments on obedience to authority were very valuable to psychologists' understanding of human behavior, but they could not be replicated today because they would violate ethical principles. Which of the following is not true about these experiments?

    a. The participants did not go through the current informed consent process

    b. The procedures used would violate current APA guidelines on deception

    c. The procedures used would not withstand today's risk/gain assessments

    d. The participants were not provided a debriefing following the procedure

92. The Principles for Professional Ethics of the NASP's Professional Conduct Manual for School Psychology lists four general principles involving Students under the Professional Relationships section. Which of the following does not correctly state one of these principles?

    a. School psychologists' professional practices should maintain children's dignity

    b. They should explain aspects of these relationships clearly and age-appropriately

    c. They should not discuss recommendations for program changes or more services

    d. They respect a child's right to voluntarily initiate, participate in, or end services

93. The Principles for Professional Ethics of the NASP's Professional Conduct Manual for School Psychology lists seven general principles for the Use of Materials and Technology under the Professional Practices section. One of these is that they maintain test security for each instrument used. Another is that they not accept any compensation in return for sharing data from their client database without first obtaining informed consent. Which of the following does not correctly state one of the other five principles?

    a. They get prior written consent or remove identifying data for public presentations

    b. Software publishers are responsible for ethical/legal use of all technology services

    c. They do not use computerized test scoring systems in which they have no training

    d. All applications of technology that will lower the quality of service are eschewed

94. The NASP's Professional Conduct Manual for School Psychology contains Guidelines for the Provision of School Psychological Services. The first of its Practice Guidelines state that school psychologists collaborate with other team members in using a decision-making process. Which of the following is not listed in the guideline as one of the purposes of this process?

    a. To identify academic problems and behavior problems

    b. To collect and analyze data to understand the problems

    c. To make decisions relative to the delivery of services

    d. To change services based on evaluation of outcomes

95. Which of the following does not correctly state one of the principles under Practice Guideline 2 of the NASP Professional Conduct Manual for School Psychology's Guidelines for the Provision of School Psychological Services?

    a. School psychologists function to maintain the status quo at all levels of the system

    b. School psychologists promote healthy learning environments by reducing conflicts

    c. School psychologists must transmit information to a large variety of communities

    d. School psychologists understand and participate in policy determination processes

96. Practice Guideline 5 of the NASP Professional Conduct Manual for School Psychology's Guidelines for the Provision of School Psychological Services includes all but which of the following principles with respect to diversity?

   a. School psychologists develop individualized academic and behavioral interventions
   b. They recognize and work to end subtle biases in themselves, others, and instruments
   c. They further practices that will enable all children to feel welcomed and appreciated
   d. Practice Guideline 5 includes all of these principles with respect to student diversity

97. Which of these does informed consent in experimental research not include?

   a. Procedures to be used, risks and benefits
   b. Commitment to complete the experiment
   c. Privacy and confidentiality of all records
   d. Voluntarily discontinuing participation

98. What is not true about the history of school psychology?

   a. School psychology's origins are concurrent with the origins of psychology
   b. School psychology is connected to both clinical and functional psychology
   c. School psychology uses educational, but not clinical, psychology principles
   d. School psychology began as part of social reforms in the 19th-20th centuries

99. Who is considered the father of school psychology?

   a. James McKeen Cattell
   b. Wilhelm Wundt
   c. Arnold Gesell
   d. Lightner Witmer

100. What is not true about HIPAA?

   a. HIPAA's administration is determined via individual states' laws
   b. HIPAA regulates the transmission of student and/or client records
   c. HIPAA regulates electronic transmittal of insurance claim records
   d. HIPAA dictates standards for protecting privacy of information

Answer Key and Explanations

1. D: Establishing a good rapport is key to creating the trust required for the respondent to share personal information with the interviewer. Establishing a relationship with the respondent will not interfere with the interview process (a). Interview questions are not most often standardized for uniformity (b). Standardization is a characteristic of survey questionnaires, but interviews are interactive dialogues. The interviewer pursues additional information by further questioning the respondent. Good interviewers do not concentrate only on information and not on social factors (c).

2. D: No one answer is sufficient. Psychological observations may focus either on the processes of behavior (a), i.e. what things the subject does and how she/he does them; or on the products of the behavior (b), i.e. the results it produces. Thus observations are not restricted to only one of these in every case. Observations of subjects may be made directly, but this is not always required (c).

3. B: Portfolio assessments would be least indicated. Portfolio assessments are performance-based and contain products of the student's learning. At the beginning of the school year a new student with no previous assessments or school records will not have a portfolio. A portfolio assessment reflects a student's progress over the school year in a given area. For problem identification with a new student who has no records, a school psychologist would administer such instruments as comprehensive IQ testing scales (a) to determine intellectual levels; personality inventories (c) to learn about the student's individual psychological makeup; tests to determine the student's social skills (d) including strengths and weaknesses.

4. C: ABA Inventory is not designed to explore a student's grades. It is designed to explore a student's activities outside of class. It covers the student's role as a member of his or her family (a); the student's role as a friend (b) with others; the kinds of games (d), hobbies, or crafts in which the student engages.

5. A: The only true statement about the CBCL is (a). The information about the child's behavior is reported by the parents. The CBCL does not assess social competencies (b). 118 CBCL items consider possible behavior problems and 20 to social competencies such as school functioning, friendships, group memberships, recreational activities, work activities, and so forth. This instrument can be self-administered by the parent(s) or administered by an interviewer (c). This checklist is standardized and cannot be individualized (d). The CBCL has a standardized format based on empirical research and has norms based on a sample of 1,300 children's parent responses which was found to be representative of the population.

6. C: The History/Transition Information Profile would be most useful for a teacher with a class of all new students who have past school records. This instrument helps teachers to learn each student's educational history by offering information about the student's abilities, interests, strengths and weaknesses, and which educational strategies and methods have worked or failed previously. "Step-up" teachers (a) and teachers with mixed-age classes who teach the same students for several years in a row (b) are less likely to need this tool after their first year with students. Teachers with all new students who have no earlier school records (d) would be less able to make use of this transition instrument. They could only use the section "from the family's perspective" to gather information from parents as well as pertinent medical records.

7. A: Alfred Binet published the first working intelligence test in France in 1905. Lewis Terman (b) of Stanford University adapted Binet's test for American children in 1916, standardized the test's administration, and later developed age-level norms. Terman's adaptation of Binet's test is called the Stanford Revision of the Binet - Simon scale. David Wechsler (c) published the Wechsler-Bellevue (for Bellevue Hospital in New York, where Wechsler worked) Intelligence Scale in 1939, adding nonverbal as well as verbal measures. It was renamed the Wechsler Adult Intelligence Scale (WAIS) in 1955. Wechsler later created the Wechsler Intelligence Scale for Children (WISC) and the Wechsler Preschool and Primary Scale of Intelligence (WPPSI) to evaluate different age groups. Raymond Cattell (d) created the Culture-Fair (or Culture-Free) Intelligence Test in 1949; in 1963 he identified the distinction between crystallized intelligence and fluid intelligence.

8. D: The TAT or the Thematic Apperception Test is a projective test used for personality assessment. The test taker is given ambiguous pictures to view and asked to make up a narrative of what s/he perceives the picture is about. The ITBS (a) or the Iowa Test of Basic Skills, the CTBS (b) or Comprehensive Test of Basic Skills, and the SAT (c) or Stanford Achievement Test, are all standardized achievement tests. These are normed tests commonly given annually to entire classes of students in elementary and secondary schools. Students' scores are compared to national standards. Results typically give age and grade equivalents for a student's scores, based on national averages.

9. B: The Digit Span subtest of the WISC evaluates short-term or working memory by asking the child to repeat a numbers series after hearing it spoken. Repetition may be in the same order or, in a harder exercise, in reversed order. The Vocabulary (a) subtest measures verbal comprehension (understanding of words) by asking the child to define given words. The Block Design (c) subtest is designed to assess perceptual reasoning ability by asking the child to assemble blocks to match an example given. The Symbol Search (d) subtest which involves matching symbols from rows to target symbols given, measures processing speed.

10. D: Being able to follow specific, step-by-step directions is not an executive function. While an inability to follow step-by-step directions represents cognitive dysfunction, following directives represents micromanagement by the director and thus does not require executive functioning from the child. Executive functions require the child to self-direct and make decisions rather than be directed at every step. Retrieving previously learned material (a), and being able to organize one's work (b) are examples of executive function, as are the ability to decide the importance of items in a group, or to assign them priorities (c). Other executive functions include emotional self-regulation; regulation of processing rate; focusing one's attention on a specific task; sustaining one's attention; making transitions from one thing to another when needed; coming up with strategies for studying, test-taking and the like; knowing how to start an assignment; presenting material in a logical order; and monitoring one's own progress.

11. C: A combination of oral and print language teaching has been found to be most effective for developing phonemic awareness. While the complexities of the relationship between phonemic awareness and the acquisition of reading and writing are not fully understood, the necessity of the former to the success of the latter has been clearly established. Oral language teaching only (a) and print language teaching only (b) have both demonstrated effectiveness in developing phonemic awareness, but using a combination of the two (c) has proven even more effective than either one alone.

12. D: The Peabody Picture Vocabulary is designed for assessing receptive vocabulary and intelligence. It is useful for younger children and those with speech or expressive language deficits as it replaces speaking with pointing at the correct picture in response to words spoken by the tester. It can indicate age/grade intellectual levels if specific deficits in receptive language ability (e.g. Wernicke's aphasia, deafness) are absent, and the student is not an ELL. Social Skills Rating System or SSRS (a) measures Positive Social Behaviors, Problem Behaviors, and Academic

Competence as rated by teachers, parents, and other students. It can be used to identify behavior problems and interpersonal skills deficits and to plan interventions. The SIB-R (b) refers to the Scales of Independent Behavior, Revised, which gives a comprehensive assessment of 14 areas of adaptive behaviors and 8 of problem behaviors. The Vineland (c) Adaptive Behavior Scales is often used to diagnose developmental disabilities by measuring areas of essential adaptive behavior, including Communication, Daily Living Skills, Socialization and Motor Skills; it includes a supplementary Maladaptive Behavior Index.

13. A: It is important to assess both a student's intellectual ability and adaptive behavior. Adaptive behavior measures will indicate more about a student's performance, but is not necessarily more important than intellectual ability (b), which indicates degree of competence. Both are needed for a complete picture of the student, and their results do not necessarily match (d). For example, high IQ scores but low school grades can identify problems in any number of areas – learning disabilities, attention deficits, behavior problems, emotional problems, mental illness, ineffective teaching strategies, inappropriate school placement, etc. Low IQ scores with high adaptive behavior ratings can indicate that a child with developmental disabilities is capable of functioning socially and academically at higher levels than might be expected given the IQ scores alone.

14. D: Elementary school students are typically in Erikson's fourth stage of Industry vs. Inferiority. For children aged 6-11, success in performing new skills leads to a sense of competence, while failure leads to a sense of inferiority. The first stage, Trust vs. Mistrust (a), is what infant's experience. When their needs are consistently met, a basic trust in the world results; if their needs are met inconsistently, a sense of mistrust develops. Children aged 2-3 are in the second stage, Autonomy vs. Shame and Doubt (b). Children emerge from complete dependency when independent activities are learned, e.g. toileting. Success results in a sense of autonomy while failure results in shame and doubt. The third stage, Initiative vs. Guilt (c), manifests in ages 3-5. Preschoolers actively explore their environment, experimenting with asserting control over it. Success develops a sense of purpose, while failure engenders guilt. The other four of Erikson's eight stages are: Intimacy vs. Isolation in young adulthood, which focuses on relationships; Generativity vs. Stagnation in middle age, which focuses on parenting and work; and Ego Integrity vs. Despair in old age, when one reflects on one's life and feels either satisfaction, wisdom, and peace; or regret, bitterness, and despair; and Identity vs. Role Confusion, when teenagers develop their own identity when successful. When unsuccessful, teens become confused, with an unclear sense of self.

15. B: Collect information to assess and describe the problem behavior. Immediately following this step, gather information to verify how serious the behavior is (d), because some problem behaviors do not require a full functional behavior assessment. Once the behavior has been identified, teachers and parents should first try standard strategies and methods. If standard measures do not work, next (c) refine the definition of the behavior. For example, the student's team can ask whether the behavior is significantly different from other students'; whether the behavior interferes with learning; whether it's the result of cultural differences; whether it's a safety threat; and whether it will result in disciplinary action if it continues. More than one 'yes' answer indicates the functional behavior assessment should continue.

16. D: Gordon Allport proposed a trait theory of personality. Allport published his research in 1937, 1961, and 1966. Hippocrates (a) posited one of the earliest theories of personality in the fifth century B.C. when he theorized that four "humors" or bodily fluids – blood, phlegm, black bile, and yellow bile, were each associated with a different temperament. In the 2nd century A.D., Galen (b) expanded on Hippocrates' theory by specifying that those dominated by blood had a "sanguine" or cheerful temperament; those dominated by phlegm had a "phlegmatic" or apathetic temperament; those dominated by black bile had a melancholy temperament; and those dominated by yellow bile had an irritable temperament. William Sheldon (c) theorized in 1942 that endomorphs with soft, round body builds were relaxed and sociable; mesomorphs with muscular, rectangular physiques were energetic, brave, and assertive; and ectomorphs, with long, thin, delicate builds were introverted, intellectual, and creative.

17. B: Psychoticism is not one of the "Big Five." Psychoticism was one of three personality traits posited by Hans Eysenck (1973, 1990), along with neuroticism and extraversion. McCrae and Costa's "Big Five" personality traits are Extraversion; Agreeableness (c); Neuroticism (a); Conscientiousness (d); and Openness to experience. Each of these five traits represents not just a quantity but a dimension. An individual's personality can be at either pole of the dimension or anywhere in between along the continuum. For example, someone who is extremely outgoing would be at one end of the Extraversion dimension, while someone who is extremely introverted would be at the other end. After a subject's relative degree of each trait/dimension is ascertained, the five dimensions are combined to yield a more specific description of that individual's personality.

18. C: The correct order of Freud's five stages of psychosexual development is (c). In the Oral stage, birth to 1 year, the infant's erogenous zones are oral – the mouth, lips, and tongue which are used for suckling, and weaning is the major developmental task. The Anal stage, age 2-3, includes the developmental task of toilet training; the erogenous zone is the anus as the child learns to control bowel movements. The Phallic stage, age 4-5, shifts the erogenous zone to the genitals as the child discovers their pleasurable aspects. The primary developmental task in this stage is resolution of the unconscious sexual desire for the opposite-sex parent, and aggression against the same-sex parent. The Latency stage, age 6-12, is when the child's sexuality becomes latent, while she/he learns about social relationships and school work is prioritized; this stage has no erogenous zones, and the development of ego defense mechanisms is the primary task. The Genital stage, age 13-18, revisits the Phallic stage; developing mature sexual intimacy is the primary task. Freud also proposed that adult fixation in any stage (except Latency) produced associated behaviors and personality characteristics.

19. A: Norm-referenced tests such as achievement tests are not used in performance-based assessments. Norm-referenced tests measure product while performance-based assessments evaluate process and product (b). Norm-referenced tests focus on separate skills, and are not integrative (c), which is another characteristic of performance-based assessments. Norm-referenced tests contain objective questions and are not constructed within the context of the class curriculum; therefore, they are not authentic (d), another criterion for performance-based assessments. Other performance-based assessment criteria specified by these researchers are that they involve constructed responses and that they require higher-order thinking skills.

20. D: It is not an advantage of curriculum-based assessment (CBA) that it need not be given often. On the contrary, it is an advantage of CBA that it can be administered frequently to maintain ongoing formative assessments of the student's progress. The probes are brief, making it practical (c) in terms of teachers' time and cost effectiveness. The objective scoring (a) of CBA is another advantage as it eliminates inconsistencies. Research has found that CBA has good validity and reliability (b), two of the most important criteria for all assessment instruments; validity means an instrument tests what it intends to test; reliability, that it can be replicated with consistent results.

21. C: Pretend play games would be most appropriate for a four-year-old. Children 2-7 years old are in Piaget's Preoperational stage. A hallmark of this stage is a developing ability to use symbolic thought, i.e. mental representations of absent objects, as evidenced in the "pretend" play of early childhood. The principles of conservation (a) are understood by the stage of Concrete Operations, from 7-11. Centration, focusing on one aspect of a situation to the exclusion of others, is common in preoperational children. For example, a preoperational child shown liquid poured from a short wide container into a tall thin container believes the taller container holds more. This stage has not developed the logic to recognize the amount is the same, only transferred to a differently shaped container. Preoperational children have achieved object permanence (b) but this answer is not as appropriate as pretend play, which emerges in the preoperational stage. Object permanence is achieved in the Sensorimotor stage, often beginning between the ages of 8 and 12 months. The ability to think logically requires abstract thought, which is reached in the stage of Formal Operations, beginning around 11 years; solving logic problems orally (d) isn't appropriate for a four-year-old.

22. D: These all are the most important criteria for high technical quality of assessments. A test should be valid (a); it measures what it is meant to measure. It should be reliable (b); its results are consistent indices of the skills tested when repeated over time, across different raters, across different items or tasks measuring the same skills. A test should be free from bias (c); any conditions that give unfair advantages or disadvantages to some students over others.

23. B: Rater consistency is not a category of evidence used to confirm test validity, but one of several measures of test reliability. How closely the test's contents match up with the standards (a) supports test validity, as is the relationship of the instrument to other measurements proven to indicate accurately the student's ability or knowledge (c). The degree to which variables that could cause inaccuracy in test results have been reduced during the student response process (d), and how much test reliability, validity, and balance of the assessment among skills, content tested, and breadth and depth of knowledge have been confirmed via the application of statistical methods are also categories concerned with test validity.

24. D: These are all main error sources that affect test reliability. Factors within the particular test being administered (a) such as a lack of consistency across items that test the same skills can cause variation in results, making the test less reliable. Factors in the particular students taking a given test (b) can have an impact on reliability if results vary among students, for example, due to linguistic or cultural differences or disabilities. Factors in scoring (c) can affect test reliability if responses to items are not internally consistent, if there is not consistency among forms of the test, or if there is inconsistency among raters doing the scoring.

25. D: These are all sources of bias in testing. Gender (a) can become a source of bias if test questions emphasize skills in which either girls or boys have less experience. Disability (b) will bias test results if test items do not give all students equal opportunities to demonstrate their proficiency, or if students with disabilities have lacked sufficient accessibility to learn the skills being tested. Language (c) is a source of test bias if the same test and administration are used with students whose competence in the language used varies (e.g., ESL or ELL students taking tests in English along with students whose first language is English).

26. A: These are all meanings for which the term "ipsative" (literally "of the self") is used. Comparing a new score with scores from previous administrations of the same test (b) is ipsative measurement. Comparing subtests of one test (c), is also ipsative, and can reveal whether the student's abilities are consistent or inconsistent across various skill sets. Another type of ipsative measurement is a statistical comparison of student scores on different scales and equating the score variance (d), called ipsatization. In this method, the average of all scores across scales is subtracted from each individual scale score, removing one degree of freedom and equalizing profiles by locating them around the same middle point.

27. C: Versatility is not included in Renzulli's three-ring conception of giftedness. In fact, Renzulli's conception explains lesser degrees of versatility in gifted students in that they can vary their levels of each attribute. This also explains why students are often not gifted across the entire range of academic areas. Renzulli's suggests giftedness is found in the intersection of the three rings of ability (a), most often measured by IQ scores—in Renzulli's theory, gifted students will likely have scores above average, but not necessarily extremely high; creativity (b)—many students may have high IQ scores but are not creative, which can be assessed by measures of divergent thinking, fluid intelligence, etc.; and task commitment, in that a student may have the ability to solve a difficult problem but not the commitment to reaching a solution.

28. B: The incorrect statement is (b). Jackie does not have moderate intellectual disabilities based on an IQ score of 67. Moderate intellectual disabilities is associated with IQ scores between 40 and 55, while mild intellectual disabilities is associated with scores between 55 and 70. Severe intellectual disabilities is associated with scores between 25 and 40; Johnny is profoundly intellectually disabled (a). Jill's score of 102 places her in the average range of intelligence (c), between 85 and 115. Albert's score of 123 defines his IQ as above average (d), between 115 and 130.

29. A: The range is not a measure of central tendency. It is rather a measure of variability. Measures of variability are statistics showing the distribution of scores around a measure of central tendency. The range is the difference between the highest and lowest numbers in a frequency distribution. The mean (b) is a measure of central tendency and corresponds to the average of a group of scores. The mode (c) is a measure of central tendency and represents the most frequently occurring score in a distribution. The median (d) is the middle score of a distribution.

30. D: The inaccurate statement is (d). No kind of correlation between variables ever indicates that one variable causes the other. Correlation does not indicate or imply causation. Correlation only indicates whether there is a relationship between the variables, and if so, the relative strength of that relationship. A correlation coefficient of 0 indicates no consistent relationship between the variables measured (a). A strong negative correlation indicates an inverse relationship, i.e. the higher the scores for one variable, the lower they will be for the other (b). A strong positive correlation means that if scores on one variable are high they will be high on the other variable as well (c), and if scores on one variable are low they will be low on the other.

31. B: Statistical significance is not a characteristic of descriptive statistics. Determining whether a difference between mean scores for two samples is a statistically significant difference as opposed to a chance variation is a characteristic of inferential statistics. Measures of central tendency (a), measures of variability around a measure of central tendency (c), correlation coefficients (d) showing if there is a relationship between variables and if so, how strong it is.

32. A: In experimental research, a chosen independent variable is manipulated by the researcher(s). The purpose is to see whether the manipulation of this independent variable will have an effect on the dependent variable (b). Thus the researchers will not manipulate the dependent variable. A confounding variable (c) is one that interferes with the experiment because it was not introduced by the researchers; it could cause effects upon the dependent variable not caused by manipulation of the chosen independent variable. Therefore, researchers seek to eliminate confounding variables.

33. C: For the scenario described, a longitudinal research design would be most appropriate. A longitudinal design studies the same individuals over a span of time, collecting data at given time intervals. A cross-sectional design (a) studies different age groups all at one time. Because it does not involve repeated data collection over a long period of time, it would not show whether gains afforded by the early intervention program were maintained five years later. A cross-sequential design (c) combines aspects of both longitudinal and cross-sectional designs in that different age cohorts are studied at the same time and are also studied repeatedly over time. For example, data from a group of five-year-olds and ten-year-olds taken at the same time and again five years later. While this design has benefits, it would not be useful in this scenario, as only one age group is being studied.

34. D: These are all types of program evaluation approaches identified by Steele. The category of kinds of data and kinds of activities (a) includes models that evaluate programs according to the types of data collected and analyzed, and the types of activities performed within the program being evaluated. The category of evaluation of program parts (b) includes models using the approach of evaluating the individual components of a program. This gives the advantage of identifying whether only certain parts of the program need to be changed as opposed to an overall program evaluation. The category of results: objectives attainment (c) includes models that focus on the results of the program, specifically whether the stated objectives of the program have been met or not.

35. D: It is false that quantitative and qualitative research methods are mutually exclusive. They can be used together in the same program evaluation; this can be an advantage as they have differing strengths and weaknesses and provide different kinds of data. Quantitative methods do make it easier to generalize findings (a) from the samples to the population. Quantitative methods make it easier to summarize findings and compare groups (b) because they use standardized measures, responses of large numbers of people to a limited number of questions or items can be measured, allowing broad sets of findings to be presented concisely. Qualitative methods make it easier to go into greater depth and detail (c), though with a much smaller group of people.

36. B: Problem-solving while important, is a cognitive skill rather than a social one. While all members of a group will need to have problem-solving skills, these are not skills specific to cooperative learning groups because all students need them to learn whether their activities are individualized or group. According to researchers in educational psychology, decision-making (a) is a social skill needed for cooperative learning groups to succeed. Trust-building (c) is a social skill required for small groups since successful interaction requires trust. Communication (d) skills are necessary for a cooperative learning group's members to participate effectively, by expressing ideas and understanding those of others.

37. D: Fostering competition among members is not a condition required for cooperative learning groups to be productive. Such groups, as their name signifies, emphasize cooperation rather than competition. Individualized learning is more likely to encourage competition with other students. Positive interdependence (a) is required for cooperative learning groups, as members succeed or fail together. Face-to-face interaction (b) is a condition for cooperative learning to succeed whereby students support each other's success. Group members teaching one another what they know, explaining problem solutions aloud, checking understanding, discussing what they are learning, and linking current studies to previous ones demonstrate face-to-face interaction. Individual and group accountability (c) are also important. The teacher can observe each member's contribution; test individuals; randomly select members to present work orally; assign members to teach what they have learned to others; and keep group size small for greater individual accountability.

38. A: The most correct choice is (a). Vygotsky's scaffolding is support that adults give children as they are learning new skills but have not yet mastered them. As a child becomes more competent at the skill, the adults gradually withdraw this support until the child is able to accomplish the task

161

independently and no longer needs it. It is provided as the child is learning, not in advance of learning something new (b). Vygotsky's concept has nothing to do with building a physical structure for children who cannot stand or walk (c). Because Vygotsky's scaffolding is temporary until the child achieves mastery, it is not provided throughout the lifespan (d).

39. C: A child who is slightly ahead in a certain subject helping another child learn in that subject is an example of Vygotsky's ZPD. Because the two children's learning levels are close, they can relate to one another. The more advanced child can remember what strategies worked at the earlier level, and the less advanced child can identify more with the other child than with an adult who mastered this level of learning long ago. It is common for teachers to assign children exercises just beyond what they have mastered (a); learning would not occur if material had already been mastered; but this is not an example of the ZPD. The ZPD does not mean that children who are at the same level help one another (b). For children to combine their findings (d) is a valuable educational exercise, but not an example of the ZPD.

40. D: Answer (d) does not correctly describe one of the points stated by OSERS to clarify IDEA regarding AT. If a student's IEP team determines that the student needs AT for home use to have a FAPE, this must be provided, not just in school. Other points which are correctly described include that the school district must supply AT to a disabled student's family at no charge (a); that the need for AT to assure a FAPE must be decided on a case-by-case basis (b); that a student's Individualized Education Plan (IEP) must include the kind of AT needed as well as how much supportive service (c) for the AT is needed.

41. A: Statement (a) is not correct; Pat and Mia do not both have performance-approach goals. Pat has a performance-approach goal (c) orientation which focuses on seeming more competent than others. Mia's goal orientation is that of a mastery goal (d). This orientation focuses on mastering new skills and information. Mia does not want the highest grade but wants to know everything possible about the subject. The reverse of performance-approach goal orientation is performance-avoidance goal orientation. This orientation focuses on avoiding negative judgment from others. Chris shows a performance-avoidance goal (b); he neither wants to seem more competent by getting the highest grade or to become more competent by mastering a subject, but is concerned with not failing the class and thus being judged incompetent.

42. C: The accurate statement is (c). Courtney and Bert both demonstrate internal loci of control by their comments. Individuals with internal loci of control attribute successes to their own effort, and failures to their own lack of effort, locating the sources of control of their outcomes within themselves. Individuals with more external loci of control attribute successes to good luck, help from others, or a teacher's help, and attribute failures to bad luck, sabotage, or an unfair teacher; locating external sources of control over their outcomes. Britney does not demonstrate internal locus of control (b). Courtney shows more internal locus of control, but Bert does not (c). Ernie shows more external locus of control, blaming his teacher and unfairness, but Courtney does not (d).

43. B: The untrue statement is (b). McClelland and others found that those with a high need for achievement actually do not work harder to achieve their goals. In fact, it was found (Feather, 1961) that those with high n Ach scores were more likely to give up on tasks represented to them as difficult (c). Some researchers think that those with high n Ach scores have a need not only for achievement but also for efficiency, i.e. attaining the desired outcome with the least effort necessary (d). McClelland et al (1976) found that sons with high achievement needs were more likely than those with low n Ach scores to exceed their fathers' employment status (a).

44. D: The factors most predictive of a child's IQ score at age 4 in this study were socioeconomic status and the mother's educational level. These were more predictive than IQ scores of both parents (a), the mother's IQ score only (b), or the mother's educational level alone without SES (c). Poverty is associated with poor maternal health during pregnancy, which often leads to low birth weights. These are both consistently predictive of lower IQ in the child. Poor children are more often malnourished, making it difficult to concentrate and remember things. Impoverished parents are also likely to have fewer resources at home such as books, computers, educational toys and games. Parents who work long hours, and especially single parents, have less opportunity to play with their children, affording less mental stimulation. All of these factors contribute to lower scores on IQ tests for children of low socioeconomic status. The mother's educational level has more impact on the child's IQ due to the typically greater amount of interaction the mother has with the child.

45. D: Manuel has different cultural values about school. Latino cultures value understanding material, respecting the authority of the teacher, and listening over talking in school. North American cultures value expressing and asserting oneself by speaking in school. The teacher's negative evaluation is most likely due to cultural difference. Manuel is probably comfortable speaking English (a) in school since he was fluent before starting school. There is no indication that the teacher is prejudiced (b), nor that Manuel is shy or socially inept (c). Manuel is most likely behaving as he was taught, by parents raised in a different culture. The teacher's negative evaluation is probably based on the teacher's Anglo standards of good school performance.

46. C: The High School and Beyond survey did not find that tracking reduced achievement differences in students of different socioeconomic status. Instead, it suggests that tracking reinforced inequities that already existed among students of different SES. However, was also found to lessen the preexisting disadvantages in achievement for girls (d) While tracking did not eliminate these inequities, the researchers found that it made them "smaller than they may have otherwise been." Tracking did "partially compensate" female and black high school students for the disadvantages they already experienced. This study also found that being placed in the college track improved students' achievement in mathematics (a) and their probability of graduating high school (b). The researchers concluded that their findings gave "qualified support" for the appropriateness and benefits of tracking.

47. D: It is false that 50% of America's ELL population speaks Spanish as a first language; 70% of ELLs in America spoke Spanish as a first language in 2006. By 2006, the population of ELLs in the U.S. had increased 169% since 1886, while the general school population only increased by 12%; this represents ELL population growth over 14 times as great as general school population growth (a). The ELL population in America as a group speaks more than 400 different languages (b). Current projections are that 30% of school-age children in the U.S. will be ELLs by the year 2015 (c). These statistics have significant implications for schools, educators, and school psychologists.

48. B: Keeping furniture setups constant once arranged is not a preventive strategy in providing positive behavioral support for the physical classroom environment. The orientation of furniture, students, and teacher should vary in accordance with the individual classroom activity. Arrangements will be different for small group activities than for whole-class presentations. Keeping areas with high traffic free of congestion (a) facilitates free movement and prevents pushing when the whole class is making a transition. Making sure the teacher can easily see the students (c) is preventive both because it is easier for the teacher to monitor the class and because students are less likely to behave inappropriately when they know they are being watched. Keeping materials and supplies handy (d) cuts down on class disruption and wasted time procuring needed materials allowing more time for teaching and learning. It also makes transitions between subjects smoother.

49. A: Classroom expectations should not be as thorough and detailed as possible. If expectations are too complex students are less likely to remember and comply. The same is true if there are too many (b); the expectations should not exceed three to five items. Expectations should be stated in positive terms (c), i.e. the teacher should communicate what s/he expects the students to do, not what s/he expects them not to do. They should be short, simple, concise statements (d). It would be hard to say a student did not follow class rules or meet class expectations if the teacher could not identify anything extrinsic that the student did or did not do.

50. D: Olweus' BPP does not have school system-level components. Although he describes his program as "a long-term, system-wide program for change," it does not actually include program components identified as school system wide. The four levels are school-level components (a), such as establishing a committee, administering a bullying questionnaire school-wide, holding meetings, introducing school rules against bullying, involving the parents, etc.; individual-level components (b), such as supervising student activities, intervening in bullying, meeting with students and parents, and developing individual intervention plans for students involved in bullying; classroom-level components (c), i.e. posting and enforcing school anti-bullying rules, holding regular class meetings and meeting with parents.

51. D: High school is the level that the Olweus program was not specifically researched and designed for, but some high schools have still used the program to address bullying as it is very effective. In addition, many schools have used this program for kindergarten classes. The program was researched at and designed for elementary (a), middle (b), and junior high schools (c).

52. D: More students from all of these categories are in schools today than in the past, creating a greater need for school safety programs. Students from dysfunctional families (a) are more likely to display dysfunctional behavior their families have modeled and are at higher risk for disruptive behaviors in school; those who are not disruptive are at higher risk for failing academically and socially because of emotional problems created by their home lives. Students from impoverished families (b) are at greater risk for poorer academic performance. Also, the pressure created by poverty can contribute to crime in schools, such as stealing and drug trafficking. Students with teenage parents (c) are at risk due to teens' generally less adequate parenting skills, lack of experience, emotional immaturity, lack of resources, and greater need for support services in parenting.

53. C: Being models of pro-social behavior equally as teaching school subjects would not be a goal for school administrators, but rather a goal for teachers in implementing a safe-school plan. Educators state that teachers should regard modeling pro-social behaviors for students as just as important as teaching academic subjects. Goals for school administrators in implementing a safe-school plan include (a) providing leadership in developing the plan, monitoring it and evaluating it; (b) creating a program wherein they can continually track school crime, report it, give feedback on it, and communicate this information to those concerned; (d) designing the school's environment to assure that traffic to, from and within the schools is kept safe. Another goal for administrators in a safe-school program is creating a school planning team or safety council to advise and decide about school crime cases, assess the safety of the school, and propose changes to the safety plan and code of discipline as needed.

54. D: All of these should be included (d). To ensure the most balanced input to a school safety council, representatives should include members of the school staff (a), students themselves (b), and parents of students attending that school (c). All of these individuals offer differing perspectives. It The social interactions contributing to school crime are complex and involve multiple sources; representing a variety of positions is essential. It is also important to see that all of the parties named are informed of and agree to school safety policies and procedures in order to enforce them.

55. A: Answer (a) is not correct. ABA has actually been found to be effective in classroom learning as well as the other areas described. Since its inception, Skinnerian behavior analysis has grown in its application until currently it is found to have a very broad range of areas in which it proves effective. Many prefer it as treatment for behavior problems related to intellectual disabilities (b), and autism spectrum disorders (c), in which it has been found to revolutionize the field, as well as for brain injuries (d).

56. B: Conducting clinical therapy 1:1 with individual students is an inappropriate activity for a school counselor. This should be done by a clinical psychologist. It is appropriate for school counselors to help individual students plan their academic programs (a); to do group counseling with small or large groups of students (c); and to counsel students who have disciplinary problems (d). School counselors can also interpret students' aptitude tests, achievement tests, cognitive tests and school records; make sure student records are maintained according to government regulations; analyze students' grades relative to achievement; counsel students on attendance and dress issues; work with teachers to present guidance curriculum lessons; give teachers recommendations for study hall management; helping the principal to identify and resolve student issues; and analyzing disaggregated data.

57. D: It is false that federal law dictates that each field has separate and exclusive programs. Federal laws (i.e. ADA and IDEA) dictate inclusion of students with disabilities, requiring that early childhood education and special education programs collaborate; their programs must interact, coordinate, and complement one another. Both of these fields stress the importance of individualized interventions and programs (a) to address the particular child's needs. Both fields agree that assessment needs to be multidimensional and naturalistic (b). For example, using the results of just one test to qualify a child for special education or to justify grade retention is rejected by both fields. Both disciplines also find that for all children, learning must be personally relevant (c). Children learn better when the materials and topics involved have personal meaning for them.

58. C: Taking charge is not one of the things recommended in conflict resolution for children. Children must work together to resolve conflict (d); having them all trying to take control would produce more conflict. Children are advised to first understand (a) what the conflict is about by allowing each child to express feelings in turn while the others listen without interrupting. Children are then advised to avoid making things worse (b) by steering clear of insults, telling secrets or dredging up past events, shouting, and physical aggression. Next, children are advised to work together (d) by using "I" statements to avoid blame and take responsibility; to take turns talking; to maintain quiet voices; to write down their perception of the problem and read what others wrote; and to use active listening techniques.

59. B: According to the CMI's training, the classroom is not a level at which crisis planning takes place. It is done at the building (a) level, typically the first level after a crisis is reported and involves such things as verifying information, informing district administrators and affected staff, delegating responsibilities and defining roles, use of support personnel, managing or changing routines, etc. It is addressed on the district level (c) to decide how crisis response team members will be shared among buildings, select team members not emotionally involved, and ensure all members have equivalent training. Since substitutes must be hired when response team members are teachers, the school board needs to approve the costs involved. On the team level (d), planning includes deciding who to contact first, notifying response team members, hiring substitutes when needed, annual training as members leave and are replaced, regular mini-trainings, regularly updating crisis response plans, and creating handouts.

60. A: All of these are school climate assessment instruments. The Education, Training, Research Character Education Survey (b) from ETR Associates has student and staff versions, with overlapping items so they may be compared. It has scales on sense of community, bonding with school, school values, student behavior, adult behavior, and intergroup relations. The Tribes Assessment Questionnaire (c) is a survey from Center Source Systems which can be filled out by students, parents, teachers, staff, and administrators. It has scales on caring and compassion, responsibility, justice and fairness, trustworthiness, honesty, doing one's personal best, and social skills. The CASE-1987 (d) is the Comprehensive Assessment of School Environments from the National Association of Secondary School Principals. In addition to a school climate survey, it includes surveys of student, teacher, and parent satisfaction. Its school climate survey includes subscales on teacher-student relationships, security and maintenance, administration, student academic orientation, student behavioral values, guidance, student-peer relationships, parent and community-school relationships, instructional management, and student activities.

61. A: Cystic Fibrosis is a genetic disease, and is not in the DSM-5. The Diagnostic and Statistical Manual of Mental Disorders, fifth edition (DSM-5, 2013) includes clinical disorders such as schizophrenia (ICD-10 code F20.9). It also includes personality disorders such as antisocial personality disorder (F60.2), and developmental disorders such as speech sound disorder (F80.0). Developed by the American Psychiatric Association, the DSM-5 is the most generally utilized classification system in the United States for psychological disorders.

62. C: Part of being a professional involves identifying gaps in one's knowledge and attempting to fill them in the best possible way. Of the options mentioned, taking a seminar would provide professional leadership, a clear curriculum, and other students for feedback. Earning a certificate would also boost the attendee's confidence that, on completing the course, he has gained the diagnostic skills needed to succeed in his work. Asking a colleague for advice (a) could be useful but will not provide all the knowledge necessary. Reading the entire DSM-5 document (b) would also be useful, but would take a long time and might not focus on the immediately practical things. Putting off the paperwork (d) is not a solution to the problem.

63. B: Although the DSM is an American invention, issues of mental health are of worldwide concern. With the country's engagement in ongoing war scenarios, more veterans than ever are experiencing physical and mental trauma on battlefields far from home during their service as well as after being demobilized. Refugees are another concern; the organizations that deal with worldwide crisis, such as the Red Cross and the World Health Organization can eliminate some confusion in communications by speaking the same psychological language. By adding the WHODAS to the DSM-5, the authors have taken an important first step in integrating American psychological diagnostics with those of the larger world. The GAF has been removed from the DSM-5 (a), (d). While the transition away from the axis system of classification (b) may be a good change, it is not related to global healthcare.

64. B: The least likely indication of substance abuse is that the student tells you about personal problems. Students abusing drugs are more likely to share few personal issues or none at all. According to the Centers for Disease Control, a sudden, sharp drop in grades (a) is a warning sign of substance abuse because it interferes with attention, concentration, memory, ability to study, and motivation. Students also often lose interest in school subjects when they are abusing drugs.

Sudden truancy or increased unexplained absences (c) is identified as a warning sign of substance abuse. The cognitive and physiological impairments caused by drugs can interfere with attendance. Depending on the drug of choice, they may also lose track of time and actually forget to go to school if their consciousness is altered enough. Or they may sleep all day recovering from the effects of alcohol, opiates, or stimulants. If a student loses interest in what have been favorite subjects (d), this is another warning sign of substance abuse. Sufficiently severe abuse may result in loss of interest in anything.

65. C: If behavior problems are serious enough, any of these would warrant requesting a behavioral consultation. The student's individual diagnosis is not the criterion for determining such a request, but the seriousness of problem behaviors resulting from the disorder or disturbance. If the behaviors are disruptive to learning, pose a threat to safety, cause physical harm, and/or have not responded to interventions already known and available within the school, behavioral consultation is indicated. Some students with autism (a) can engage in serious problem behaviors, especially when frustrated by changes without adequate transitions, an inability to communicate verbally, or as a reaction to sensory stimuli. Students with bipolar disorder (b) are subject to mood swings from mania to depression, especially if they are unmedicated or the medication is not effective. Severely bipolar individuals can suffer from delusions and/or hallucinations, resulting in unpredictable behavior; and severe depression can lead to suicidal behavior. Students with ADHD (d) cannot learn if their attention deficit is severe enough, and hyperactive behavior can be extremely disruptive to others.

66. A: It is false that mental health consultants in early childhood programs do not conduct direct therapeutic interventions. MH consultants use play therapy and/or other developmentally appropriate therapeutic interventions with the children as indicated. One role of MH consultants in early childhood programs is to give information, instruction, and support to teachers and administrators to help them deal more effectively with children with problem behaviors or developmental delays (b). Another is to consult with teachers or case management teams to resolve problems with an individual child and/or family (c). Yet another role of MH counselors in early childhood programs is to coach parents on ways to interact more effectively with their children when they are at home (d).

67. D: According to UM's lab for IC teams, the goal of IC teams is to enhance, improve, and increase the performance of students and staff. Goals are more global while objectives are specific instances of how to achieve that goal. The objectives of IC teams according to the UM lab are: (a) to establish a systematic network of support, to include a trained IC team, in every building; (b) to improve or enhance teachers' skills in and use of instructional best practices in both assessment and delivery; and (c) to develop norms to be used throughout the school for collaborating and solving problems.

68. C: According to the Indiana School Boards Association, the incorrect statement is that (c) school board policies should tell administrators how to do what they should do. School board policies should tell school administrators what they should do (b), but not how they should do it. Policy helps to guide decisions and should be clear, but is written in general terms. This allows administrators to choose their own methods for accomplishing what policy requires. School board policies should give schools a definite course of action to pursue (a). In some cases, these policies have been dictated by laws (d).

69. B: The hippocampus is the largest structure in the limbic system and has the most involvement of the structures listed here in forming new explicit memories. The hypothalamus (a) regulates motivated behavior such as eating and drinking, maintains homeostasis, or internal equilibrium, and regulates the actions of the endocrine system. The cerebellum (c) coordinates body movements, controls body posture, and maintains the body's equilibrium or balance. It is also involved in the learning and performance of sequences of body movements. The amygdala (d) regulates emotional states, aggression, and the acquisition of emotional memory.

70. A: Although no one lobe of the brain exclusively controls any one function, the most likely lobe to be damaged when these problems exist is the frontal lobe. The frontal lobe, at the front of each hemisphere, is involved in cognitive functions such as planning, making decisions, and setting goals, and controls motor functions. The parietal lobe (b), at the upper side of each hemisphere, handles the sensations of touch, temperature, and pain, so problems with the executive functions described would not be attributable to parietal lobe damage. The temporal lobe (c), at the lower side of each hemisphere handles the hearing process; no executive functions occur there. The occipital lobe (d) controls visual processes and would not be the area damaged if executive cognitive functions are impaired.

71. C: It is not true that neither emotional reactivity nor environmental stressors were found to affect schizophrenia symptoms. Researchers (Docherty et al, 2008) found that schizophrenics had increased delusions and hallucinations in the presence of both high emotional reactivity and stressful life events. Neither those that had more intense emotional reactions but no stressful events in their lives, nor had those who experienced environmental stressors but had lower emotional reactions increased symptoms. Only those with both showed increases in symptoms over a nine-month period. Research by Gottesman (1991) found that while the risk of schizophrenia in the general population was 1%, the risk for children whose parents both had schizophrenia was 46% (a), and also that the probability of identical twins having schizophrenia was around three times higher than for fraternal twins (b). Barkataki et al (2006) found through magnetic resonance imaging (MRI) schizophrenics often have larger ventricles (channels that cerebrospinal fluid flows through) in their brains than do normal brains (d). Kuperberg et al (2003) found that schizophrenics had thinner areas in the frontal and temporal lobes of their cerebral cortex, indicating loss of brain tissue.

72. D: Research has identified all of these as factors associated with higher rates of schizophrenia. People who live in cities (a) have higher rates than those in rural or suburban areas. People with financial problems (b) experience higher rates of schizophrenia than those with fewer or no money problems. People who have emigrated from one country to another (c) demonstrate higher rates of diagnosed schizophrenia than those who did not migrate.

73. A: A student with Wernicke's aphasia will have difficulty understanding what you say. Damage to Wernicke's area in the temporal lobe interferes with receptive language, the ability to process spoken language. Those with Wernicke's aphasia can speak fluently (b), but don't understand what is being said. Because they never understand both parts of conversations, eventually what they say has increasingly less meaning. They may speak logically in response to visual stimuli. Many patients with this disorder hide it by developing stock expressions; for example, if asked a question they may respond "How nice you look today!" or "Is it still raining out?" While irrelevant to the conversation, they make sense on their own and can distract you from your question. Wernicke's aphasia is not associated with deafness (c); but is an inability to process spoken language and understand meaning. Such individuals have no difficulty with spelling and grammar (d) if they did not have trouble with them before the aphasia.

74. D: A short attention span is not a common characteristic of autism spectrum disorders, but of attention deficit disorders. Many students with autistic disorders focus on one activity for long periods, and tend to have a very narrow range of solitary interests as they have difficulty with social interactions (b). Their intense focus on an activity is not easily disrupted; hence they need sufficient transition from one activity to the next. Psychologists have theorized that autistic children have difficulty with social interaction because they cannot understand others' feelings (c). According to researchers, autistic children do not form the "theory of mind" that other children do at young ages—the understanding that others have different points of view. Recent research indicates that autistic individuals can learn to identify social cues such as facial expressions which they otherwise cannot interpret. Neuropsychologists believe that such training rewires the brain, bypassing dysfunctional areas. Autistic individuals frequently engage in repetitive and ritualistic behaviors (a), such as arranging objects in symmetrical patterns, which are soothing activities. Autistics also commonly display hypersensitivity to sensory stimuli—sounds are too loud, lights and colors too bright, scratchy clothes painful. The combination of sensory hypersensitivity and difficulty with social activities means that situations with noisy crowds are very stressful for them and may precipitate behavioral problems.

75. B: The only correct statement with reference to Pavlov's classical conditioning is (b). The food was an unconditioned stimulus; no learning or conditioning was required to elicit the response of salivation in Pavlov's dogs; salivation was automatic. (a) The food was not an unconditioned stimulus, nor was the tone paired with the introduction of food (c) because it did not cause salivation by itself. But once the dogs had been repeatedly exposed to the tone accompanying food, they salivated at the sound because they associated it with food. The tone then became a conditioned stimulus. It is false that salivation was always an unconditioned response (d) or always a conditioned response. It was both at different times in the experiment.

76. C: It is false that classically conditioned and operant responses are elicited by particular stimuli. Operants (behaviors emitted by an organism that affect, or operate on, the environment) are not elicited by certain stimuli. Operant conditioning can increase or decrease the probability of an operant behavior recurring in the future by manipulating its consequences (d). In other words, changing what happens following the behavior (the consequence) will cause the organism to do it more or less. If a child does something and receives a reward immediately afterward, the child is more likely to do that thing again. Rewards are called reinforcement because they reinforce the probability that the behavior will be repeated. If a child does something and the behavior either receives punishment or is ignored (extinction), the likelihood that the child will repeat the behavior is diminished. It is true that classical conditioning was developed earlier than operant conditioning (a). Pavlov began his experiments in classical conditioning in the late 1920s and Skinner began his experiments in operant conditioning in the 1960s. It is true that operant conditioning involves voluntary behaviors and classical conditioning involves involuntary ones (b). Classical conditioning conditions reflex behaviors to occur in the presence of previously neutral stimuli while operant conditioning changes the frequency of behaviors that are not automatic.

77. A: Psychologist G. Stanley Hall is the only researcher listed who viewed adolescence as a period of "storm and stress" (1904). Cultural anthropologists (b) Margaret Mead (1928) and (c) Ruth Benedict (1938) studied different cultures in which adolescents did not seem to experience any major upheaval but gradual transitions instead. More recent research by (d) psychologist Jeffrey J. Arnett (1999) confirms that the adolescent experience varies according to culture.

78. B: This example illustrates displacement. Displacement is releasing pent-up feelings – usually of hostility – onto someone or something less threatening than the original cause. The teacher is an adult authority figure, so Charlie could not yell back at her. But his little sister is not a threat to him, so he took out his anger at the teacher on her, which was safer. Projection (a) is attributing one's own impulses to others or blaming them for one's own problems. A man that desires a woman who rejects him might insist that she wants him. Regression, (c), is reverting to an earlier developmental level. Children who envy all the attention a new baby is getting may regress to babyish behavior in

169

an attempt to compete. Sublimation, (d), is channeling unacceptable impulses into socially acceptable activities. Random aggression is not acceptable in society, but becoming a professional boxer or wrestler can channel aggressive impulses into acceptable forms.

79. D: The theory of Carl Rogers is not a cognitive theory of personality but a humanistic theory of personality. Humanistic theories are phenomenological, emphasizing the individual's subjective point of view and the also the need for self-actualization or realizing one's potential. Rogers pioneered person-centered or client-centered therapy and emphasized the importance of unconditional positive regard by parents in child rearing and by therapists in counseling. The social learning theory of Albert Bandura (a) is a cognitive theory. Bandura pioneered the concept of self-efficacy, or the belief that one has the competence to perform successfully in a given situation; the concept of reciprocal determinism, meaning that the individual and the environment mutually affect one another; and the concept of observational or vicarious learning, meaning that an individual can learn by observing others' experiences without having to have the experience directly oneself. The cognitive-affective personality theory of Walter Mischel (b) emphasizes the understanding of behavior as a function of interactions between persons and situations. He defined variables, such as encodings; expectancies and beliefs; affects; goals and values; and competencies and self-regulatory plans, which determine how a person will behave in given situations. The social intelligence theory of Nancy Cantor (c) is a cognitive theory of personality. She defined three dimensions of individual differences: choice of life goals; knowledge relevant to social interactions; and strategies for implementing goals. According to Cantor, these three interact to form the different behavior patterns that form personality.

80. D: Socialism is not one of Batson's motivations for pro-social behavior. Socialism is a group of theories of social, political, and economic organization. Altruism (a), or acting for the benefit of others, is one of the motivations Batson identified. Egoism (b), or helping others to benefit oneself, is another. Some people will help others in exchange for a return favor or to receive a reward. Collectivism (c), or helping for the benefit of a group such as a family, a political party, or an organization, is a third motivation proposed by Batson.

81. A: Spearman and Gardner formed, respectively, the most reductionist and most expansionist theories of intelligence. Charles Spearman (1927) theorized a factor of general intelligence called g that underlies all intelligence performance. He also identified domain-specific skills, or s; s is less a separate type of intelligence as a group of specific subsets of abilities related to areas of knowledge while g still underlies all intelligent performance. Howard Gardner (1999, 2006) formulated a theory of multiple intelligences, expanding the definition of intelligence beyond the measurements of IQ tests. He defined eight types of intelligence, later adding a ninth. Raymond Cattell and Robert Sternberg (b) fall in the middle. Cattell (1963) used factor analysis to conclude that Spearman's idea of general intelligence could be divided into two independent parts: crystallized intelligence and fluid intelligence. Crystallized intelligence is learned knowledge together with the individual's ability to retrieve that information. This component of intelligence enables management of concrete and routine or recurrent tasks in life. Fluid intelligence is the ability to solve problems and identify complex relationships, and permits addressing abstract and novel tasks. Robert Sternberg (1999) formulated the triarchic theory of intelligence. Analytical intelligence provides information-processing abilities needed to problem-solve familiar tasks. Creative intelligence is the ability to solve novel or unfamiliar problems. Practical intelligence is tied to specific contexts and allows adaption to various contexts, select appropriate ones, and shape the environments to meet needs.

82. D: Noam Chomsky is not known for subscribing to the idea of linguistic relativity. Chomsky postulated the existence of a language acquisition device (LAD) he said was inherent in all humans irrespective of teaching or other environmental factors. He also theorized a universal grammar, an innate body of linguistic knowledge. Edward Sapir (a) proposed that differences in languages create differences in thought, a radical concept at the time. Benjamin Whorf (b) was a student of Sapir's. They studied different cultures and concluded that the language people speak influences how they think. For example, people of the Dani culture in Papua New Guinea have two words for colors meaning black/dark and white/light, while English uses eleven basic color terms. Sapir and Whorf are known for their principle of linguistic relativity. Based on the Sapir-Whorf Hypothesis, as the linguistic relativity principle is often known, Roger Brown (c) distinguished between weak linguistic relativity, wherein language limits thought, and strong linguistic relativity, wherein language determines thought.

83. D: These all represent limitation in self-report measures. Children too young for speech, deaf and some autistic individuals, others who are nonverbal, and students with delayed and/or limited language development (a) cannot respond to written surveys or oral interviews as others can. Some people with mental illnesses (b) may be unable to understand and/or respond appropriately to self-report measures; for example, those with disorganized thinking, delusions, hallucinations, and other symptoms can have altered perceptions of reality and/or disordered expressive language. Validity of the measurement (c) can be questionable as respondents may misunderstand questions, inaccurately remember what they are to report, give untrue or misleading responses manipulatively, be embarrassed to tell the truth about some items, or may lie to meet some end, such as to be hired by an employer or to be released from a mental hospital.

84. C: Jean Piaget made extensive use of naturalistic observation of children in the research that formulated his theory of cognitive development. He unobtrusively observed the behavior of children as they played, exploring and acting on their environment, so as not to influence their behaviors. He also used case studies to develop thorough profiles of the individual children he studied. Sigmund Freud (a), the father of psychoanalysis and psychiatry, primarily used interviews, free association, and dream interpretation and analysis to formulate his psychoanalytic theory. He did not observe people in their natural settings but rather asked them questions and/or listened to them talk in his office. B. F. Skinner (b), pioneer of behavior modification through operant conditioning, originally experimented with animals in his laboratory, manipulating the consequences of their behaviors to change the probability of those behaviors in the future. He used operant chambers or "Skinner boxes" and other devices. He later worked with humans as well, but he still manipulated consequences to increase or decrease the probability of their engaging in certain behaviors. His purpose was see how he could change behavior by manipulating conditions in a lab setting, not to observe the subjects in their natural settings. Since (c) Piaget is the only correct answer, answer (d), all of these is incorrect.

85. B: A student with Broca's aphasia can be expected to have trouble expressing themselves in words. This type of aphasia involves damage to Broca's area, a part of the brain in the left hemisphere discovered by Paul Broca that is responsible for the processing of expressive language. Individuals with this disorder have difficulty retrieving words they already know, hampering their expression as they struggle to find words they cannot locate to communicate with others. They can also have difficulty ordering words into sentences and other functions of expressive language. Because Broca's aphasia is a disorder of expressive language, it does not normally affect receptive language, so those with Broca's aphasia can understand what you say to them (a). A disorder of receptive language is Wernicke's aphasia, which affects Wernicke's area, the part of the brain responsible for processing the spoken language that is heard. A student with Broca's aphasia would not have trouble understanding what she sees (c). Such a problem would be related to damage in the occipital lobe, which processes visual information. A student who has problems with motor coordination (d) is more likely to have damage in the cerebellum, which is responsible for motor coordination, balance or equilibrium, and body position or posture.

86. A: Content validity means that a test measures the complete range of the domain being tested. For example, testing students on their satisfaction with school would not provide information about their satisfaction with life; that would require testing their satisfaction with family, friendships outside school, leisure activities, etc. Criterion validity (b) means that a test's results correlate positively with another criterion for what the test measures. A student's scores on an achievement test that correlate highly with the student's class grades, indicates criterion validity, with grades being the criterion. Criterion-referenced tests employ this principle. Predictive validity (c) is simply another term for criterion validity. Construct validity (d), as its name implies, means that a test does a good job of measuring the construct underlying it. For example, such abstract qualities as anxiety, depression, or aggression do not have a single perfect criterion, so psychologists create constructs, or theories, about them. A test will have construct validity if its scores correlate highly with validated measures of the characteristics used to define the construct.

87. C: Split-half reliability is one measure of internal consistency, which is a measure of reliability related to the degree of consistency of the responses within one test. This can be demonstrated by comparing a student's scores on odd-numbered items with scores on even-numbered items; this is called split-half reliability. Split-half reliability is not measured using parallel test forms (a); these are different versions of a test. Using parallel forms is another way to evaluate a test's reliability as it mitigates a practice effect in students who take the identical form of a test repeatedly and may remember items. In the case of survey questionnaires asking for opinions, where there are no correct or incorrect answers, parallel forms can also decrease the effects of a respondent's wish to demonstrate consistent responses to the same items over repeated administrations. Split-half reliability is not an indicator of test-retest reliability (b). Test-retest reliability measures of how highly the scores correlate between two administrations of the same test to the same individuals; people who got the highest and lowest scores the first time will do so the second time if there is good test-retest reliability. The higher the correlation coefficient between the two administrations of the test, the more reliable the test is.

88. D: The researchers concluded that this discrepancy was due to an unfair cultural bias in the test's items. To privileged white children, social conventions taught that a cup and saucer went together. But poorer black children's families typically did not have sets of china with cup-and-saucer pairs. In their homes, a cup was simply set on the table. Thus, for their cultural background, their choice of "table" as the correct answer was logical. This revelation prompted the development of "culture-free" or "culture-fair" tests, such as Cattell's, as well as a test specifically oriented to black culture by Robert L. Williams, Ph.D., which he jocularly named the B.I.T.C.H test: Black Intelligence Test of Cultural Homogeneity. It contains items such as "Deuce-and-a-quarter is: (a) money; (b) a car; (c) a house; (d) dice;" the correct answer is (b) a car—deuce-and-a-quarter was black slang for the Oldsmobile 225, a luxury model auto. Williams called attention to the cultural bias in favor of whites by turning it on its head with this test. Hence the black children's incorrect answers on the white-designed test were not due to cognitive impairment (a), inadequate vocabularies (b), or disparity in intelligence between the races (c).

89. B: It is not one of the general principles under the Professional Competency section of the Principles for Professional Ethics of the NASP (National Association of School Psychologists)'s Professional Conduct Manual for School Psychology not to inform clients of their education and experience. One general principle is to represent competence levels, training, education, and experience accurately to clients in a professional manner. Another is to (a) recognizing the strengths and limitations of one's training and experience. Psychologists should not undertake practices unless qualified, or they should seek referrals to, consultation with, or supervision by other specialists as needed. Another general principle is (c) not using their affiliations with individuals, professional organizations, or universities and other institutions, to over-represent their levels of competence. Pursuing continuing professional development to stay current in their field (d) is another of these general principles.

90. D: All of these statements represent additional APA guidelines regarding deception. APA guidelines state that the topics for study and the hypotheses proposed must be found important enough to the advancement of education and science to justify the use of deception (a); that the researchers must show there are no other procedures without deception that will work as well as the procedures involving deception (b); and that after the study is finished, researchers must explain the deception to participants (c). This part of the process is called debriefing.

91. D: It is false that the participants were not provided a debriefing following the procedure. Milgram and his team debriefed participants by explaining they were not actually shocking people. By today's APA guidelines, they would not have been allowed to deceive the participants because of significant emotional distress. The participants in these experiments did not go through the current informed consent process (a). Research participants must now be informed about procedures and the risks and benefits of participating, and then sign a document giving their consent to participate. They must also be told they may withdraw from the study at any time with no repercussions. Milgram's researchers repeatedly told participants who complained when they heard screaming that they "must continue" to "shock" the "learners." The procedures in Milgram's experiments would violate today's APA guidelines on deception (b) as well, because participants were misled about the chances of physical or emotional distress being caused by the research, to both the "learners" and to themselves. Milgram's procedures also would not pass the risk/gain assessments mandated today (c), which dictate that risks in any study be minimized, that participants be informed first of the risks, and that appropriate precautions be taken in the event of strong reactions.

92. C: The incorrect statement is (c). School psychologists should discuss recommendations for program changes or additional services, including available alternatives, with the appropriate persons. Moreover, (a) school psychologists' professional practices should always maintain the dignity and integrity of their clients, with sensitivity to the intimacy and confidentiality of such services. School psychologists should explain significant aspects of their professional relationships in a clear, understandable, and age-appropriate way (b). These significant aspects include the reasons services were requested, who will be given information about the services, and what outcomes are possible. These principles also state that school psychologists will respect a child's right to initiate services, * participate in them, or terminate them voluntarily (d). (*The manual states elsewhere that school psychologists must also seek parental support, that children's rights to initiate services without parental consent can vary, and that consequently, the pertinent local, state, and federal laws and ordinances.)

93. B: The incorrect statement is (b). Software publishers are not responsible for ethical/legal use of technology services; the principle states that school psychologists who use the technology services are completely responsible. School psychologists who publicly give lectures, present papers, or publish books or articles should first get written consent or remove identifying data before presenting their work (a). School psychologists should not use computerized test scoring systems unless trained (c). School psychologists should not use technology that ultimately lowers the quality of service (d).

94. D: This guideline in the NASP manual does not list changing services based on outcome evaluation as one of the purposes of the collaborative decision-making process. It lists the identification of academic and behavior problems (a); the collection and analysis of information for understanding these problems (b); and that a purpose of this process is to aid in making decisions about service delivery (c), e.g. what kinds of services should be provided and how they will be delivered.

95. A: The incorrect statement is (a). School psychologists do not function to maintain the status quo at all levels of the system. A principle of this Practice Guideline is that they function as agents of change at the student, classroom, building, district, local, state, and federal levels. Promoting healthy learning environments by using their skills in conflict resolution (b), and negotiation are other principles of this guideline, as is transmitting information in a relevant, organized way to a large variety of communities (c) composed of parents, teachers, school boards, policy makers, business leaders, and fellow school psychologists. Guideline 2 also states that school psychologists understand and participate in the policy determination process (d). They can promote organizational change and development by applying decision-making strategies to public policy decisions.

96. D: Practice Guideline 5 includes all of these principles with respect to diversity. School psychologists design academic and behavioral interventions, understanding that the most effective ones will be tailored to the individual student's qualities and needs (a). They are able to identify subtle biases with regard to race, class, culture, and gender in themselves, in others, and in the assessment and intervention instruments and techniques that they use, and how these biases can affect teaching, decisions, behavior, and long-term outcomes for students; and work to decrease such biases (b). They endorse and use practices that allow all children, regardless of their background, to feel welcomed and appreciated in the school and in the community (c).

97. B: Informed consent does not include commitment to complete the experiment. When participants in experimental research sign written consents, they are not giving consent to finish the study. In fact, informed consent includes the provision that they can leave the study at any time (d) without being penalized in any way. Before signing, participants are to be informed of the procedures that will be used in the experiment(s), and also of the possible risks and benefits to them (a). They are assured that all records of their participation are kept private and confidential (c); these records may not be made public unless the participant gives approval.

98. C: It is false that school psychology uses educational psychology principles but not clinical psychology principles. School psychology's origins were concurrent with the origins of the field of psychology (a) itself, i.e. it began as early as the field of psychology did. It also has connections to both clinical psychology and functional psychology (b). Functionalism was opposed to structuralism and was founded by William James. Some scholars claim clinical psychologists want to know what occurs with children and how it occurs, while functional psychologists also want to know why; school psychologists take their orientations from both. School psychology began as a part of the social reform of the late 19th and early 20th centuries (d). When child labor laws were passed prohibiting minor children from working in factories, compulsory education laws were also passed. Both laws were due to the focus on children in social reform movements. Because of these laws, children with disabilities attended school. Educators realized these children needed alternative teaching methods. In the early 1900s a number of schools created small special education classrooms, and educators saw a need for experts to select children for special education. This need resulted in the birth of school psychology.

99. D: Lightner Witmer is founded the first psychological and child guidance clinic at the University of Pennsylvania in 1896, and advocated for children with special education needs. Witmer studied under both James McKeen Cattell (a), who helped establish psychology as a legitimate science, and Wilhelm Wundt (b), who is regarded as the father of experimental psychology. Arnold Gesell (c) a pediatrician and psychologist, was the first American school psychologist, and worked as such in Massachusetts.

100. A: It is false that HIPAA is determined via individual states' laws. HIPAA is a Federal law. HIPAA stands for the Health Insurance Portability and Accountability Act. This 1996 law was sponsored by Senators Edward Kennedy (D-Massachusetts) and Nancy Kassebaum (R-Kansas). HIPAA also dictates the standards for protecting the privacy of a client's or student's health records, including therapy records (d). Title II of this law mandates the creation of national standards for electronic health care transactions and national identifiers for health insurance plans, providers, and employers. It regulates the electronic transmission of student/client records (b) as well as information used in health insurance claims (c).

How to Overcome Test Anxiety

Just the thought of taking a test is enough to make most people a little nervous. A test is an important event that can have a long-term impact on your future, so it's important to take it seriously and it's natural to feel anxious about performing well. But just because anxiety is normal, that doesn't mean that it's helpful in test taking, or that you should simply accept it as part of your life. Anxiety can have a variety of effects. These effects can be mild, like making you feel slightly nervous, or severe, like blocking your ability to focus or remember even a simple detail.

If you experience test anxiety—whether severe or mild—it's important to know how to beat it. To discover this, first you need to understand what causes test anxiety.

Causes of Test Anxiety

While we often think of anxiety as an uncontrollable emotional state, it can actually be caused by simple, practical things. One of the most common causes of test anxiety is that a person does not feel adequately prepared for their test. This feeling can be the result of many different issues such as poor study habits or lack of organization, but the most common culprit is time management. Starting to study too late, failing to organize your study time to cover all of the material, or being distracted while you study will mean that you're not well prepared for the test. This may lead to cramming the night before, which will cause you to be physically and mentally exhausted for the test. Poor time management also contributes to feelings of stress, fear, and hopelessness as you realize you are not well prepared but don't know what to do about it.

Other times, test anxiety is not related to your preparation for the test but comes from unresolved fear. This may be a past failure on a test, or poor performance on tests in general. It may come from comparing yourself to others who seem to be performing better or from the stress of living up to expectations. Anxiety may be driven by fears of the future—how failure on this test would affect your educational and career goals. These fears are often completely irrational, but they can still negatively impact your test performance.

> **Review Video: <u>3 Reasons You Have Test Anxiety</u>**
> Visit mometrix.com/academy and enter code: 428468

Elements of Test Anxiety

As mentioned earlier, test anxiety is considered to be an emotional state, but it has physical and mental components as well. Sometimes you may not even realize that you are suffering from test anxiety until you notice the physical symptoms. These can include trembling hands, rapid heartbeat, sweating, nausea, and tense muscles. Extreme anxiety may lead to fainting or vomiting. Obviously, any of these symptoms can have a negative impact on testing. It is important to recognize them as soon as they begin to occur so that you can address the problem before it damages your performance.

> **Review Video: 3 Ways to Tell You Have Test Anxiety**
> Visit mometrix.com/academy and enter code: 927847

The mental components of test anxiety include trouble focusing and inability to remember learned information. During a test, your mind is on high alert, which can help you recall information and stay focused for an extended period of time. However, anxiety interferes with your mind's natural processes, causing you to blank out, even on the questions you know well. The strain of testing during anxiety makes it difficult to stay focused, especially on a test that may take several hours. Extreme anxiety can take a huge mental toll, making it difficult not only to recall test information but even to understand the test questions or pull your thoughts together.

> **Review Video: How Test Anxiety Affects Memory**
> Visit mometrix.com/academy and enter code: 609003

Effects of Test Anxiety

Test anxiety is like a disease—if left untreated, it will get progressively worse. Anxiety leads to poor performance, and this reinforces the feelings of fear and failure, which in turn lead to poor performances on subsequent tests. It can grow from a mild nervousness to a crippling condition. If allowed to progress, test anxiety can have a big impact on your schooling, and consequently on your future.

Test anxiety can spread to other parts of your life. Anxiety on tests can become anxiety in any stressful situation, and blanking on a test can turn into panicking in a job situation. But fortunately, you don't have to let anxiety rule your testing and determine your grades. There are a number of relatively simple steps you can take to move past anxiety and function normally on a test and in the rest of life.

> **Review Video: How Test Anxiety Impacts Your Grades**
> Visit mometrix.com/academy and enter code: 939819

Physical Steps for Beating Test Anxiety

While test anxiety is a serious problem, the good news is that it can be overcome. It doesn't have to control your ability to think and remember information. While it may take time, you can begin taking steps today to beat anxiety.

Just as your first hint that you may be struggling with anxiety comes from the physical symptoms, the first step to treating it is also physical. Rest is crucial for having a clear, strong mind. If you are tired, it is much easier to give in to anxiety. But if you establish good sleep habits, your body and mind will be ready to perform optimally, without the strain of exhaustion. Additionally, sleeping well helps you to retain information better, so you're more likely to recall the answers when you see the test questions.

Getting good sleep means more than going to bed on time. It's important to allow your brain time to relax. Take study breaks from time to time so it doesn't get overworked, and don't study right before bed. Take time to rest your mind before trying to rest your body, or you may find it difficult to fall asleep.

> **Review Video: <u>The Importance of Sleep for Your Brain</u>**
> Visit mometrix.com/academy and enter code: 319338

Along with sleep, other aspects of physical health are important in preparing for a test. Good nutrition is vital for good brain function. Sugary foods and drinks may give a burst of energy but this burst is followed by a crash, both physically and emotionally. Instead, fuel your body with protein and vitamin-rich foods.

Also, drink plenty of water. Dehydration can lead to headaches and exhaustion, especially if your brain is already under stress from the rigors of the test. Particularly if your test is a long one, drink water during the breaks. And if possible, take an energy-boosting snack to eat between sections.

> **Review Video: <u>How Diet Can Affect your Mood</u>**
> Visit mometrix.com/academy and enter code: 624317

Along with sleep and diet, a third important part of physical health is exercise. Maintaining a steady workout schedule is helpful, but even taking 5-minute study breaks to walk can help get your blood pumping faster and clear your head. Exercise also releases endorphins, which contribute to a positive feeling and can help combat test anxiety.

When you nurture your physical health, you are also contributing to your mental health. If your body is healthy, your mind is much more likely to be healthy as well. So take time to rest, nourish your body with healthy food and water, and get moving as much as possible. Taking these physical steps will make you stronger and more able to take the mental steps necessary to overcome test anxiety.

> **Review Video: <u>How to Stay Healthy and Prevent Test Anxiety</u>**
> Visit mometrix.com/academy and enter code: 877894

Mental Steps for Beating Test Anxiety

Working on the mental side of test anxiety can be more challenging, but as with the physical side, there are clear steps you can take to overcome it. As mentioned earlier, test anxiety often stems from lack of preparation, so the obvious solution is to prepare for the test. Effective studying may be the most important weapon you have for beating test anxiety, but you can and should employ several other mental tools to combat fear.

First, boost your confidence by reminding yourself of past success—tests or projects that you aced. If you're putting as much effort into preparing for this test as you did for those, there's no reason you should expect to fail here. Work hard to prepare; then trust your preparation.

Second, surround yourself with encouraging people. It can be helpful to find a study group, but be sure that the people you're around will encourage a positive attitude. If you spend time with others who are anxious or cynical, this will only contribute to your own anxiety. Look for others who are motivated to study hard from a desire to succeed, not from a fear of failure.

Third, reward yourself. A test is physically and mentally tiring, even without anxiety, and it can be helpful to have something to look forward to. Plan an activity following the test, regardless of the outcome, such as going to a movie or getting ice cream.

When you are taking the test, if you find yourself beginning to feel anxious, remind yourself that you know the material. Visualize successfully completing the test. Then take a few deep, relaxing breaths and return to it. Work through the questions carefully but with confidence, knowing that you are capable of succeeding.

Developing a healthy mental approach to test taking will also aid in other areas of life. Test anxiety affects more than just the actual test—it can be damaging to your mental health and even contribute to depression. It's important to beat test anxiety before it becomes a problem for more than testing.

> **Review Video: Test Anxiety and Depression**
> Visit mometrix.com/academy and enter code: 904704

Study Strategy

Being prepared for the test is necessary to combat anxiety, but what does being prepared look like? You may study for hours on end and still not feel prepared. What you need is a strategy for test prep. The next few pages outline our recommended steps to help you plan out and conquer the challenge of preparation.

STEP 1: SCOPE OUT THE TEST

Learn everything you can about the format (multiple choice, essay, etc.) and what will be on the test. Gather any study materials, course outlines, or sample exams that may be available. Not only will this help you to prepare, but knowing what to expect can help to alleviate test anxiety.

STEP 2: MAP OUT THE MATERIAL

Look through the textbook or study guide and make note of how many chapters or sections it has. Then divide these over the time you have. For example, if a book has 15 chapters and you have five days to study, you need to cover three chapters each day. Even better, if you have the time, leave an extra day at the end for overall review after you have gone through the material in depth.

If time is limited, you may need to prioritize the material. Look through it and make note of which sections you think you already have a good grasp on, and which need review. While you are studying, skim quickly through the familiar sections and take more time on the challenging parts. Write out your plan so you don't get lost as you go. Having a written plan also helps you feel more in control of the study, so anxiety is less likely to arise from feeling overwhelmed at the amount to cover.

STEP 3: GATHER YOUR TOOLS

Decide what study method works best for you. Do you prefer to highlight in the book as you study and then go back over the highlighted portions? Or do you type out notes of the important information? Or is it helpful to make flashcards that you can carry with you? Assemble the pens, index cards, highlighters, post-it notes, and any other materials you may need so you won't be distracted by getting up to find things while you study.

If you're having a hard time retaining the information or organizing your notes, experiment with different methods. For example, try color-coding by subject with colored pens, highlighters, or post-it notes. If you learn better by hearing, try recording yourself reading your notes so you can listen while in the car, working out, or simply sitting at your desk. Ask a friend to quiz you from your flashcards, or try teaching someone the material to solidify it in your mind.

STEP 4: CREATE YOUR ENVIRONMENT

It's important to avoid distractions while you study. This includes both the obvious distractions like visitors and the subtle distractions like an uncomfortable chair (or a too-comfortable couch that makes you want to fall asleep). Set up the best study environment possible: good lighting and a comfortable work area. If background music helps you focus, you may want to turn it on, but otherwise keep the room quiet. If you are using a computer to take notes, be sure you don't have any other windows open, especially applications like social media, games, or anything else that could distract you. Silence your phone and turn off notifications. Be sure to keep water close by so you stay hydrated while you study (but avoid unhealthy drinks and snacks).

Also, take into account the best time of day to study. Are you freshest first thing in the morning? Try to set aside some time then to work through the material. Is your mind clearer in the afternoon or evening? Schedule your study session then. Another method is to study at the same time of day that you will take the test, so that your brain gets used to working on the material at that time and will be ready to focus at test time.

STEP 5: STUDY!

Once you have done all the study preparation, it's time to settle into the actual studying. Sit down, take a few moments to settle your mind so you can focus, and begin to follow your study plan. Don't give in to distractions or let yourself procrastinate. This is your time to prepare so you'll be ready to fearlessly approach the test. Make the most of the time and stay focused.

Of course, you don't want to burn out. If you study too long you may find that you're not retaining the information very well. Take regular study breaks. For example, taking five minutes out of every hour to walk briskly, breathing deeply and swinging your arms, can help your mind stay fresh.

As you get to the end of each chapter or section, it's a good idea to do a quick review. Remind yourself of what you learned and work on any difficult parts. When you feel that you've mastered the material, move on to the next part. At the end of your study session, briefly skim through your notes again.

But while review is helpful, cramming last minute is NOT. If at all possible, work ahead so that you won't need to fit all your study into the last day. Cramming overloads your brain with more information than it can process and retain, and your tired mind may struggle to recall even previously learned information when it is overwhelmed with last-minute study. Also, the urgent nature of cramming and the stress placed on your brain contribute to anxiety. You'll be more likely to go to the test feeling unprepared and having trouble thinking clearly.

So don't cram, and don't stay up late before the test, even just to review your notes at a leisurely pace. Your brain needs rest more than it needs to go over the information again. In fact, plan to finish your studies by noon or early afternoon the day before the test. Give your brain the rest of the day to relax or focus on other things, and get a good night's sleep. Then you will be fresh for the test and better able to recall what you've studied.

STEP 6: TAKE A PRACTICE TEST

Many courses offer sample tests, either online or in the study materials. This is an excellent resource to check whether you have mastered the material, as well as to prepare for the test format and environment.

Check the test format ahead of time: the number of questions, the type (multiple choice, free response, etc.), and the time limit. Then create a plan for working through them. For example, if you have 30 minutes to take a 60-question test, your limit is 30 seconds per question. Spend less time on the questions you know well so that you can take more time on the difficult ones.

If you have time to take several practice tests, take the first one open book, with no time limit. Work through the questions at your own pace and make sure you fully understand them. Gradually work up to taking a test under test conditions: sit at a desk with all study materials put away and set a timer. Pace yourself to make sure you finish the test with time to spare and go back to check your answers if you have time.

After each test, check your answers. On the questions you missed, be sure you understand why you missed them. Did you misread the question (tests can use tricky wording)? Did you forget the information? Or was it something you hadn't learned? Go back and study any shaky areas that the practice tests reveal.

Taking these tests not only helps with your grade, but also aids in combating test anxiety. If you're already used to the test conditions, you're less likely to worry about it, and working through tests until you're scoring well gives you a confidence boost. Go through the practice tests until you feel comfortable, and then you can go into the test knowing that you're ready for it.

Test Tips

On test day, you should be confident, knowing that you've prepared well and are ready to answer the questions. But aside from preparation, there are several test day strategies you can employ to maximize your performance.

First, as stated before, get a good night's sleep the night before the test (and for several nights before that, if possible). Go into the test with a fresh, alert mind rather than staying up late to study.

Try not to change too much about your normal routine on the day of the test. It's important to eat a nutritious breakfast, but if you normally don't eat breakfast at all, consider eating just a protein bar. If you're a coffee drinker, go ahead and have your normal coffee. Just make sure you time it so that the caffeine doesn't wear off right in the middle of your test. Avoid sugary beverages, and drink enough water to stay hydrated but not so much that you need a restroom break 10 minutes into the test. If your test isn't first thing in the morning, consider going for a walk or doing a light workout before the test to get your blood flowing.

Allow yourself enough time to get ready, and leave for the test with plenty of time to spare so you won't have the anxiety of scrambling to arrive in time. Another reason to be early is to select a good seat. It's helpful to sit away from doors and windows, which can be distracting. Find a good seat, get out your supplies, and settle your mind before the test begins.

When the test begins, start by going over the instructions carefully, even if you already know what to expect. Make sure you avoid any careless mistakes by following the directions.

Then begin working through the questions, pacing yourself as you've practiced. If you're not sure on an answer, don't spend too much time on it, and don't let it shake your confidence. Either skip it and come back later, or eliminate as many wrong answers as possible and guess among the remaining ones. Don't dwell on these questions as you continue—put them out of your mind and focus on what lies ahead.

Be sure to read all of the answer choices, even if you're sure the first one is the right answer. Sometimes you'll find a better one if you keep reading. But don't second-guess yourself if you do immediately know the answer. Your gut instinct is usually right. Don't let test anxiety rob you of the information you know.

If you have time at the end of the test (and if the test format allows), go back and review your answers. Be cautious about changing any, since your first instinct tends to be correct, but make sure you didn't misread any of the questions or accidentally mark the wrong answer choice. Look over any you skipped and make an educated guess.

At the end, leave the test feeling confident. You've done your best, so don't waste time worrying about your performance or wishing you could change anything. Instead, celebrate the successful completion of this test. And finally, use this test to learn how to deal with anxiety even better next time.

> **Review Video: 5 Tips to Beat Test Anxiety**
> Visit mometrix.com/academy and enter code: 570656

Important Qualification

Not all anxiety is created equal. If your test anxiety is causing major issues in your life beyond the classroom or testing center, or if you are experiencing troubling physical symptoms related to your anxiety, it may be a sign of a serious physiological or psychological condition. If this sounds like your situation, we strongly encourage you to seek professional help.

Thank You

We at Mometrix would like to extend our heartfelt thanks to you, our friend and patron, for allowing us to play a part in your journey. It is a privilege to serve people from all walks of life who are unified in their commitment to building the best future they can for themselves.

The preparation you devote to these important testing milestones may be the most valuable educational opportunity you have for making a real difference in your life. We encourage you to put your heart into it—that feeling of succeeding, overcoming, and yes, conquering will be well worth the hours you've invested.

We want to hear your story, your struggles and your successes, and if you see any opportunities for us to improve our materials so we can help others even more effectively in the future, please share that with us as well. **The team at Mometrix would be absolutely thrilled to hear from you!** So please, send us an email (support@mometrix.com) and let's stay in touch.

> **If you'd like some additional help, check out these other resources we offer for your exam:**
> **http://MometrixFlashcards.com/GACE**

Additional Bonus Material

Due to our efforts to try to keep this book to a manageable length, we've created a link that will give you access to all of your additional bonus material.

Please visit http://www.mometrix.com/bonus948/gacescpsych
to access the information.

185